Canoeing for
Disabled People

Geoff Smedley

Canoeing for Disabled People

Geoff Smedley

photographs by:

Geoff Smedley

illustrations by:

Ron Brown

cover design:

Sue Ryan

First Published 1995

ISBN   0 900082 08 9

Printed in Great Britain by:

BPC Wheatons Limited

Hennock Road, Marsh Barton, Exeter EX2 8RP

ACKNOWLEDGEMENTS

A number of people have given me support and advice in the production of this book. Many are listed in the text at the appropriate section. Others I would like to mention are:-

Janet Zeller and Anne Worthem Webre the authors of *"Canoeing and Kayaking for People with Physical Disabilities"* published by the American Canoe Association, for permission to use information from their book.

Nederlandse Bond Voor Aangepast Sporten for letting me use some of the ideas in their book *"Kader Informatie Map"*.

The Canadian Recreational Canoeing Association for permission to refer again to their book, and the source of my original inspiration, *"A Resource Manual in Canoeing for Disabled People"*.

I must also acknowledge the advice and support of the following people.

Howard Bailey	*Roger Biggs*	*Yann le Carre*	*Steve Devlin*
Geoff Good	*Clive Gritton*	*Tricia Harris*	*Everett Haughton*
Brian Hunter	*Carol Jobson*	*Gordon Neale*	*Puffin Pocock*
Ken Roberts	*Keith Ripley*	*Simon Scandrett*	*Mark Southam*
Gina Southey	*Stuart Turnbull*	*Karin Wilkinson*	

and my wife Margaret for her patience and support.

NOTE: Whilst every effort is made to ensure the accuracy of the information in this publication, it is provided without any liability on the part of the contributors or the British Canoe Union and readers should satisfy themselves as to its accuracy before placing reliance thereon.

Readers will note that an attempt has been made to reflect the commitment of the British Canoe Union to equal opportunity issues. I believe it is a clumsy strategy to use terms such as *him or her*, or *him/her* or even *s(he)*. Therefore, all references are of one gender and should be assumed to include both genders whenever they appear, unless stated otherwise. The use of either gender is random and should not be interpreted as an implication that some references are particularly male or particularly female in their orientation.

Geoff Smedley
Coventry 1995

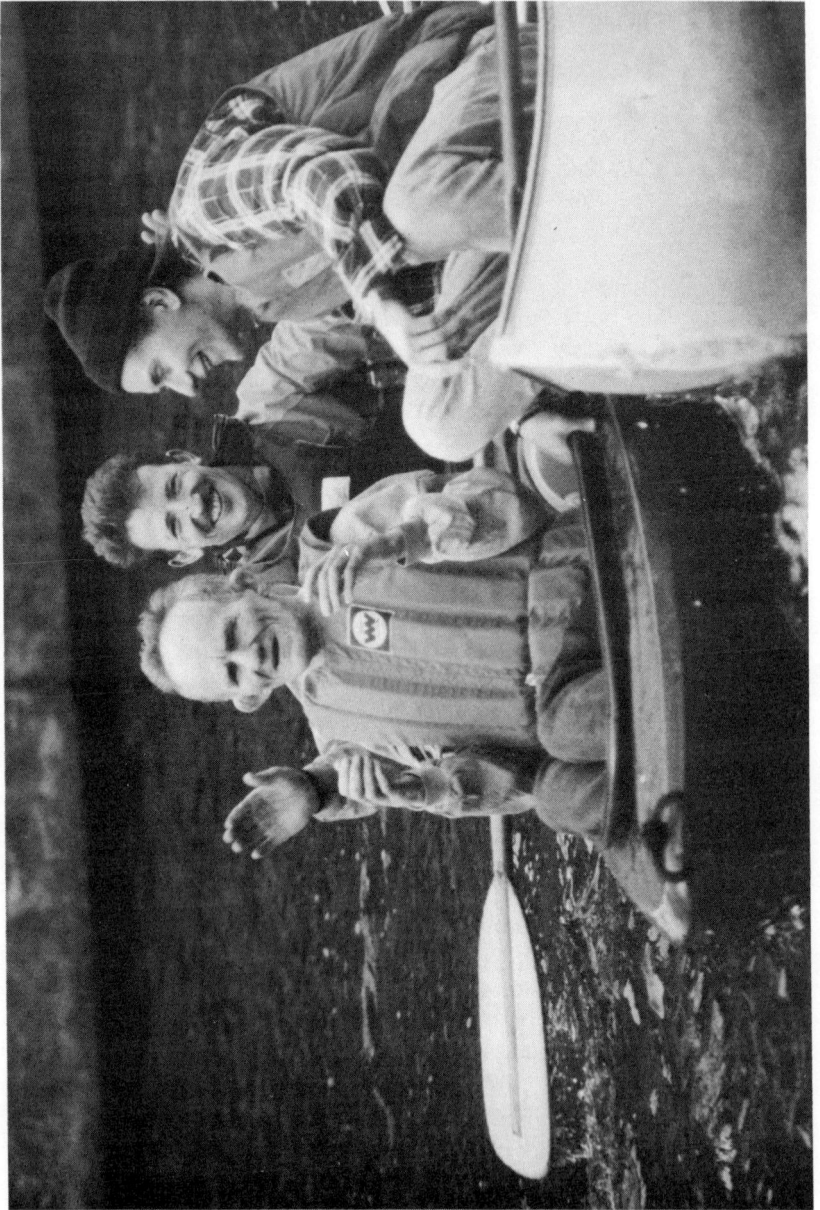

Plate a: *Canoeing is for disabled people*

CONTENTS

CHAPTER ONE

INTRODUCTION - THE CANOEIST WITH A DISABILITY

The Special Need.

Not all people with a disability have *special needs*, it has been successfully shown that many disabled people have been able to participate in canoe-sport without requiring any *special* considerations. They are able to access and benefit from all the existing resources of the B.C.U. When coaching these canoeists the coach, similarly, has all the coaching resources of the B.C.U. to call upon and will probably not have the need to refer to a book such as this.   This is why the reader will not find many references to the teaching of paddling skills, except where the pupil's impairment may require a special coaching strategy. The best coaching advice is obtained from the BCU's excellent *"Canoeing Handbook"*.

However, there are some people with disabilities who, even if only at the introductory stages of involvement, do need special consideration, concerning both resources and programmes, if they are to access and benefit fully from the opportunities that canoe-sport has to offer. This book has been compiled for these people, and their coaches.

Perceptions of Terminology

If you were to ask members of the general public to give you a word to describe people who are somehow different in terms of their physical, sensory or intellectual ability, you would be given a range of descriptive words across a spectrum of acceptability.   I am not going to elaborate on those considered to be generally unacceptable, these are words or phrases that have largely become derogatory or insulting even though some have a medical origin, albeit long since discontinued.

Nevertheless, for those words that are generally socially acceptable there is still some confusion regarding their appropriate use from a variety of stand-points.   It is impossible these days not to be aware of the value placed upon politically correct terminology.   However, as with any political statement, the interpretation of what is correct depends upon the viewpoint taken.

Whatever interpretation this book adopted would find critics from another viewpoint.   I have made a serious attempt to avoid insulting the integrity of any group. If I have not succeeded I hope the reader will not allow the terminology to prejudice their use of the book, but will consider the value of the content since it is the content that is paramount to the success of the sport for all those who participate.

The Terminology of this Book

Opinion appears to be divided between using *disabled people* and *people with a disability*. People with a disability is used particularly in a specific context, i.e. people with a visual impairment or people with learning disability.   However, when referring generally, and including all such specific groups, the term used is disabled people.

Handicap is generally used to describe the restrictive or adverse effect of an environment, a resource or attitude that inhibits or even prevents a disabled person from access to a building, type of canoe or sporting opportunity.

Our aims as coaches should be to enable people with disabilities to participate fully and remove all effects of the environment, resources or attitudes that would handicap potential canoeists.

Impairment is used to describe an individual's condition in which they have restricted use of a faculty, such as a Visual Impairment when a person does not have full vision. There is with all impairments, a range within it that, for example when considering vision, extends from people who have no sight at all, to people who may have a minor impairment that is adequately corrected by wearing glasses.

The Focus

Regardless of the ability of the person being introduced to canoeing, along with other considerations, the coach will need to observe the capabilities of the individual to determine an appropriate coaching programme.   Similarly, if it is necessary to give consideration to the special needs of a disabled person, knowledge of the impairment is important to draw up a coaching needs profile. However it must be born in mind that it is generally more helpful to examine what the individual can do, rather than make assumptions based on a medical category or condition.

Each person is an individual with individual strengths and needs.

It has been observed that when people without disabilities coach people with disabilities for the first time, one significant problem these people face is their own anxiety. This anxiety can cause a coach who is inexperienced at coaching disabled people unnecessarily to restrict his coaching programme.

Working in partnership with the disabled person is the best possible way ultimately of devising a programme that will give the maximum opportunity to the person and also maximise the expertise of the coach.

Some Guidelines for Consideration

1. Discuss the coaching programme with the person and, if appropriate, those people who provide her day to day support and care.

2. Familiarise yourself with the relevant implications of her disabilities. Find out what the special individual needs are for her, and how she manages them.

3. Relate what you learn from 2. to the coaching programme you consider offering. You will need to take into account, transport, access conditions, instructor support, equipment, water conditions, temperature, and weather. There is further guidance and information regarding these considerations in later chapters.

4. Have a well thought out, and rehearsed, strategy for dealing with emergencies.

5. Know what drugs, medical aids or special diets may be necessary, and under what conditions they are to be administered.

6. Have any medical or personal information forms on hand to refer to, giving due regard to the confidentiality of these forms and the information they contain.

Positive attitudes of the instructor to people with disabilities, their special needs and their ability to take part in the canoeing programme, are essential for re-assurance to the individual, and, if necessary, to their family or carers.

A Note of Caution.

It is a fact that, because of the complexities of the problems faced by people who have physical or sensory impairments, much of the information contained within this book appears to be directed towards these people. It is relatively easy to write about the physical needs of people and the development, adaptation or modification of equipment to facilitate participation. It is considerably less easy to describe the modification or adaptation of attitudes that will facilitate the participation of all people with disabilities, especially those people with learning disability.

However, it would be a serious mistake to consider the information to be specific to one impairment or another. In many instances the advice offered may be considered to be applicable and pertinent to a variety of impairments within a number of contexts and environments.

The importance of attitudinal awareness for special coaching needs and for those impairments often called "invisible" (that is those medical conditions such as epilepsy, diabetes or asthma), is not ignored in this guide and there are sections referring to these to be found in later chapters. Furthermore, the understanding of these conditions with physical, sensory and learning disabilities, and the ways in which they are all affected by attitudes is an important part of the *B.C.U. Disability Awareness Training Course* that is featured in Chapter 15.

CHAPTER TWO

GETTING STARTED

Two disciplines

Introducing people with disabilities to the sport of canoeing involves two disciplines. It requires both the expertise of teaching the skills of canoeing and an understanding of the effects of specific special needs on the canoeist, especially where these may have implications for the well being of the individual and the integrity of the canoeing programme.

The breadth of knowledge necessary to understand the implications of all impairments is probably beyond the ability of any one individual. Just as it is unlikely for any canoeist to be qualified across the range of all canoe-sport activities. This book assumes that a team approach will be applied to the coaching situation in which the canoe instructor will liaise with the person with special needs to determine the most appropriate approach. However, do be aware that a large number of people with impairments will enter canoe-sport without the necessity for any special considerations.

It would be over ambitious of the canoeing instructor to assume that, armed with this book, he could commence coaching people with special needs without any previous experience of doing so. Equally, it would be inadvisable for any person to consider coaching canoeing armed only with the British Canoe Union "*Canoeing Handbook*"

This book should be seen as an aide memoir. It contains the basic information and references that should be supplemented by the experience and expertise of the instructor within the context of the knowledge of the disabled person. To facilitate this objective I would refer the reader, once again, to the B.C.U. *Disability Awareness Training Courses*, run throughout the country, that aim to raise levels of awareness and impart basic skills in the area of canoeing for people with special needs.

Liaison is the key to success. By utilising the experience of the canoeing instructor, within the context of the individual's special needs, there is every possibility that each individual will realise his full potential in the sport with the minimum of risk and the maximum satisfaction and enjoyment.

The Contents

The various chapters of this book will discuss the implications of a number of impairments, physical, sensory and mental in nature. They will also refer to the implications of canoe sport for people with disabilities They will consider attitudes as well as the physical and organisational needs implicit in developing a suitable programme.

The information contained in this book has been gathered from a variety of sources, and from a breadth and depth of experiences. Therefore, it should be interpreted as a summation of experience. It presents not the "right way" but some useful guide-lines that have worked in practice. Take from it that which you find useful and use that to assist in the development of strategies that will bring canoeing to disabled people.

I hope that my aim in writing this book and your aim in reading it may be similar. That is, to give access to the sport of canoeing to as many people as possible. As a canoeist myself, I have in mind as the potential reader primarily, experienced canoe instructors who are looking to extend their expertise to enable them to coach people of all abilities. Furthermore, I am very conscious of the fact that some instructors may themselves be disabled.

I also expect this book to be of value to the disabled person who may be considering canoe sport and needs some advice regarding this. In addition, I hope carers, enablers and facilitators working for people with disabilities will draw from this book the inspiration to include canoeing as one of the sporting and leisure opportunities they organise.

This book is not intended to give expertise to the inexperienced, no matter how well intentioned. Canoeing is a sport that contains, perhaps more than most, an element of risk.   The experienced canoe instructor has the expertise to reduce this risk to an acceptable level - this is paramount to the success of the sport and to the involvement of all people.

Finally, I believe that the sport can be enjoyed at a wide diversity of levels and expertise. Some individuals will gain tremendous satisfaction from the wild water kayak trip, but equally there will be those who get the same thrill from sitting in a canoe in a quiet backwater. What is important is the achievement as expressed by the individual canoeist when participating, perhaps for the very first time in a new and exciting sport.

CHAPTER THREE

PROGRAMME - DEVELOPMENT

The process of developing a suitable programme requires three basic stages.

- **PREPARATION**
- **EDUCATION**
- **PARTICIPATION**

There are a number of questions that need to be answered in the following sections. Your ability to answer them, or recognise the right answers, will depend on your experience or training. Therefore, it may be necessary to read the rest of this book, and, or, to attend a *Disability Awareness Training Course,* before you are ready to apply the suggestions in this chapter to your situation.

PREPARATION

Accessibility

Can participants get to the site,

- into the changing rooms and toilets,
- into and out of the canoes or kayaks,
- out of the water if necessary?

Specific aspects of access are covered in Chapter 19 and potential solutions to the accessibility of certain craft are discussed in Chapter 9. You will need to assess your situation and if you envisage problems of accessibility, either to the canoeing base, or from the bank to the boat, you will need to study these chapters and apply the information therein.

Physical needs

Are the participants

- confident in the water,
- suitably dressed,
- suitably equipped?

The ability to swim is not a prerequisite to the participation of people with disabilities in a canoeing programme. Of more importance is the participant's confidence in the water. In this respect the suitability of their clothing is important.

Clothing needs to be able to keep the individual comfortable in their craft yet be appropriate for the activity, giving both protection and ease of movement. If the individual should be in the water which, in this country, is likely to be cold, clothing should insulate and kept them as dry as possible.

The equipment should include a buoyancy aid appropriate to the swimming ability of the participant. These and other items of equipment are fully discussed later.

Is the course

- adequately staffed,
- resourced for emergencies, and first aid,
- capable of meeting individual or group needs?

Communication systems.

Again there is more information about these needs and possible solutions offered later.

Will it be necessary to provide a preparation programme to develop strength and fitness?

People with disabilities sometimes have a lifestyle in which they do not have the same opportunities to exercise as people without disabilities . Most people can achieve some level of exercise in their usual daily routine. However, if you require a wheelchair for your mobility, or you have a learning disability or are visually impaired, you may need support in order for you to leave your home and undertake any journeys. Under these circumstances, exercise is less frequent and as a result the level of fitness and strength may be under developed. In order to participate in a canoeing programme some preliminary work to improve fitness or strength may be necessary.

Social Needs

Is a "confidence" session required?

Canoeing has a mythology of being both a high risk sport and one in which it is necessary to get very wet. Whilst some canoeists do undertake adventurous activities where the level of risk is high, many canoeists enjoy their sport in relatively safe situations. Of course it is the former that attracts the camera; and the media is more likely to present this viewpoint than it is to present the latter.

Similarly, some canoeists venture into activities where they appear to spend as much time with themselves and their craft partially or totally submerged as on the surface. However, these people, whilst engaging in perfectly legitimate and enjoyable aspects of the sport, do not represent the majority for whom the objective is to stay upright and dry.

With these considerations in mind it is sometimes necessary to reassure beginners that their introduction will be with the risk levels at a minimum and with the intention of keeping them as dry as possible.

Does everyone know what the nature and aims of the programme are?

As leaders we are often guilty of asking of participants information about themselves, which is often requested in the interests of organising appropriate activities and of making the activity safe. We are not so good at providing participants with the information they might need to make decisions about what to wear, what to take and, most importantly, what to tell you about their specific needs which, if appropriately addressed, would make their experience more enjoyable and your job easier.

Risk

Of course, risk is a variable concern for everyone but it is often exaggerated by impairment. For some the element of risk is the adventurous edge to the sport that gives the participant a sense of satisfaction and raises their self esteem. The element of risk must be determined according to the needs of the individual, but careful planning will ensure that there is no undue risk.

If disabled people are to enjoy the same quality of life as everyone else, then they must have the right to choose what they do. The decision to be involved in risk activities is an undeniable right for all, as long as they do not put other people at risk in the process or in the aftermath.

Safety

This has featured in all the other aspects of PREPARATION but it does no harm to keep it as a separate heading to double check. In particular it is necessary to bear in mind
- confidence in the water
- proper clothing and suitable equipment
- adequate experienced supervision
- the physical and mental readiness of the individual
- emergency and first aid procedures
- an acceptable level of risk.

EDUCATION

The participant

Start by considering the question "why canoe?". Then ask yourself "Why not!" Canoeing opens up a whole range of opportunities and new experiences for us all.   The quality of life for us all is enhanced as we enjoy the fun, sport, adventure and sense of personal achievement

Other canoeists

All canoeists, disabled or not, need to have an empathy with one another. Each needs to understands the needs of the other, not to patronise or to encourage sentimentality, but to understand the fundamental difference between when someone needs the help of another, and when a person wants to be left to achieve the objective unaided.

> *A problem is not a problem if the individual does not perceive it as such. At times a problem shared is effectively a problem halved. It is important to know the difference.*

Participant's parents, teachers or other carers

The vast majority of people with disabilities lead independent lives. However, some people need to rely in part on others for their day to day care and support, this may be for transport, escorting or for their domestic needs. The people who provide this care can show concern and may need some reassurance from you that everything implicit in the canoeing experience will be done with proper regard to the needs, and safety, of the disabled person.

Instructors and helpers

It would be reasonable to assume that these people would have a positive commitment to the programme structures and ideals that intend to meet the needs of people with disabilities. Their attitudes and responses must reflect the same positive attitude and confidence of the course leader.   It is important that they see their role as promoting the involvement of disabled people in canoeing.

Time needs to be devoted to the training of all support staff, both those on and those off the water, to give them awareness and insight into the special needs of the paddlers with disabilities in their group. They need to foster a team attitude in which everyone, including the participants and their carers, is working toward common goals where each recognises his own role and respects the roles of others.

Staffing Ratios

The number of qualified leaders you may need for a particular group is a very variable factor. It needs to consider the abilities and experience of the people and the resources available. Consider also the input that can be made by people who may accompany participants who have a disabilities. However, once on the water my advice would be to start from at least a 1:1 instructor ratio, and sometimes a 2:1 ratio, and only relax this when it seems appropriate.

Finally

The successful programme needs an atmosphere that is positive and encourages success.

PARTICIPATION

Appropriate facilities.

A crucial aspect of participation for any person is the level of support that he or she may need.

If individuals are totally independent, mobile and confident then they will be perfectly able to join any club situation along-side all its other members.   There are many successful examples of this.

In addition, there are a number of people with impairments who are also able to join a club without the need for individual support where the club conditions are appropriate.

For example, the club that is on one level from car park to waters edge, and where members with special physical needs can be given preference in the allocation of canoe racks at a low level, does allow people in wheelchairs the potential to be independent.

There are some excellent examples of where this has happened. Club members can arrive at reserved car spaces close to the club, move in their wheelchairs through the changing rooms to the canoe-store, put their craft onto a portage trolley and, still in their wheelchair, travel down to the waters edge for embarkation.

Similarly, for people with visual impairments, good lighting, the positioning of handrails, clear or tactile signs, the avoidance of sharp edges to walls and furniture, removing objects that may clutter the floor, making sure that boats and paddles are stored in such a way that they cannot be walked into, especially at eye levels, and the use of different floor surfaces to indicate changes of levels, steps or doors, can facilitate their independence in the club situation.

Of course, for many impairments, such as learning disability or medical conditions like epilepsy or diabetes, then the most important facility any club can offer is an attitude based on the principle of ensuring equal rights and opportunities.

Many changes and modifications can be made with minimal cost implications. For more ideas about improving access see Chapter 19. For information about contacts and strategies for fund-raising see Chapter 21.

Club Styles

At the other end of the scale is the need for some people with disabilities to have an environment that is much more geared to their specific needs and therefore, possibly, outside the range of activities or resources of the usual canoe club.

There are those people who need the security of a special environment in which they can gain confidence and skills at their own pace, with the opportunity to explore ways and means of meeting the demands of accessing the sport in their own way. In some cases they may require specific equipment, resources or coaching needs, not usually provided within a club. Such people gravitate towards the Special Needs canoe group.

The formation of Special Needs groups may be made for a number of reasons, but often they can be divided into two categories, closed groups, and open groups.

Closed groups are often formed within Institutions or Organisations, such as schools or day centres, and are intended to offer a specific opportunity to their members. Often instructors outside the organisation are co-opted to run canoeing sessions, perhaps in a swimming pool. In these situations the motivation for the formation of the group may come either from the people themselves or from their carers.

Open groups are more likely to be created by coaches, perhaps motivated by a desire to extend current club activities, or because they perceive the need positively to encourage people with disabilities. These groups look to provide for groups or individuals coming to them for the canoeing activity. Some of these groups have developed from closed groups.

The differences, advantages and disadvantages, between Mainstream and Special Needs clubs will be discussed in the next chapter.

For this discussion let us accept that what has been described thus far are the two ends of what should be a continuum of provision, between the totally integrated club and the totally segregated club.

The factors that help the individual to move from the Special Needs to the Integrated Club, if they wish to do so, are confidence and skill acquisition.

The reason why many disabled people choose to start canoeing with a Special Needs group is because they need, or perceive a need, to explore the potential of the sport and how they might adapt to it, and how it may be adapted to them. As will be seen later in this book these perceptions of different needs are often either unfounded or believed to be greater than the reality.

Nevertheless, once the individual has begun to acquire canoeing skills they may wish to consider the move towards the mainstream situation, and we as coaches should be encouraging this move. The key feature of this transition is the level of support.

Individual needs

To meet individual needs this support may take a number of different forms. It may be in terms of a person, or persons, giving individual support to the participant. It may be advisory support to the club regarding its response to the disabled person, this may come externally, that is from the British Canoe Union, or it may come internally, perhaps from a member of the Coaching Team who has been on one of the *B.C.U. Disability Awareness Training Courses.*

Support may also take the form of special or adapted craft that enable the person to follow the activity with the maximisation of their abilities and the minimum discomfort.

Of course the transition from Special Needs to Mainstream club may also be a gradual process with elements of the Special Needs club retained as the individual joins the Mainstream club. For example, one of the Special Needs club coaches may go with the individual to the Mainstream club to offer support until it is no longer required, the important consideration being that the disabled person is the best person to decide.

The programme may be based on joining, at first only for selected activities, then later to make more regular contact. Throughout this process consideration should also be given to establishing social contact with members of the club. Sometimes this essential contact is missed because of constraints brought about by difficulties that a person with a disability may face in, changing their clothes, before and after the activity, or perhaps by the need to organise special transport that arrives later and leaves earlier than everyone else.

Equal opportunities

Today, the principles of equal opportunities are well known, if not always applied. In any club, either Special Needs or Mainstream, consideration should be given to ensuring that its management reflects its membership, in terms of proportional representation. That is, the club whose members are predominantly people with disabilities should be in the majority on its management and policy making committees.

Whilst the achievement of this ideal may require some planning for its fulfilment there is no reason why all clubs and organisations should not make a statement of intent immediately. By making such a statement there is an explicit invitation to people with disabilities to come forward.

CHAPTER FOUR

PROGRAMME - PLANNING

Philosophy

Before the commencement of any programme; instructors, helpers and the participants need to meet to discuss aims, objectives and the subsequent the nature of the programme.

First, and foremost, the programme should be designed to meet the needs and aspirations of the participants, although it is recognised that, until people have experienced canoe sport in at least some of its aspects, they may not appreciate its full potential and therefore be unable to determine what they want to do in any great detail.

Initiation by capsize!

It is still a fact that the introduction to canoe sport for many people may have been one that scarcely encouraged them to try again. I refer to those who may have been introduced via the closed deck "slalom" type kayak in which the first necessary skill was that of the capsize.

After being turned up-side-down to exit the kayak, which in the U.K. is often into cold murky water, it is hardly surprising that many people decided their first experience of canoe sport was also their last.

It is even more unfortunate that some of these people have also spread their concern to others, causing them shy away from the sport in the belief that the first requirements of the coaching programme is that they must fall out and get both wet and uncomfortable, before anything else can happen. In the past, instructors have allegedly, but not always necessarily legitimately, justified this practice in the interests of safety.

The sensible alternative

In these more enlightened days, when the use of stable craft with wide cockpits make the practice of such drills unnecessary, we are able to give all beginners a virtual guarantee that their first experience of canoe sport need be neither wet nor uncomfortable without having to sacrifice any of the important aspects of safety.

However, to make this promise and ensure it is not broken, does require the instructor to have the knowledge and awareness of these craft and the appropriate coaching programmes that go with them.

Resources

Fundamental to the question of resources, is the nature of the club. Is it a Special Needs or Open club?

The Open Club

This club will have a range of equipment for the use of its members. However, most clubs only participate in a selected number of the potential aspects of canoe-sport. It is worthwhile enquiring if what the club offers meets the aspirations of the potential new member. If what is offered is acceptable it is usually the case that, whatever the style of canoeing, much of the standard equipment will be usable by people with disabilities with little, or no, modification.

The club is also likely to have a range of club equipment which individual members will be able to borrow. By utilising this facility members will be able to evaluate the use and fitness for purpose of equipment, before making a firm decision about which equipment they want to purchase for themselves.

However, should club members with disabilities ask the club to purchase a particular piece of equipment that will meet their special needs, the bid may have to take its place with bids from other, perhaps larger, sections of the club's membership. However, I would expect that in keeping with the BCU's policy of promoting canoeing for disabled people that priority will be given to establishing a core of essential equipment that will facilitate their involvement.

The presence of people with or without disabilities in the same club is not automatically integration. Integration requires a positive commitment from all the participants for it to be successfully achieved. However, the establishment of intent and the participation together of all the members is a move towards mutual understanding and is a good start towards successful integration.

The presence of enthusiasts in a club can be a motivation to all members, including those with a disability, to look for and take up new challenges. However, care must be taken to ensure that enthusiasm so generated is not equally effectively dampened by an inappropriate coaching pace.

Paddlers with disabilities sometimes require specialist help that has the potential of moderating individual enthusiasm and channelling it within the limits of acceptable risk as determined by an experienced coach. Unfortunately, in an integrated situation it can be difficult to accept this constraint, no matter how necessary it be, whilst around you other paddlers are doing what you have been denied.   This can be a frustration and limitation of choice that may not be apparent in the specialist group where there may not be the same contrasts in ability levels.

Experience has demonstrated that many disabled people can join canoeing activities without special considerations. Currently, they participate in all aspects of competition, the coaching scheme and in other activities such as touring and expeditions. An impairment in itself must not cause any individual needlessly to be denied opportunities.

The Special Needs Club

In this club specialist equipment can be bought and specialist resources developed specifically for people with special needs. Individuals can then try out and experiment with equipment to determine how best to maximise their abilities.   This is especially important for them to experience before they buy equipment of their own.

In a similar way, groups of paddlers with disabilities can benefit from having their coaching or activity programmes planned with their special needs in mind.

Some people prefer the confidentiality and sensitivity that can be generated when the group consists solely of disabled paddlers since they feel they would be embarrassed to be seen following these strategies described in the previous paragraph in front of "able" people. They prefer to make their mistakes in a potentially more sympathetic environment than that perceived in an integrated club, and only move to an integrated club when they have mastered the basic skills. Whilst one could contend that this is not always a legitimate argument it is a feeling held by many that should be respected.

For some groups, for example people with a hearing impairment, the motivation for a special group may have arisen due to the need for the group to communicate. Sign language is a skill that cannot be learned quickly, yet without this skill, communication with a deaf person is extremely difficult.

Geoff Smedley   Canoeing for Disabled People

There is a danger that the specialist group may become inward looking and lack regular contact with the main body of the sport. This can lead to outdated practices and also to a regression of standards. This can be offset if the leaders make it a practice to keep their coaching skills up to date and if the members of the club are encouraged to participate in the B.C.U. personal tests schemes. Working towards, and achieving these individual awards can lead to an improved self image, whilst the potential to achieve in the same way as all other paddlers can boost both standards and confidence.

Special Needs clubs also tend to have fewer members than open clubs. This can have a serious effect on its ability to raise funds from its membership. However, whilst the direct income may be limited, the Special Needs club will probably be more likely to attract outside charitable funding than the Open club.

Programme Components

People need to live life as fully as possible regardless of their impairments. To this end, sport and recreation are invaluable tools. The following are suggested components of your programme to enhance it especially for people who may have a disability.

- Observation

- Preparation

- Practical Coaching

        fitness
        learning skills
        demonstration
        feedback
        memory
        transfer of skills

- The "Buddy" system

- Integration

Observation

There are tremendous differences in ability and motivation between individuals with disabilities as there are with any group of people. Clearly then, before setting about devising training programmes or sessions, or thinking about which activities would be appropriate for any individual, it is important to learn something about that person.

Each individual may react differently to the same situation or problems, and sometimes in ways you may not expect. Whilst, again, recognising the dangers of generalisation, it is a fact that some people with learning disability are not always aware of the hazards that some situations present, or the risks that are involved in taking certain courses of action. These problems can be exacerbated for people who also have a reduced awareness of pain.

Personality is a very individual thing and whilst the majority of people respond is a fairly consistent way, sometimes individual responses to a given situation can also range from volatile to withdrawn. You will only appreciate the personality of any individual by careful observation. Although you will need to make these observations yourself, you should also call upon the experiences of the individual and others who have been directly involved with them.

Personal opinions, observations and decisions are very important, never be afraid to discuss programmes or activities with the individual person directly. Most individuals will have some idea of why they want to participate and what they hope to achieve through participation.

Observation of the individual is essential in preparing programmes. Nevertheless, as a coach, you will probably make certain assumptions based on previous experiences in the same situations. However, when working with some people with learning disability these assumptions are not always reliable.

For example, you should avoid the assumption that because a person can pull the paddle through the water on one side of the craft they can do the same on the other side; an action related to the first skill but with the other hand dominant. People with learning disability sometimes lack the ability, and experience, to transfer skills from one context to another.

On the other hand, by allowing participation, with only the lowest level of intervention to minimise risk, and observing what happens you may well discover that the individual has skills and capabilities that were not anticipated. Such abilities may form the basis for further development of specific skills.

An important part of your role is the recording of these observations. Sometimes improvements and progress can be so small as to be almost unnoticeable. Records are important to assess progress and give encouragement.

Preparation

Your preparation for providing an appropriate programme for people with disabilities fundamentally the same as for any group. The key features are:

- Treat them as you treat other people in any other group that you coach or lead.

- Give careful consideration to environments and conditions that are safe and re-assuring and will give the maximum confidence.

- The keys to success and confidence are familiarity and security. Build these concepts into your programme from the beginning.

- Take into account any medical considerations or any particular aspects relating to the safety of the individual.

Practical Coaching - fitness

Although public attitudes are changing, it is still a fact that many people , because of their impairment, are unable to enjoy the same access to sporting and fitness opportunities as the rest of the population. They may also be restricted in the usual play activities of young people such as walking, or cycling to school or playing street games with their peers in the community.

Therefore, it is likely that such people coming to canoeing may well be less fit than their non-disabled peers.

In addition, it is recognised that some quite ambulant people with learning disability have a poor posture and gait. It is not understood why this is so but it is due, on part, to the lack of opportunities mentioned previously.

With this in mind you may have to introduce a programme of general fitness looking at basic muscular development and cardio-vascular function before embarking on the coaching programme itself.

Practical Coaching - learning skills

When you start the coaching programme you will need to break down skills into the basic steps and be prepared to go over them again, and again, if necessary. Each new skill should be drawn from observed existing skills and once learned should be linked into the next skill. This process is called "chaining" skills.

Details of this process can be found in Chapter 8, Programmes and Individual Targets.

Lack of understanding can lead to frustration and sometimes even the most apparently simple instruction uses confusing language. For example, there are amongst the most able of us those who confuse instructions involving "left" and "right". Try using practical demonstrations as the main teaching aid.

When success is achieved, give opportunities to repeat the activity several times to "get the feel of it" and give encouragement so that the individual experiences the joy of achievement. Within your programmes remember that a little training and a lot of play makes a good recipe for both enjoyment and success.

Practical Coaching - demonstration

Demonstrations play an important part is coaching skills and are used frequently to support verbal explanations. However, do not use demonstrations as an alternative to verbal explanation, use them to support what you are saying. By using more than one channel of communication you are increasing the possibility of being understood.

Focus the attention on particular aspects of movement, not only be inviting the individual to look, for example, at the position of your hands, but also by placing their hands in the correct position. Do not be afraid to touch, this can be the most direct form of communication for many people.

Often you can help a person learn a particular skill by placing your hands on top of theirs whilst you guide them through the movements. Just as for chaining you can let your control lead or follow their control as you feel they are learning to execute the skill themselves.

Practical Coaching - feedback

In the early stages of learning a skill or movement, some people may not be able to judge for themselves whether they are performing it correctly. Direct and understandable feedback may be required from you. The most obvious form of feedback is re-assurance or confirmation that the skill is being performed correctly.

Always endeavour to make this feedback positive. Even the most badly executed skill will have a part that is correct, or nearly so and sufficient for you to be able to give positive reinforcement. You will find that certain people respond best to certain forms of positive recognition. This can vary from a smile at the right moment to a joyful shout and a "high-five" style of response. Find out what works best and use it often especially recognising each success no matter how small.

Constantly seek opportunities to give praise and positive recognition, learning will generally be much quicker and more effective if you do.

Finally, do not neglect the more permanent forms of recognition. Whilst some B.C.U. badges or certificates are there to work towards, because of the time it may take some people with disabilities to reach the end of the assessment process, seek some form of intermediate reward. You can invent your own "stage" or "modular" certificates which represent parts of the award and can be accumulated until all the parts of the award or test have been covered. In this respect see also chapter 14 on Personal Tests and Awards.

Practical Coaching - memory

It is often assumed that people with learning disability are forgetful and no matter how much effort you put into teaching them something one day, they will have forgotten all about it by the next day. Like the rest of us, some people with learning disability may well be forgetful, but do not assume that they will all be. Initially they may have difficulty learning certain skills, but with careful coaching and plenty of practice, skills will be retained over a period without a significant degree of loss.

Strategies such as those explained in chaining skills mentioned earlier, or the use of the modular system of recognising achievement, contribute to successful skill achievements.

Practical Coaching - transfer of skills

As discussed earlier you will need to be aware that skills taught in one situation may not easily be transferred to another situation even though you may think that the difference between the two is very small. This happens sometimes when people identify activities closely with the environment in which they are performed. If you change any elements of the activity, its surroundings or the equipment, or the usual pattern of arrangements, you may create some confusion for the individual.

Similarly, if the individual is confident with one instructor or buddy, the change to a new one may need some preparation. This situation can be eased if individuals are not always coached exclusively by the same person. Making the occasional change may help to avoid the apparent reliance on one instructor or buddy thus facilitating these changes when the more regular person cannot be there.

When it is necessary, or appropriate, to make changes, treat each situation as a new one and coach accordingly, do not assume that skills will transfer from previous experiences.

The "Buddy" system

When an individual needs support, either in a physical sense, or when the ability to understand or perceive danger may be impaired and there is a concern that moves the balance of risk from acceptable to unacceptable, then the best way to support is the "buddy" system. This is the pairing of the person that needs support with a person known to be competent in the given situation.

However, such a buddy system needs preparation and the person needs to get to know his buddy well. If the buddy can be someone who already knows the person to be supported all the better. If there are likely to be communication difficulties, it may be advisable to have someone who does know the person being buddied well close at hand.

This person can often interpret what the instructor wants to convey to the disabled person in a way that they understand best.

The attitude of buddies is paramount to a successful relationship. It must be based on a balance between:

- sensitivity and firmness
- friendliness and authority
- enthusiasm and security
- small steps yet not boredom
- challenge that is not frustrating

However, instructors and buddies should not just assume responsibility and leave it at that, they must also draw the attention of the person to the skills being learned or to impending risk situations in such a way that the learner will be able to recognise such skills and situations themselves in time.

When successful as a strategy, the buddy system is an ideal first stage towards integration as discussed earlier in this chapter.

In Conclusion

These are but a few observations and are all open to appropriate interpretation. The concern must always be for the needs of the individual. Ideally one would hope that irrespective of the nature of the group or club, with appropriate planning all the stages of PARTICIPATION could be catered for within the organisation of the sport.

Such a positive start at the *FOUNDATION* level of the sport is more likely to encourage people with disabilities to take the parallel stages of *DEVELOPMENT* and *PERFORMANCE* and perhaps then the final stage of *ELITE* participation be it in competition or expedition or by becoming active members of the Coaching Scheme and thus training others, including those with disabilities.

These ideas and their potential development are discussed further in Chapter Seven.

CHAPTER FIVE

PROGRAMMES

PREPARATION

Before any canoeing commences, all the participants, helpers, instructors and the course leader need to meet.   The programme should be explained to all and each stage of PREPARATION, EDUCATION AND PARTICIPATION be discussed. The basic outline of the programme should be given to each participant for use, when deciding what to wear and bring.   For some people with physical impairments this information can be valuable if they are having physiotherapy since the canoeing programme can support this.

Safety, and any potential risks involved, should be discussed openly, whilst bearing in mind that participants, and sometimes parents and care staff will need re-assurance about the organisation of the activities and the competence of the organisers.

Discussion should take place with each individual regarding his or her abilities and how to maximise these to the benefit of the individual. In addition it is important that all involved are aware of, and sensitive to, the individual's special needs. You may find that the content of Chapter 20 is of benefit in gathering and sharing information.

The various chapters that follow contain references to a wide variety of programme opportunities, craft and equipment. It is quite possible that you may not have all these to hand.   The art is to match your programme to the resources that you have.   It is not advisable to compromise your programme if, without the proper equipment, you cannot deliver it safely.

A good example of this is the need for CO_2 inflatable buoyancy aids for paddlers who may be subject to epileptic seizures.   Without these buoyancy aids you just cannot take people with epilepsy on the water with any degree of confidence. (This is explained fully in Chapter 17.)

Therefore, simply start with the equipment you have, and if you do not have the resources for a particular activity do something else until you have. Consequently, supposing someone who may have an epileptic seizure wants to canoe and you do not have any CO_2 buoyancy aids. Explain the situation, tell them you will try to beg, borrow or buy one and in the meantime you will teach them all you can about the sport, by restricting the canoeing sessions to the swimming pool. Then, when the CO_2 buoyancy aid is available they will be better prepared to start training for paddling on open water.

However, fundamental to any programme are the people who wish to canoe or kayak. Without the participants all your efforts will be to little avail. Chapter 7 outlines the many ways in which a programme can be developed and includes strategies to encourage people to come along. Often the difficulties arise in ensuring that the programme continues to meet individual needs, and encourages people to come back having tried the sport once.

Most of us can recall a time when we found ourselves in a new, and perhaps slightly threatening, situation. We were uncertain about what to do or say in case we unwittingly broke some rule or inadvertently caused some offence. Usually, these concerns are based upon our anxiety, lack of knowledge or understanding of the situation, and once we become familiar with it we are much more confident and happy.

Sometimes, coming to a canoeing or kayaking opportunity for the first time, and perhaps bringing along the kind of apprehensions that I have referred to earlier, is very daunting. Some re-assurance on the part of the organisers can make all the difference to a successful experience.

To address this potential problem, Puffin Pocock adapted a programme that she devised as a teacher. It is repeated here in a form that has been used successfully by individual instructors and organisations for many years now.

VISITOR INTRODUCTION SESSION

Aim

On the occasion of their first visit, to bring new people into your group in a positive way that will encourage and give them the confidence and desire to come back again.

Process

Letting people know that you have a resource that you want everyone to enjoy is sometimes difficult. You must make it clear in your publicity that you welcome everyone. From time to time you will probably have "open" days or "come and try it" sessions. Such events will bring people to your facility for the first time.   These are your visitors.

Preparation

Your preparation for this positive experience will involve making sure you have sufficient equipment and helpers.   It is important that your helpers must know what their roles are, for example:-

- who will meet the participants and introduce them to the instructors and helpers,
- who will show them what the facilities are,
- who will support them in changing
- who might be "buddying"
- who will be the instructors

The important objective in all this is to ensure that not only do people understand what their role is but that they are confident in it.

An Invitation

To make the first contact a positive one, I believe it is worth sending out invitations. Such a process enables you to be fully prepared and the prospective participant to feel that if they come someone will welcome them. With this in mind you should ensure that they are welcomed on arrival.

Even though you may send out invitations and even get a response it is still difficult to predict the actual numbers who will turn up. Nevertheless, if it is your intention that prospective participants will join in, your invitation will have made clear what they need to bring and you will have arranged for the appropriate equipment to ensure that they can participate safely.

The Welcome

In order to make people welcome you should consider the need to have someone who will be at the point of entry, the car park or the club gates, so that the newcomers are met.

Having been met they can be put at their ease and reassured that they are indeed welcome and the hosts would like them to participate, enjoy themselves and, if they wish, to come back again.

The Programme

You will have decided beforehand what you will be doing when your visitors arrive. This will be based primarily on the resources you have, although you should also consider borrowing resources if they will enable the activities to proceed more successfully.   Some BCU Regions now have a regionally based trailer and boats specifically to support canoeing for people with disabilities.

More ideas for the content of the programme will be later in this section and in other parts of the book.

The Farewell

Do not forget to say good-bye to your visitors.   Sometimes a good experience can be spoiled by the fact that it peters out in a rather inconclusive way.   A good close to the session is to arrange for everyone to meet after changing for refreshments and a chat.

Finally, you should be prepared for, and expect, any people you invite to come back again.   Perhaps to another special session or perhaps to a general club session.   Either way you should consider whether giving people an experience which they might enjoy and wish to repeat is appropriate if you have no intentions of giving them that opportunity.

CONCLUSIONS

In general, having completed your preparation, you must determine:-

- the needs and abilities of your group,
- what resources you have, human and physical.

The detail of the coaching programme should then be planned under:-

- **Environment**

- **Aims and Objectives**

- **Individual Targets**

- **Craft**

- **Resources**

CHAPTER SIX

PROGRAMMES - ENVIRONMENT

Under the general heading of Environment this chapter will look at;

- Transport
- Access - to the water's edge
- Access - getting into and out of the boat
- Instructors
- Helpers
- Water Conditions
- Weather and Temperature

Transport

People without disabilities, and many people with disabilities, may be able to walk, ride a bike, catch a 'bus or a train, in addition many people travel independently using wheelchairs, buggies or cars, and some have friends or family who give them lifts.   However, the inadequacy of our public transport systems often mean that some people encounter considerable difficulty in travelling even comparatively short distances. Be aware that some people who have visual impairments or learning difficulty, depending upon the individual's disability, or the degree of their dependence upon others may not be able to travel independently.

Therefore, it may be necessary for you to give consideration to the transport needs of your students as a part of your programme planning, just as you would have to consider a transport "ferry" if organising a river trip. Much can be done by asking other students or their transporters to assist those without the means. However, it may be necessary for you to look to providing the transport.

There are a number of ways you can tackle this. Some clubs have their own minibus. This not only serves the needs of people with disabilities, but other groups looking for cheap communal transport such as youth sports teams. You may, in return for an offer of coaching opportunities, be able to borrow a minibus from a school, youth club or other organisation.   Be persistent in your search.   Enlist the local City, Borough or Council Leisure Services or Social Services Departments. Also enquire of the local charities, Gateway Clubs, PHAB groups, Rotary and Round Table Organisations sometimes have minibuses.

Your local public library will probably have a list of these organisations.

Access - to the water's edge

This is not the usual question of *"have I permission to use this stretch of water?"*; I must assume that you have already negotiated this aspect of access.   Rather this is the question, *"can the participants actually physically get into the clubhouse, toilets, changing rooms or down to the water?"* If inappropriate, access into and around the clubhouse may be difficult to modify. The provision of accessible toilet facilities for people, hand rails, Braille signs, ramps and doors wide enough for wheelchairs can be expensive and, in some cases, involve re-construction of buildings. However, even the most inadequate access can be overcome if the attitude and adaptability of the membership is positive.

I visited a club in Hull where the club-room could only be accessed by an external steel fire escape, yet it had a flourishing membership of people with disabilities. With these members established, and having adopted a variety of means to overcome the difficulties of the stairs, the club was converting an area on the ground floor, previously only suitable for storage, to an accessible changing room, shower and toilet. With this level of commitment the next stage of a lift to the club-room on the first floor seemed almost an inevitability.

Access - getting into, and out of, the boat.

The majority of people with sensory or learning disabilities will be able to acquire the skills of getting in and out of the boat in much the same way as non-disabled people. However, for some people with a physical disability this skill may require either support from helpers or by using specific resources.

Often the most convenient resource to assist someone to get into their boat is that of the helpers. This resource has the advantage of being flexible in use, able to adapt to different people and different situations, and as a lifting aid, not usually requiring expense or special materials for its construction. However, helpers are an easily damaged resource and potential lifters would be well advised to seek expert, qualified instruction in lifting, both general rules and those which apply to people, before attempting to lift people with a physical disability.   There are further references to helpers later in this chapter. Refer to Chapter 16 for specific advice about lifting aids, jetties and other methods of getting in and out of boats.

Instructors

Most clubs that welcome people with disabilities can trace the start to one person.   This may have been an instructor keen to open the membership to people of all abilities, or it may have been a disabled person joining the club and giving the incentive for others to follow.

Whatever the start, many clubs have successfully developed their provision and coaching team by gathering expertise and experience, and have supported this for current needs and for the future by looking at a programme that identifies aspiring instructors, and encourages them to also consider the needs of people with disabilities.

The *BCU Disability Awareness Training Course* has proved to be a worthwhile course to give those instructors working with people with disabilities some skills and awareness to enable them to maximise their skills.   It has also proved to be inspirational to those who have not previously worked with disabled people to start doing so.   It is important to identify instructors willing to coach disabled people, and having done so to cherish their commitment and use it to encourage others.

Helpers

When working with people with disabilities the need for helpers becomes quite important.   Assistants who can carry boats to the water, assist in the changing rooms and help people in and out of boats are invaluable.

They do not have to be canoeists themselves and so it is possible to enlist parents, brothers and sisters or other volunteers.   However, be warned! In my experience it is only a matter of time before such helpers become active canoeists and in some cases instructors, thus leaving you with the problem of recruiting more helpers who are able to stay off the water and help on the bank-side.

Water Conditions

When you study the implications of some disabilities with respect to the ability of the individual to keep warm or cool, it becomes apparent that the temperature of the water is more significant that "how big is it?".

You will also have to give more consideration to the cleanliness of the water. Whilst no-one relishes the prospect of inhaling dirty water, for some people the requirement to keep unhealthy water away from their skin or from any stomas (see the chapter on medical implications) becomes very important.

Temperature/Weather

Just as the temperature of the water may have more than the usual implications for people with disabilities, so too can the weather and associated air temperature. Remember particularly the effects that wind chill and wetness has on temperature, but also the effect that exercise has on raising the temperature of the body. Consider also the effects that being in the outdoors and subjected to the effects of pollen and dust may have on people with respiratory conditions such as asthma.

Being comfortable is very important. The cold person, or the overheated person, will not enjoy your programme as much as if they were happy about their temperature. Therefore, give careful thought to your activities and equipment and good advice to the participants regarding their clothes.

CHAPTER SEVEN

PROGRAMMES - AIMS AND OBJECTIVES

Intended Outcomes

When putting your programme together, and wherever possible in consultation with those for whom the programme is intended, you will need to make decisions about what you, and the participants, wish to get out of your programme.

There are a number of principal objectives that you might have. None of them is mutually exclusive, neither should they be seen as having any particular priority.   Rather they should be viewed as potential opportunities with specific objectives in mind.

Objective - Awareness

We should be aiming to give the participants of any programme we devise an awareness of the enjoyment that can be gained from canoeing and how diverse a sport it is. Even in their first experience it is possible for the participant to experience both kayaking and canoeing, and to see that a craft may be propelled by one blade or two, by one person or by two, or more.

It is this range of craft and propulsion methods that has proved to be so beneficial in finding an appropriate branch of the sport for people with disabilities. Whatever the disability there is usually a craft, a paddle or a style of paddling that can be used, often without any adaptation of the standard, to enable success.   We will look at these craft and other resources in more detail later.

Objective - Skills

For even the briefest of sessions it is possible to introduce some canoeing skills. In fact if we are to expect people to want to try again after an introductory session, the learning of even the simplest skill gives the feeling of achievement that encourages people to want to do more. It is not necessary for skills taught to be mastered immediately. Showing someone how to get in and out of the craft may only be possible for them to achieve with considerable support from the instructor and others who will not only be assisting the entry but also maintaining the craft's stability.

Nevertheless it is worth doing rather than lifting the individual in and out without offering them the opportunity to participate in the process.

Objective - Application

All opportunities and skills lead the participant to consider the question, "Now I have this opportunity or skill, what should I do with it?"

At this point we should now be considering the possible programme processes we can use to introduce people with disabilities to canoe sport. There are many variations but essentially the process probably follows this path:-

- sampling (or "try-it") sessions
- regular fun based activities
- a recreation programme
- competition
- awards - personal
          - coaching

Whilst these programmes are not necessarily progressive we should aim to make sampling sessions open ended to encourage people to want to canoe again. Furthermore, if we make the very first experience a positive one we stand more chance of people returning to the sport and enjoying the opportunities provided.

Preparation for this needs to be thorough and carefully considered and in this respect the format for the Visitor Introduction as suggested in Chapter 5 is recommended.

PROGRAMME FORMATS

Sampling

This is an activity that all of us have undertaken at some time and probably in a variety of sports. Sometimes we are motivated to try a new sport by seeing in on television or being told about it by a friend.

Whatever the reason we often try out a sport to see if we would like it even before we seek to discover whether or not we would be any good at it.

I have mentioned previously the common misconceptions that people have about canoeing related often to poor experiences of their own in the past, or of other people who have described their own poor experiences. There is much we can do to make the first experience an enjoyable one that will not discourage the participant from wishing to try again.

To further these objectives we should adopt sensible approaches to the first experience such as:-

- preparing well and having all the appropriate equipment and resources to hand,
- finding a friendly environment
- ensuring that no-one gets unnecessarily wet,
- seeing that people enjoy themselves,
- making it clear that it is possible to enjoy the sport as a regular activity and not just as a one-off.

In providing this activity it is valuable to gather together a variety of craft, canoes, kayaks and inflatables in order to give the participants the maximum opportunity to try craft that best suit their needs. You should also try to organise as many instructors and helpers as possible to ensure that participants have the support that will give them confidence to have a go.

At this stage of participation you should be prepared for some people to join the activities but not be active in their craft, they would rather participate passively as passengers. As long as you have assured yourself that they have been given the opportunity to participate actively let them enjoy the activity as they want, many reluctant people become successful paddlers having started at this passive stage and after they have gained confidence both in their own abilities and those of their instructors.

Finally, you should be prepared for those who will want to come back and canoe or kayak again and perhaps consider it as their sport, or one of their sports. In this respect you should be able to give participants information about regular sessions to enable them to fulfil their aspirations. I feel very strongly that sampling sessions should not be offered if the provider has not considered this latter requirement very seriously. It is building false expectations among people if sampling sessions do not have the potential for regular activity.

Fun

If we give people a positive sampling session of the sport we may expect them to come back.   To many people the sport of canoeing is addressed purely as a fun activity.   Whilst we would hope that all canoeing is fun whatever the other objectives might be, for some fun and games is the key objective.

Bear in mind people who come infrequently and barely have time to re-learn the skills they have forgotten from the last time.   Give them the opportunity to enjoy the sport and progress through the acquisition of skills at their pace remembering what a major logistical exercise it might have been to get to the programme venue.

Recreation

I would suggest that once an individual has made the decision to take up canoeing, the first period of skill acquisition is similar whatever the ultimate aim might be.   Therefore, if the emphasis is initially geared to recreational canoeing, this does not preclude the opportunity to develop the basic skills for touring, expeditions or competition in addition to furthering recreational activities.

Whilst the element of enjoyment will be still important, once a person makes a decision to adopt a sport as a recreation activity she has usually made decisions that include:-

- regular commitments,
- membership of a club or organisation,
- the obtaining of some personal equipment, such as a paddle or buoyancy aid.
- the desire to learn the skills of the sport and seek opportunities to use these skills,
- a view of it being a progressive activity with certain goals in mind, such as a canoeing holiday, an expedition or to enter a race,
- the opportunity to share experiences and take part in the social life that often comes with membership.

The pace at which people will want to progress their canoeing skills will be varied. Some people will be content for some time to learn only the most basic skills necessary to assist the propulsion of a double kayak or canoe, but rely on a partner to have the expertise to keep the canoe on course. Whilst others may go solo but be content with forward and reverse paddling and turning skills, the basic minimum for maintaining a simple course.

In time, and with the right encouragement, most people will master the basic skills and move onto the more complex skills of control. At this stage the most appropriate programme to follow would be that suggested by the content of the BCU Personal Skill Awards.

These awards provide the essential strokes at graduated levels that progressively introduce all canoeing, or kayaking skills. For people with disabilities there are specific suggestion regarding the examining of these awards in Chapter 14.

It is at this level of participation, when people have made a commitment, that many exciting opportunities are possible. We will look at competition and the working towards awards, both personal and coaching, but for recreational paddling the possibilities of applying skills to go on trips or expeditions gives the paddler with mobility difficulties the often unprecedented freedom to travel relatively independently.

The canoe or kayak as a means of transport, with its wide variety of propulsion methods (including these days, and increasingly so, that of sail) offers people unique opportunities. The leader or instructor can encourage and facilitate this by giving good advice such as which club to join, what kinds of activity can be pursued, where to obtain appropriate personal equipment etc.

The arguments that surround the decision, whether to join an integrated or special needs club are discussed elsewhere, nevertheless advice from the leader or instructor at the sampling or fun sessions will be valuable in helping the individual to come to a decision.

Sub-Objectives

For many people the decision to take up a recreational activity may have at its core a number of underlying or sub-objectives. Some of these such as the social opportunities, or canoeing as a means to reach a goal, an expedition or a race, were referred to earlier. However, there are other possibilities. The desire to become physically fitter may be one, another may be the opportunity to travel independently through the countryside, an activity sometimes denied to people who rely on wheelchairs for transport.

Sometimes these sub-objectives are suggested by those people who support the individual as being valuable for the personal development of the individual. Parents, carers and social workers, sometimes have responsibility for the well-being of people who need someone to act for them as advocates or enablers.

In these situations the objectives are often related to social goals, such as developing confidence, as well as the physical ones. Discussions with the person and the parent or carer can determine the reasons behind the choice of canoeing for the recreation activity and this can assist in making the experience as fulfilling as possible for all concerned.

Competition

Not everyone who participates in a sport wants to do so competitively. However, for those that do the BCU offers a wide range of opportunities catering for the novice through to the World Championships in a wide variety of paddle sport formats.

Many of these competitions are regularly entered by people with disabilities. In fact there are probably more people with disabilities taking part in open competitions than there are taking part in competitions devised especially for disabled people.

I am aware of significant successes by paddlers with disabilities in Slalom, Sprint Racing and Marathon as well as in long distance races such as the Devizes-Westminster Race.

Whilst these people will continue to compete successfully in open competition, there are a large number who, whilst they enjoy the open events, will always be disadvantaged in such events by their disability. For these people it is desirable to develop some parallel competitions, exclusively for people with disabilities, classified in such a way that they can compete with a fair opportunity to be successful.

For those people with disabilities who wish to compete in what may be termed mainstream sport, all of the various competitions are open to them as for any other person. People taking this line will find all the help they need within the structure of the various disciplines and would be advised to contact these for further information.

Plate 7:a   *Paddler in an International 'Handykayak' Sprint*

However, for those people with disabilities who cannot, or choose not to, compete in open events it is necessary to consider alternative competitions. Canoeing, as yet, is not a Paralympic sport although in time this will probably change. Meanwhile, the BCU in collaboration with the Italian Canoe/Kayak Federation does have international competitions under the heading of *"Handykayak"*, although the BCU prefers to call this *"Paddle-ability"*. A description of this competition is given in more detail in Chapter 13.

Notwithstanding the potential future for Paddle-ability, there is a need to develop fair and equal opportunities for all people within all the competitive committees of the BCU. Such developments can only come from the committees themselves, and then only if sufficient encouragement is given to them from appropriate sources.   This encouragement should come primarily from disabled people, although there is no reason why this should not be supported by their coaches.

Experience gained from Paddle-ability should assist in the evolution of competition in the other disciplines and the expertise that exists within the BCU Coaching Scheme will further assist the development.

Expeditions

The range of expeditionary opportunities for people with disabilities is growing quickly. Expeditions that were once considered the exclusive domain of a few fit and skilful of paddlers, are now being tackled successfully by groups comprising people of all abilities.

Plate 7:b   *Expeditioning*

As yet, I am not aware of any expeditions organised exclusively by and for people with disabilities but I feel sure that it is only a matter of time before people with disabilities take the initiative.

When planning an expedition it might be appropriate to consider the Information Form details in Chapter 20.

AWARDS

Working towards awards may not be the sole programme objective but it will often provide the motivation for a sense of achievement that forms the reward for working at the development and mastery of canoeing skills.

Awards of Personal Ability

Awards can be those of personal achievement in learning and applying skills such as the BCU Star Awards, or the Touring Awards.

Whilst these awards are progressive, for some people the acquisition of all the parts necessary to achieve the award may take quite a long time. For this reason it is possible to use a "Modular" form of assessment. In this process the participants are awarded an interim certificate based on the parts rather than the whole test.

Therefore, a participant could be given a certificate for "Paddling Forward" they could then work towards a certificate for "Paddling Backwards". Over a period of time such a student would acquire all the certificates that constitute the whole of the BCU One Star Award. Whilst this process may have taken a long time the presentation of interim certificates has kept the interest alive.

Of course for some people parts of some awards may not be possible for them. This will not prevent that person from taking and receiving that award. The process for this is explained in Chapter 14.

Coaching Awards

Many people with disabilities are also able to qualify for awards which enable people to pass on their skills within the Coaching Scheme.

As long as the person is able to show that they have the skills and qualities expected of a member of the coaching scheme they are encouraged to work towards these awards.

Sometimes a person with a disability cannot assume the responsibility for the safety of the group he may be coaching. In these circumstances some sensible agreements for the working practice is agreed, such as ensuring there is always additional suitably qualified people assuming responsibility for the safety of the group.

IN CONCLUSION

The development and delivery of appropriate programmes and activities will ensure that the BCU's principle of "one Union for all regardless of ability" is maintained, and give all people equality of opportunity and participation at all levels of the sport.

Plate 7:c *A sport for everyone*

CHAPTER EIGHT

PROGRAMMES - INDIVIDUAL TARGETS

Introduction

Whatever programme is decided upon as appropriate for the people you will be paddling with, together you should determine individual targets for each person. Just as you will be treating each person as an individual so too should you treat their programme in an individual way. Therefore, in consultation with the individual these are suggestions of how you might proceed.

From Aims and Objectives decide:-

1. Intended Outcomes and any Sub-Goals.

2. Draw up a programme:-
   subdivided into Stage Targets,
   with Time Scales for each stage.

3. Always be prepared to modify, adjust and be flexible.

Case Study Example

Barry is a novice paddler. He has decided that he would like to improve his skills to the point where he can paddle his kayak on a short trip.

He has difficulties walking and getting into and out of his kayak. Upper body control is quite good and he has the potential to perform all the basic strokes, although up to this time he has not been particularly active and, therefore, is not very fit. He is still at school and receives regular physiotherapy.

From Aims and Objectives

Barry and his instructor discuss what Barry will need to achieve to realise his goal.

- To learn the skills necessary to manage his kayak appropriately.
- Be safe in his kayak, or in case of a capsize, be safe and confident in the water.
- Be strong enough to paddle the required distance.

Intended Outcomes

To paddle from the club house for 3 miles on the river to an adjacent car park where the group will be ferried back to the club house.

Sub Goals

Currently, Barry is using a club boat and club equipment. However, this means that he has to negotiate each time he comes to the club to obtain equipment. This is a good social exercise since for most of his life he has not had to share very much at all. As an incentive his mum has promised she will buy him his own boat if he achieves his goal of paddling this trip.

In the meantime Barry is saving to buy his own paddle since this is a very personal piece of equipment. Of necessity club equipment is sturdy and correspondingly rather heavy, whereas Barry would benefit from a lighter paddle adjusted to a length appropriate to him.

Objectives

- To reach the One Star level of Personal Performance.
- Work on fitness levels to be able to sustain the effort required for the trip.
- Practice capsize drills and being rescued.
- Paddle more frequently and use his paddle at home
- practice all the skills whilst sitting down.
- Barry talks to his physiotherapist about some exercise he can do to enable him to get fitter.
- Do some work to earn the money to buy his paddle.
- Draw up a progressive programme of coaching

Barry is encouraged to come to the club each week at the river session and also to attend weekly at the pool sessions.

Together with his instructor Barry decides that he should be able to reach the required standard for the trip in 10 weeks.

Stage Targets

Barry is given a weekly programme. This comprises some new targets, some previous targets that need regular practice, and occasionally a check on targets that have been mastered to ensure that they have not been forgotten.

Also included will be the acquisition of skills appropriate for Barry to be rescued safely, such as capsize drill. His instructor will be practising his rescue strategy for Barry, not with Barry initially, but with another able kayakist who can simulate Barry's disability and give valuable feedback to the instructor about the strategy as the rescue is practised. Only after this process, and when the strategy seems to be successful should Barry be involved in its rehearsal and then only in the swimming pool initially.

Whilst a draft scheme for the 10 weeks was prepared, the weekly programme was worked on a week at a time until a reasonable assessment of Barry's rate of progress could be made so that the programme moves on at an appropriate speed, not too slow thus risking boredom, and not too quickly leading to frustration.

At the appropriate time the instructor will progress those skills from the programme, that have been successfully achieved in the swimming pool, onto the river.

Finally

Throughout, the instructor will have assessed Barry's progress and modified the programme accordingly with the aim of reaching a successful conclusion. However, should it appear that the objectives will not be achieved within the ten weeks or that they will be achieved earlier than anticipated, the instructor will adjust the times scales accordingly and explain this to Barry.

The Development of Similar Strategies.

In using this model to prepare programmes for other people the following advice may be useful.

Give the weekly programme some variety. Always include elements of:-

- introducing new skills,
- practice skills for mastery,
- practice of previously mastered skills to ensure that they are not forgotten.

Balance practical work with some theory, the purposes of skills and canoeing practice can be explained to all paddlers at a level appropriate to their learning ability. Introduce the skills for safety, such as capsize and rescue, in a safe environment before progressing to the environment in which they will be necessary.

Always make the learning enjoyable, there are lots of games that can be used to make learning fun.   See the book by Dave Ruse in the bibliography.   Finally, the acquisition of skills can often be facilitated by the use of chaining.

Plate 8:a *Hands on coaching*

Chaining

Chaining is a process of linking together the various sub-skills that are a part of a complete skill. For example the forward paddling stroke, for a kayak paddler, contains the skills of:-

1. holding the paddle correctly,
2. putting the paddle into the water at the correct angle,

3. moving it through the water,
4. lifting it out at the end of the stroke,
5. repeating the stroke on the other side, and finally
6. returning the paddle to a position to begin the stroke again.

This description implies the use of an unfeathered paddle. I have introduced students to paddling with an unfeathered paddle who, having learned how to paddle successfully with this, have then successfully learned how to feather with the appropriate wrist rotation.

The pre-requisite skills are that the paddler :-

*   sits safely and balanced in the kayak,
*   uses an unfeathered paddle,
*   holds the paddle correctly.

The instructor needs to be behind the paddler being coached to adopt a hands-on approach. A good way to achieve this is to use an open canoe or an open decked two person kayak.

Forward chaining

In this process the instructor would assume a "hands on" position with the students. The student is taken through the whole stroke with the instructor leading, making sure that the student's hands are also on the paddle.

Then the instructor focuses the learning on the student performing skill 1 unassisted. Once this has been achieved the instructor replaces her hands on the paddle and leads the student through the other skills to complete the stroke, again ensuring that the student's hands remain on the paddle.

This can be repeated until the instructor feels it is appropriate to teach skill 2. After going through the whole stroke again with the student, the students performs skill 1 and is taught skill 2 to follow it. Once again the instructor then places her hands on the paddle and completes the stroke.

This can be repeated until the instructor feels it is appropriate to teach skill 3. Similarly, after going through the whole stroke again with the student, the students performs skills 1 and 2, and is taught skill 3 to follow it. Once again the instructor then places her hands on the paddle and completes the stroke.

This can be repeated until the instructor feels it is appropriate to teach the skill 4. This process is repeated until the complete stroke has been learned and the student can achieve it unaided.

Reverse chaining

In this process the instructor would again assume a "hands on" position with the students. The student is taken through the whole stroke with the instructor leading, making sure that the student's hands are also on the paddle.

Then the instructor leads the student through the stroke again, but this time stops before the final skill, skill 6 and focuses the learning of the student on performing this skill unassisted.

Once this has been achieved the instructor replaces her hands on the paddle and leads the student through the first 5 skills, again ensuring that the student's hands remain on the paddle, but leaves the student to complete the stroke by performing the last skill unaided.

This can be repeated until the instructor feels it is appropriate to teach skill 5. The instructor then leads the student through the stroke again, but this time stops before skill 5 and focuses the learning of the student on performing this skill and linking it to skill 6, unassisted.

This can be repeated until the instructor feels it is appropriate to teach skill 4. After going through the whole stroke again with the student, the instructor repeats the stroke up to skill 4, and focuses the learning of the student on performing this skill and linking it to skills 5 and 6, unassisted.

This can be repeated until the instructor feels it is appropriate to teach skill 3. This process is repeated until the complete stroke has been learned and the student can achieve it unaided.

In Conclusion

This technique can be applied to any major skill that can be broken down into sub-skills. The process was developed for people with learning disability since it contains many of the strategies valuable for skill acquisition such as repetition, reinforcement, feedback and success.

CHAPTER NINE

CRAFT and EQUIPMENT

Introduction

The use of the word "canoe" to describe craft that are either canoes or kayaks is fairly common practice in the UK.   Therefore, the words "canoe" and "canoeing" have thus far been used in this book to mean craft or a sport that could be using either canoes or kayaks, or both.

However, in this chapter the words canoe and kayak will be used specifically. In addition I will also be referring to craft that appear to be neither, yet have characteristics of both. These craft I will be calling open decked kayaks. Finally, there is a growing use of inflatable craft. I will also be making reference to these.

This chapter will look at:-

- **Craft**

- **Equipment**

- **Flexible Resources**

CRAFT DETAILS

The best advice generally can be found in Chapter 2 *"Design and Selection of Equipment"* by Frank R Goodman, in the BCU's *"Canoeing Handbook"*. With this in mind the advice in this chapter will focus upon the selection of craft as a means of making the most of the abilities of people with impairments.

There are a number of factors that need to be taken into account when considering which would be the most appropriate craft for any individual. The design of any craft is determined very largely by the purpose for which it will be used. This makes the categories of canoes and kayaks very different, but also gives rise to a wide, and sometimes confusing, variety of styles and designs within each category.

All paddlers are advised to try a number of different craft before they decide on one to buy. One of the best ways to do this is to join a club. Most clubs have a selection of craft available for members. However, it is well to remember that many clubs have a specialised membership. Members may be oriented towards canoe or kayak, flat or wild water, inland or sea, recreation or competition, or a combination of some, but probably not all, of these.

Although the coaching programme will always focus on the abilities of the individual, if those abilities are to be realised fully the choice of craft and equipment will be important.   Therefore, to avoid creating frustration that comes from trying to use unsuitable equipment some assessment of any special need must be made.

If the paddler has an impairment there may be factors of choice that need to be considered initially. For example; if balance is an issue then the craft needs to be stable, if strength or direction ability is a problem then the boat needs to have the ability to track well (go straight), if the person needs to have a "buddy" then the craft must be suitable for two people.

However, many of these initial decisions are likely to be only temporary. Given time and good coaching some of the early difficulties of balance, strength and independence may be resolved. Experience has shown that, whilst some people with disabilities may need additional considerations to enable them to begin canoeing, they have ultimately developed canoeing skills that are comparable with those of canoeists who do not have disabilities.

For this reason any use of a craft, such as an open decked kayak where the design is outside the usual specification, or any modifications of standard craft, should be seen as a temporary measure. Only when it is shown conclusively that a particular craft or modification is essential to an individual's success as a canoeist should this become the regular craft for them to use and develop skills for.

To help the paddler or the instructor identify the most appropriate craft I have listed the main types in this chapter. In the next chapter are suggestions regarding which of their characteristics are appropriate for the special needs of people with impairments.

TYPES of CRAFT

Once again let me establish that I am looking at craft with the special needs of people in mind. All of the craft described in this section would be called "general purpose" craft. Anyone who does not have a special need should study the advice in Chapter 2 of the *"Canoeing Handbook."*

Under this heading I will be looking at:-

- Construction

- Canoes

- Kayaks

- Open decked kayaks

- Inflatables

In each section I will make reference to some examples, although this does not imply a particular preference. At the time of writing I am aware of certain craft that are available and that are in use. However, new craft are developed annually and the reader should investigate the market fully to identify appropriate craft. The annual International Canoe Exhibition held in the UK during February is a good opportunity to see what is available.

Construction

For all but the inflatable craft, canoes and kayaks are made of a variety of materials. Wood, wood and fabric, glass reinforced plastic (grp), aluminium and many types of moulded plastic have all been used for production. Whilst grp is still used for many types of craft the only craft with this construction that we will consider later is the Caranoe. Although grp and aluminium are also used, versions of all the other craft are available in plastic.

There are advantages and disadvantages of plastic as a construction material. The principle disadvantages are that it is relatively heavy and that it tends to deform and ripple over time. However, as the technology improves these disadvantages are being resolved. The main advantage of plastic is that it is considered to be "friendly". That is, it is warm to the touch and has no sharp or hard edges. This friendliness is important for people with reduced skin sensation.

Plate 9:a   *The open canoe*

Canoes

Whilst canoes can have either a closed, or open deck, for this chapter I am only looking at open canoes.   The advice which will apply later for closed decked kayaks can be applied generally also to closed decked canoes.

Canoes vary in size from 4 metres to 7 metres and are capable of carrying 1 to 4 people (although there some that carry 20 paddlers). They are paddled by a single blade paddle with the paddlers either sitting or kneeling. Open canoes make excellent craft for expeditions since they are capable of carrying large amounts of equipment.

<u>Advantages</u>

- They are usually quite generous in their dimensions with large seats and room for people's legs.
- They are stable and track well.
- To increase stability it is possible to raft two or three canoes together.
- Open canoes are easy to get into and out of.
- Those capable of carrying more than one paddler enable people who cannot paddle solo to participate.
- In the event of a capsize paddlers can usually exit without even wetting their hair!

<u>Disadvantages</u>
- The seats do not give support to the sides or back.
- Sitting on the seat can cause some people to feel unstable, however when in the most stable position, sitting in the bottom of the canoe, it is impossible to paddle.

Fig 9:1   *Canoes rafted together for stability*

Examples

There are a great many craft that are suitable, both made in this country and imported. Look especially at those made from a plastic sandwich since this offers all the features of comfort with durability and flotation. It is always worth trying canoes to investigate their stability, tracking and manoeuvrability. Mobile Adventure are just one of the dealers who will give you advice regarding the most appropriate canoe for you.

Kayaks

There is a very wide range of kayaks designed for specific purposes. However, we will be considering those classified as "general purpose". Kayaks vary in size from 3 metres to 7 metres. They can be paddled solo or tandem, with the paddlers sitting and paddling with a double bladed paddle.

Kayaks can be designed to be manoeuvrable, or to track well. It is impossible to have a boat that is good at both and so most general purpose boats tend to be a compromise. With the general purpose kayak this compromise might tend towards the manoeuvrability or towards the trackability, with an element of the opposite for more flexible use.

Fig 9:2 *The double kayak*

Very manoeuvrable kayaks are designed for use on white water rivers or for sea surf. Therefore, another aspect of their design is a small cockpit to keep the water from swamping them. These kayaks have a beam wide enough to make them stable, but being short they do not track well and take some practice to paddle them in a straight line.

Those kayaks designed to go fast in a straight line are long and narrow. This makes them more difficult to manoeuvre and they tend to be rather unstable. They need practice to be paddled without the paddler falling out, especially at slow speeds. The cockpits are large to allow the knees to be bent and able to move up and down since this is more efficient for racing.

Purpose designed touring kayaks are designed to track well whilst retaining some manoeuvrability and stability. They have much larger cockpits and are consequently easier to get in and out of.

Advantages
- Kayaks are more practical than canoes for people who wish to paddle solo.
- Seats can be modified relatively easily to enable people with physical impairments to be supported.
- Stability and tracking can be improved by the addition of external, temporary modifications. These are described later.
- Double kayaks enable people who cannot paddle solo to participate with another paddler.
- Kayaks are more practical than canoes in the swimming pool.

Disadvantages
- Even kayaks with a large cockpit can pose some difficulties of entry and exit.

- Space is often limited especially for people who need room for legs that do not bend easily.

- Those made from grp (glass reinforced plastic) have to be carefully maintained to avoid loose glass fibre strands projecting. This is especially true inside the kayak where such strands are less likely to be seen and more likely to damage the legs of the user.

Examples
There are many examples of touring craft available from manufacturers. It is worth trying them to determine their stability, tracking and manoeuvrability.

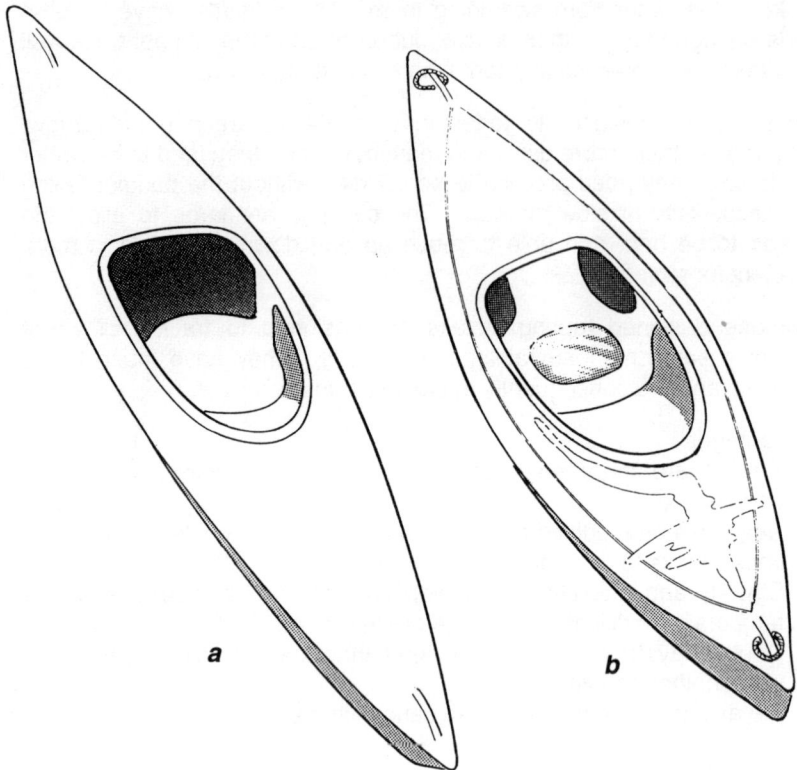

Fig 9:3a *The Poly Pippin*   **Fig 9:3b** *The Kiwi*

The Poly Pippin Fladbury Canoeing, has very good tracking, is quite quick and is very stable, has a large cockpit but the seat gives very little support and it does not turn easily.

The Kiwi, from Perception, has good tracking and is manoeuvrable but is not very quick and could be tiring on long trips, although the seat is very comfortable and gives excellent support. It is very stable with a large cockpit. It also has a small extra seat for a child that can be fitted to both the singe seat and double seat versions.

Both of these craft are made from plastic.

a   b

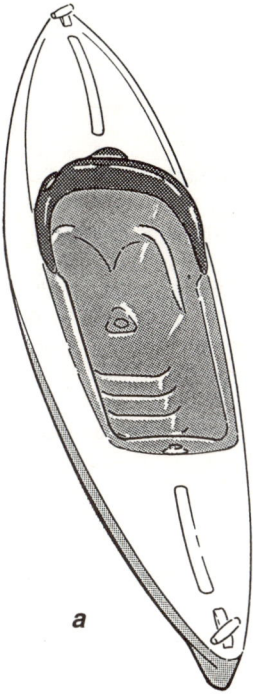

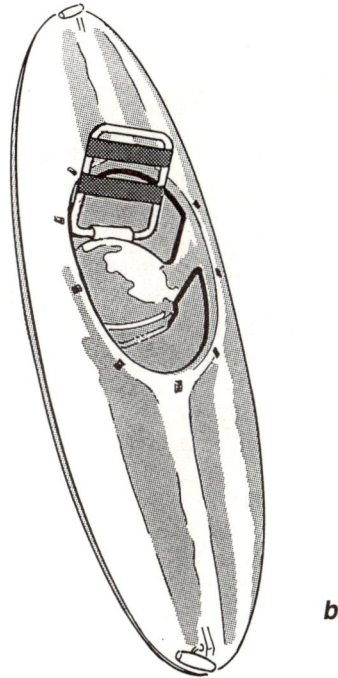

Fig 9:4a The Rob Roy   **Fig 9:4b** The Caranoe

The Caranoe, from Valley Canoe Products, has been a popular kayak for many years.   It is extremely stable with good tracking and manoeuvrability. Whilst the seat does not offer much support backrests are easily fitted. Although the Caranoe is made from grp the cockpit edge is rolled inwards which makes getting in and out comfortable. However, this feature also means that a spray deck can only be fitted by means of Velcro tabs which makes it less secure than one fitted to a cockpit rim. A rim can be fitted but this reduces the previously friendly inward rolled edge.

Another disadvantage of the Caranoe is that it has come to be known as a kayak for people with disabilities. Indeed its unusual shape for a kayak draws attention to its difference. This is not conducive to a policy of integration and avoiding "special" attention.   Nevertheless, it is an excellent kayak with excellent characteristics for paddlers in the early stages of skill development.

Open Decked Kayaks

These kayaks are either those designed for sea surfing or for general leisure use.   In this country the open deck surf kayak is a very specialised craft and not appropriate for consideration in this section.

The open decked leisure kayak is sat on, rather than in, making entry and exit easy.   They are usually a reasonable compromise between trackability and manoeuvrability being neither very good or very bad at either. Their width makes them quite stable in use.

Open decked kayaks are usually paddled with a double blade paddle from a sitting position.

Advantages
• Having an open deck makes them very suitable for use in the swimming pool, or in sheltered waters when capsizing of the individual is a high risk.
• Not having their legs inside the boat gives many people more confidence and fewer fears about being trapped during a capsize.

Disadvantages
• Bracing the body for some paddle strokes is difficult since the bottom and the heels are the only contact points.
• Being open these kayaks do not offer much protection from cold, wet or wind to the user.
• Sitting in a balanced position is difficult and putting in modifications for extra support is hard since there are few points for fixing or wedging such aids.

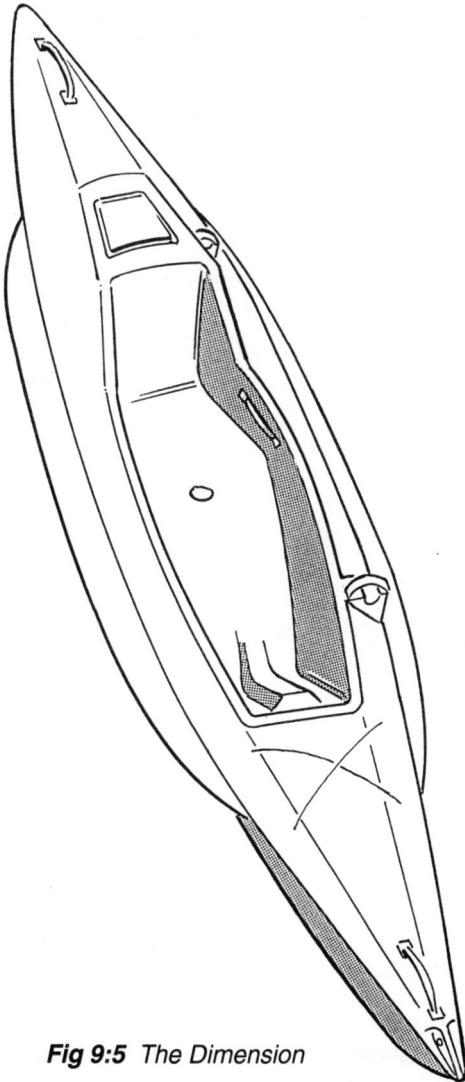

Fig 9:5 *The Dimension*

Examples

The Rob Roy, from Piranha, is probably the most well known of these craft. (Fig 9:4a). It has a double skin construction which means it is unsinkable. If it is capsized it can simply be rotated in the water to empty it. There is an optional backrest which is essential for anyone who needs back or side support. The footrests provision is rather inadequate. The improved version has a keel which helps with tracking. However, it should be considered a fun craft, best suited to the swimming pool and not extensive open water use.

Other open kayaks, such as the Dimension, are available, most from North America. However, because they have to be imported they tend to be rather expensive. Plastimo import many of these kayaks.

Inflatables

Inflatable craft are usually of two main types. Large rafts for 6 to 10 people or smaller rafts for 2 or 3 people. They are paddled with single blades. Large rafts are usually paddled from a sitting position. Smaller rafts may be paddled either sitting or kneeling and using either single or double bladed paddles.

Plate 9:b *Rafting*

The majority of rafts are very manoeuvrable and stable. Small long rafts where the paddlers sit in line astern track better than those with a much smaller length to beam ratio.

Large rafts can accommodate inexperienced paddlers but do need experienced paddlers in control and the helm (the person who steers) must be taken by someone qualified especially on white water.

Advantages

- There are no sharp edges and the tubes from which they are constructed are both warm, soft and capable of giving support.

- Many people can paddle together, giving the opportunity for those who cannot paddle well to be supported by others who can. However, all those in a raft can contribute to the manoeuvring.

Disadvantages

- Giving support to people with balancing problems is not possible unless they sit on the floor of the raft. However from this position it is impossible to paddle.

Fig 9:6 *The Rapid Runner*

Examples

Inflatables are expensive and therefore usually purchased by large organisations or commercial groups. However, being largely handmade it is possible to have a raft built to an individual specification without a significant increase in cost. Anyone contemplating a purchase would be well advised to consult with a manufacturer, and other raft users, before making a decision about designs and what type to purchase.

EQUIPMENT

Whilst it is now true that a number of manufacturers have recognised the need to develop resources that are accessible to people with disabilities, the primary objective for everyone is to use equipment and resources that are standard.

In this way people with disabilities have access to mainstream equipment without incurring the extra costs that are often associated with specialised equipment.

This also facilitates the objectives of the instructor, when considering the aspirations of the student, whatever the ability or disability. Together they can explore the possibilities offered by what is these days a very wide range of styles and types of equipment.

Equipment Details

In this section I will be looking at:-
* Clothing
* Buoyancy Aids and Life-jackets
* Paddles
* Helmets
* Spraydecks

Clothing

The need

The need for clothing appropriate to the circumstances is very important for all canoeists. When people with disabilities are canoeing there may also be additional considerations to be made with respect to comfort and protection.

The chapter on the implications of impairments will describe the need for skin care and warmth for some people, this has an obvious influence on the selection of clothing.

The principle need for all participants in this country is to ensure that they do not get cold. It is especially important to provide protection for the upper part of the body which has less protection than the lower part when in a kayak, similarly, but to a lesser extent, in a canoe. At the same time it is necessary for clothing to give freedom of movement to allow the individual to paddle.

Consideration must also be given to changes in temperature. Not only those which are a result of the weather, temperature and wind, but those changes of the body temperature of the individual between paddling and resting. In the swimming pool, or on those rare occasions outdoors when warmth is not a problem, many paddlers will still need some protection to the skin.

A clothing list

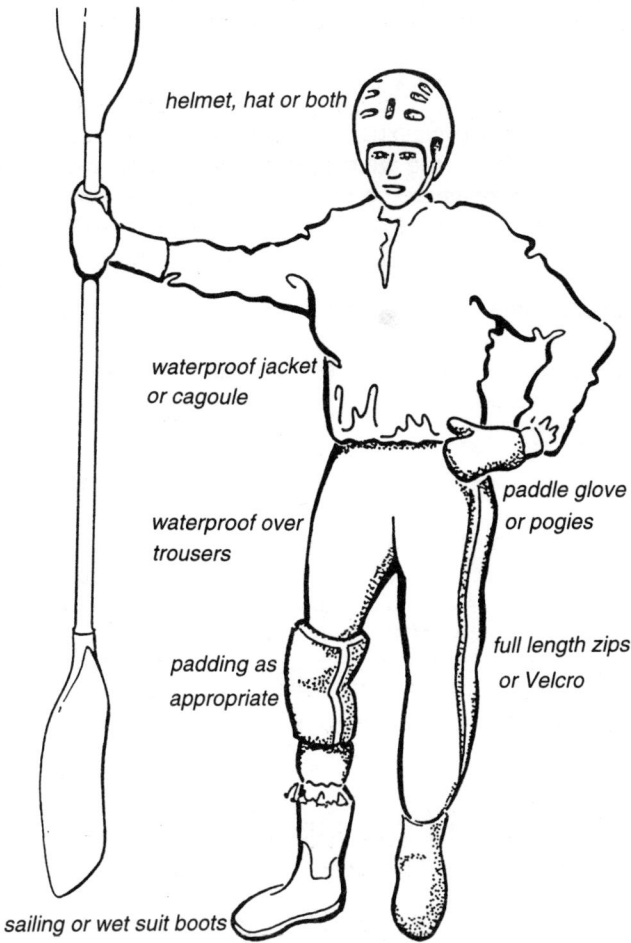

helmet, hat or both

waterproof jacket
or cagoule

paddle glove
or pogies

waterproof over
trousers

padding as
appropriate

full length zips
or Velcro

sailing or wet suit boots

It is always valuable to give potential paddlers a clothing list with suggestions about appropriate and suitable clothing. The first experience can be ruined if the person is not dressed properly and is uncomfortable and cold. Furthermore, the possibility of undetected hypothermia is higher for people who have reduced sensation in their limbs since this impairment may mask symptoms such as shivering or feeling cold.

Fig 9:7 Clothing

When it is warm a T shirt, shorts and footwear may be appropriate. However, for those people who need to take care of their skin, lightweight long trousers will be better than shorts. Footwear is essential both in and out of the craft.

Clothing worn in addition to the above really needs to provide two things:-

• A warm insulating layer to keep body heat in. Several thin layers of clothing are preferable to one thick layer. This makes for less bulk and easier movement. It also allows for the removal of a layer if the person overheats.

• A waterproof/windproof layer to keep the cold and wet out.

Many manufacturers now produce clothing made from fleecy or furry fibrepile materials.   These fabrics are warm to wear and dry quickly, although even when wet they retain some warmth.   They have some elasticity which makes them easy to get on and off.   They can also be fitted with zips, or Velcro fastenings to make changing even easier.

On top of this a waterproof jacket to keep the wet and the wind out is important if the inner layer is to work efficiently. This should be generously cut to ease taking on and off, rather than having zips which can let in wet and wind. There are some fabrics that allow condensation to escape whilst keeping the wet out.

Trousers are also obtainable in fibrepile materials.   For comfort it is better to have salopettes.   This design has a high front with braces to keep them up.   They are more comfortable than trousers with a waist fitting especially when sitting down.   Look also for those with a generous leg width or which have long zips in the legs if the wearer has an impairment which affects the mobility of the lower body.

Some manufactures, such as Buffalo and Chang, have produced garments than combine a fibrepile lining with a waterproof outer layer. Some of these also have long zips to make changing easier.

In cold weather an additional underlayer with long sleeves and legs can be worn.   Modern synthetic fibres have the ability to draw perspiration away from the body thus reducing the chilling effect of wet skin.

When selecting clothing, wool is a good fibre but cotton should be avoided.   On the whole synthetic fibres provide the most suitable garments since they stay warm even if wet, and dry out quickly.

Remember that a buoyancy aid will also give some warmth to the torso area of the body.

<u>Wet Suits</u>

Wet suits are also very popular with recreational paddlers.   These are close fitting garments made of a synthetic rubber. They are excellent if the paddler is to get very wet since they trap warm air against the skin. They are made of fairly thick spongy material which does have the additional advantage of providing protection from minor knocks and abrasion. They also increase the buoyancy if in the water.

However, they are difficult to get on and off and do need to fit well to be effective, although it is relatively easy to have extra zips put into wet suits. Anyone considering a wet suit should investigate their ability to get in and out of one before buying.   People wearing a stoma bag might find difficulties with a wet suit due to its tight fit.

Dry Suits

Dry suits work by keeping water away from the body completely. To do this they have very tight cuffs at the necks, wrists and ankles. They are fairly easy to put on since the usual closure is a long zip across the shoulders. They offer good protection with easy of movement and generally unrestricted use of a stoma bag. However, they are very expensive and not the kind of item to buy unless you anticipate using it frequently.

Footwear "footwear"

Footwear can vary a great deal. Its purpose is to protect the feet when walking and sitting in the boat, and also to keep the feet warm. Keeping the feet warm is relatively easy. Neoprene, fibrepile, or wool socks with training shoes or tennis shoes that have a good gripping sole work well. Some of the modern sailing boots with draw string tops are also warm and comfortable. These boots should not be confused with traditional Wellington boots which are not suitable.

Hats

A hat is valuable since keeping the head warm is very important; a large percentage of the body's heat can be lost through the head. Hats also help to keep the head dry in the rain or spray.

Of equal importance is the use of a hat to protect from the sun and keep the head cool, and subsequently help to cool the body.

Gloves

Similarly, the hands should be kept warm. Wearing gloves is not easy for wet activities, there are very few that keep the hands warm and allow a good grip on the paddle. Some paddlers have found washing-up gloves to be effective.

The most effective covering for the hands are paddle mitts. These are nylon covers that loosely enclose the hands and the paddle shaft in one, fastening with Velcro. They keep the hands fairly dry, but of more importance they protect from the wind. For extra protection that can also be lined with fibrepile.

Buoyancy Aids and Life-jackets

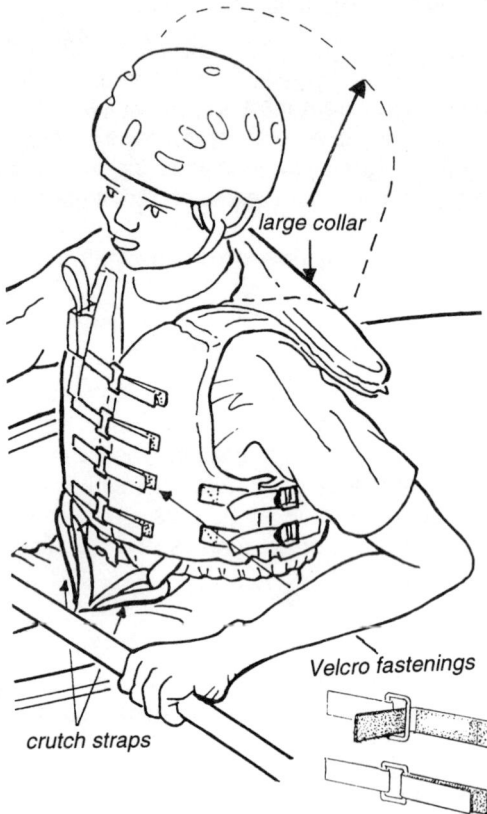

Fig 9:8 Buoyancy aid

Paddlers on open water, and sometimes in the swimming pool, should wear a buoyancy aid or life-jacket, the fitting of which should be checked by a qualified leader, since even the best aid is useless if not fitted correctly. A buoyancy aid should fit close to the body. Too loose and it will ride up in the water and too tight it will restrict movement.

Normally canoeists should be able to swim 50 metres in light clothing. However, discretion may be exercised in accordance with the leader's training and experience for disabled people. Some non-swimmers may be safely introduced to canoeing by trained instructors, in a controlled environment, as a means of encouraging water confidence. The wearing of a buoyancy aid is essential at all times, both on and off the water, for non swimmers.

The specification

Life-jackets to B.S.I. 3595/81 or buoyancy aids approved B.M.I.F. or

B.C.U./B.C.M.A. Standard B.A. 83 are normally suitable, although the new European Standards *CE* Mark will soon be obligatory. You should look for the CE mark and the *50 Newtons* as the standard.

On open water, the sea, you should wear a life-jacket. This has built-in buoyancy and in an emergency further buoyancy can be added by putting air into the life-jacket. (CE 150N)

If you have epilepsy it is advisable to wear, in addition to a CE 100N buoyancy aid, a life-jacket that will be automatically inflated by a CO_2 bottle to an additional 150N should you fall into the water. This is because a buoyancy aid is not self righting, whereas the life-jacket is. For further information about this see Chapter 17.

Fig 9:9 a & b   The CO_2 Buoyancy Aid

Implications

Wearing a buoyancy aid or life-jacket affects the attitude of the person in the water. To be able to swim wearing either requires a specific technique. For people with physical impairments it is advisable for them to experience being in the water with a buoyancy aid in the safety of the swimming pool so that they can accustom themselves to the feel and effect.

Geoff Smedley   Canoeing for Disabled People

Anyone wearing a wet suit or clothing that makes the legs buoyant will generally float on their backs more easily than on their front.

Features

Buoyancy aids come in a wide variety of styles.   Some features are particularly useful for people with disabilities.

Slab buoyancy where a single piece of buoyancy foam makes up the back of the aid is especially useful for people who need support to their back.

Zips can make it easier to take the aid on and off. However, there are Velcro or buckles that snap together that may be easier for people who find zips difficult to manage. Zips can be made easier to manage if large pull rings or balls are fitted to the slider and bottom of the zip for more grip.

Collars give people in the water a feeling of security and confidence. They also reduce the effects of waves which might otherwise splash over the person's face.

To help the aid fit more comfortably, adjustable side straps and crutch straps are useful. This is particularly true for people who have physical impairment which means their spine is bent or irregular.

Paddles

The paddle is essentially a blade which goes into the water to propel the craft and a shaft onto which the blade is fixed. In general, canoes have a paddle with a single blade on one end of the shaft and a hand grip at the other end, whilst kayak paddles have a shaft with a blade at each end.

For something which is comparatively simple in concept there is a bewildering range and variety of paddle combinations available. Blade shape, size and contour can vary with the shaft thickness, length and shape, along with choices of materials affecting strength, flexibility and weight.

This potential variety can be used to effect when trying to find the most suitable paddle for any individual.   This selection is illustrated in the next chapter. At this stage the best advice is for the paddler to select the paddle appropriate to the task. The instructor is the best person to advise on features such as length, weight and shape.

Thereafter, the paddler should try as many different types as possible to see which is the most comfortable and effective.

Length

David Train in Chapter 7 of *"The Canoeing Handbook"* gives the following advice.

> *For general use or touring, the usual length for a paddle is determined by standing up with the paddle vertical. For a kayak paddle the arm is fully extended upwards to the paddle blade with the fingers just curling over the tip of the blade. For a canoe paddle the handle reaches the chin of the standing paddler.*

Ideally the length of the paddle is also determined by the craft to be paddled, but for a paddler with a physical disability these recommendations have to be flexible; for example to accommodate people whose lower body is shorter than would be expected for the upper body length.

A longer than usual paddle can be useful when people need to:-

- Give weaker muscles more leverage.
- Compensate for restricted arm movement by giving more reach.
- Allow more reach when the seat has been lowered for stability.

However, do not use paddles that are too long since there is a point at which they become unwieldy.

Weight

Paddles made of lighter materials are useful when people:-

- Have weaker muscles.
- Get tired easily.

However, lightweight materials are usually more expensive. Making paddles lighter by reducing their size also makes them weaker. Paddles lightened in this way need clear identification to avoid them being broken by a stronger paddler.

Shape

Smaller blade areas are useful:-

* For people who have weaker muscles or who tire easily.
* Where the wind effect may be significant.
* For people who have arm, hand or wrist impairments

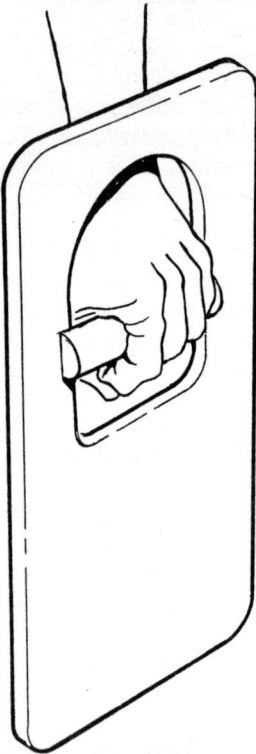

Fig 9:10 Hand Paddles

Feather

Traditionally, kayak paddles are "feathered" that is the blades are set at 90 degrees to each other. This requires the paddler to rotate the paddle with the wrist for each stroke. However, even amongst the serious competition fraternity this tradition has been challenged and paddles with a feather as low as 50 degrees may be seen. For beginners of all abilities I believe early success in paddling can be achieved by using an unfeathered paddle.

The use of jointed paddles makes feathering or unfeathering a paddle quite easy. Some joints, such as that produced by Ainsworth, are infinitely adjustable giving great flexibility of use.insworth paddle joint"

Removing or reducing the angle of the feather is valuable for people who:-

* Have hand or wrist impairments.
* Have weak muscles or tire easily.
* Have difficulty in co-ordinating the wrist action for feathering.

Special Paddles

Some people have found it advantageous to use unconventional paddles. Of these the most commonly used are the hand paddles. These are quite simply wooden paddle blades modified so that they are gripped by the hand.

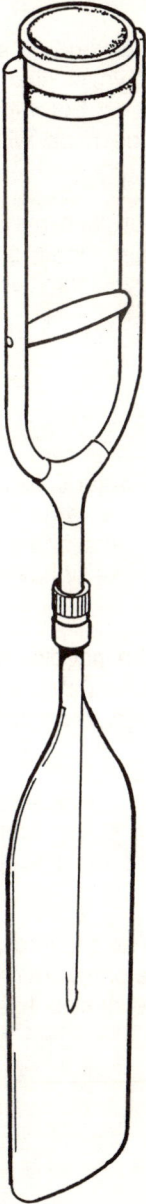

They are suitable for people who have difficulty in co-ordinating the use of a double blade paddle, for those people who find even a light weight paddle difficult to manage, and for people who find the best position for them is kneeling on their haunches. The comfort and weight are variable by the use of different materials for construction and by appropriate padding.

Commercial versions of hand paddles are made by some sailing dinghy manufacturers as emergency aids in breakdown or no wind situations.

Another adaptation involves the addition of a paddle blade to a conventional medical crutch. This enables someone with one arm to paddle. Best suited for canoe use, the length and the pitch of the blade needs to be adjusted to the individual.   "crutch paddle"

However, length adjustment can be retained from the original crutch whilst a paddle joint such as that made by Ainsworth Paddles can be use to vary the pitch.

A more comprehensive description of the various features available for paddles is included in the next chapter which looks at suggestions for matching resources to individual needs.

Fig 9:11 Crutch paddle

Helmets

It is essential to wear a safety helmet when on white water and on surf. The purpose of the helmet is to protect the head, however, like the buoyancy aid it can be useless if not fitted correctly.   Sometimes helmets are worn when there is a danger of hitting the head with a paddle or another boat when playing games.

If you decide that a helmet is appropriate for a person who may be more at risk because of a particular impairment, do ensure that in doing so you are not making this person more conspicuous in situations where no-one else is wearing a helmet.

Spraydecks

A spraydeck is worn to stop the kayak swamping, from water splashing over the deck into the cockpit, when paddling it on the sea, large lakes with waves or white water rivers. Some canoes and rafts and most kayaks, with the exception of open deck kayaks are capable of having a spraydeck fitted.

Whilst they do add considerably to the comfort of the paddler they should only be used when the paddler is capable of making a safe exit from the craft. For this it is usually necessary for the paddler to practice the capsize drill, preferably in the swimming pool initially.

To assist in the removal of the spraydeck, it should have a release loop, which must be large enough for the hand to grasp and easily found if upside down, which will break the seal on the cockpit rim and allow it to be removed.

Spraydecks, such as that fitted to the Caranoe, can also be secured with Velcro. When this is done do ensure that the "loop" side of the Velcro is attached to the deck rather than the "hook" side since the hooks are more abrasive on the skin.

Flexible Resources

Many craft that are suitable for people with disabilities are also suitable for people who do not have disabilities. Open canoes have great potential use by all groups including families. The Poly Pippin is a versatile kayak for beginners but also for K1 and C1 sprint training. The Kiwi 1 and 2 are very flexible in use being suitable for beginners, short trips and families.

Split paddles are an obvious illustration of equipment that is flexible in use being either feathered or unfeathered.

Buoyancy aids can also be purchased with adjustable side straps that can be used as standard aids by canoeists within a range of sizes yet still offer the ability to adapt to the needs of canoeists with disabilities.

Whenever choosing equipment there is value in selecting that which gives the greatest benefit to the most people likely to use it whatever their ability or disability.

Remember also that most people, whilst they may start their paddling in a stable, good tracking craft, may want to change to a more specialist craft that possesses neither of these characteristics. Therefore, beware of building up a fleet of craft that are only suitable for beginners, build into your range of craft the potential for progression.

Finally

Bear in mind that this chapter has covered the basic requirements. Some people will need to have their equipment adapted or modified to meet their specific needs. These are featured in the next chapter

Plate 9:c   *The Caranoe and spraydeck*

CHAPTER TEN

FUNCTIONAL ADAPTATIONS or MODIFICATIONS

Introduction

This chapter looks at examples of functional impairments for people with disabilities and makes suggestions regarding potential craft and equipment with adaptations and modifications that can be made. However, whilst it looks at a number of functional impairments it is impossible to cover all the possible combinations. Many people will have a complexity of impairments which necessitate the prioritising of the needs and then a search for the best possible match from the suggestions. Therefore, someone with a leg amputation may need to consider getting in and out, balancing and rescues, in addition to their specific needs in terms of canoeing with one leg.

The models use are based largely on function and not the medical condition. Information about the latter is covered in Chapters 11 and 12 to be studied as appropriate.

Furthermore, no particular coaching advice is given in this section. Readers should refer to:-

- Chapters 7 and 8 for general information,

- Chapter 11 for information about people with;
  > appliances
  > hearing impairments,
  > sensory impairments,

- Chapter 11 also considers the implications of;
  > asthma,
  > diabetes,
  > epilepsy.
  > medication side effects

- Chapter 12 for information about people with impaired behaviour.

- Chapter 17 for information about programmes for people with epilepsy,

- Chapter 18 for people with learning difficulty.

Use this information in conjunction with the following suggestions.

A Cautionary Note on Adaptations and Modifications

Only if the special needs of the individual are such that the standard equipment is inappropriate should modifications or adaptations be considered. Even when such changes are made they should be as temporary as possible.

It has been shown that, whilst such changes are important at the early stages of the sport, many people learn how to develop the skills to manage without them and progress to standard equipment.

A simple illustration of this is the use of unfeathered paddles for early coaching. These take the strain from weak wrists or remove the additional complication of rotation to present the feathered blade at the right angle, but as strength or skills develop the paddler will often be able to progress to the more usual feathered paddle.

CONTENT

- This section will look at the following functional impairments:-

- Unfounded anxiety

- Getting in an out of the craft   - upper body impairment
-                                      - lower body impairment

- Sitting without support

- Maintaining balance

- Directional Stability

- Difficulties when capsizing and exiting

- Difficulty holding a paddle

- Lack of strength   - upper body
                         - lower body

Unfounded Anxiety

I am grateful to Puffin Pocock for drawing my attention to this effect and for suggesting some of the strategies described.

Canoeing for Disabled People   Geoff Smedley

As has been mentioned previously there still exists with some people a mythology that associates all canoeing or kayaking with getting wet. Furthermore, some people with disabilities have been subjected to the opinion that sports such as canoeing are hazardous and therefore generally unsuitable for them.

For these reasons, people who come to canoeing with some of these concerns may develop a functional impairment derived from their individual perceptions of the situation and not the reality. For example, some people have a fear of capsize, which they have come to believe is synonymous with canoeing, this causes them to be anxious irrespective of the fact that they may be in a very stable craft. Whilst this, or any other unfounded anxiety, remains it will be difficult to progress any participation or coaching for these people.

The sensitive instructor should address this anxiety and respect the concerns whilst trying to alleviate them. The aim must be to identify the fear, and its basis, and then present persuasive arguments or demonstrations that show the basis of the anxiety is unfounded.   If persuasion or demonstration is not sufficient then another strategy such as distraction may be useful.

Sometimes, by drawing the attention of the individual to another aspect of the experience they will "forget" the anxiety in the effort of addressing the new focus. After a period of time their attention may return to the original situation with such reassurance as "see, you can do it" or "that all seems OK now".   Care must be taken to ensure that these reassurances are seen to be genuine acknowledgements of achievement and not just patronising comments.

Sometimes, the anxiety may reappear, and the instructor may need to repeat this strategy a number of times until it is completely alleviated.

Getting in and out - General

The first consideration must be the design of craft to be used. Whilst many people will be able to choose from any of the craft mentioned in the previous chapter, some people may not be able to get into and out of some closed deck kayaks without compromising their safety when on the water. Difficulty getting in could indicate difficulties in getting out in the event of a capsize. Although it may be appropriate to consider that when upside down gravity will assist exiting, many of the capsize problems occur before the craft reaches the upside down position and when paddlers try to exit at any of the intermediate stages.

To establish confidence and safe practice, it is recommended that people who have difficulties getting in and out should also practice capsize drills in the warmth and safety of the swimming pool before going on open water.

There are a number of suggestions for aids and support to help someone to get in and out of their craft in Chapter 16. However, most of these involve the use of specific, and often static, resources such as hoists.   Thus the paddler can only leave from, and return to, the same place.

The following are suggestions for the individual or the modification of their craft that require only minimal resources and can be achieved virtually anywhere.

<u>Additional Support</u>

It is often helpful if, in addition to a steadying hand on the bank side, a second canoe or kayak is placed on the water parallel to the first canoe or kayak so that a helper can support the paddlers craft from the water side.

<u>Handles</u>

Handles or straps can be fitted at appropriate points on the canoe or kayak for the person to pull, or push, against. These can be made from domestic plastic handles or constructed from foam blocks. Take care not to put them where they will get in the way during paddling or when exiting in a capsize.   Cover or pad any fittings on the inside of the craft.

<u>"Seal" Launches</u>

The person can be helped into their craft whilst on the bank and then they and the craft slid into the water. With appropriate end loops this process can be repeated for getting out.

Waxing the hull of the boat, or using a sheets of plastic, or old carpet under the hull makes it easier to launch and retrieve the boat and also reduces wear and tear on the hull.   It is sometimes easier to launch the boat in reverse.

Alternatively, if the paddler has some short handles, such as shortened ski sticks, they can propel themselves into the water. However, these will probably not be sufficient for assisting an exit from the water.

A number of paddlers with disabilities I know get into their kayak whilst on the bank and with it parallel to the water.   They then launch themselves sideways into the water with a strong support stroke.

Fig 10:1 *The "seal" launch*

Reinforcing the rear deck of the kayak is often necessary so that people can use this as a midpoint in the transfer from bank to seat.

If the person is transferring from a wheelchair to the craft:-

• Try to do this with the craft on the bank.

• Position the wheelchair close to the craft.

• Place a stool or similar (old plastic milk crates are quite good) to give a half way level between the wheelchair and craft to reduce the height difference. The person can then make the transfer in two stages.   Steve Devlin has used "Nautibins", these have the additional value of also being good for storage.

- Cover this stool and the rear of the kayak with padding or towels.

- Ask the person in the wheelchair how best you can support them during the transfer. They will be able to advise you on what they can do and what they need assistance with. If you are going to support them take great care not to hurt the person by gripping too hard, or by squashing them or possibly their stoma bag.

- Be aware also of the need to protect yourself and do not strain your back.

- Follow the advice for lifts and transfers outlined in Chapter 16.

All strategies should be practised in safe comfortable situations.

Getting in and out - Upper body impairment

The main difficulty here is that of maintaining balance and the stability of the canoe (or kayak). Stability is improved if the canoe is supported by another craft on the water side and a "transfer board" (a plank with a smooth surface and edges about 40 cm wide and 170 cm long) positioned between the paddler's canoe and the bank.

The paddler sits on this and slides along until they can slide forward into their seat.   This method gives some stability and the legs can sometimes be used to assist the movement.   Make sure that the board is held very steady during this operation.   There is more information about transfer boards in Chapter 19.

Getting in and out - Lower body impairments

Rolling in and out

Getting into a kayak can be quite difficult.   Whilst the best solution is to use a stable kayak with a large cockpit the following method is successful in many cases where the paddler is using a kayak with a smaller cockpit. By placing a carrymat, blanket or towels on the ground beside and on the rear deck of a kayak, the person can roll in.

The following method was devised by a young lady with Spina Bifida.

- The movement starts with the paddler sitting (sometimes with support from behind) on the bank or landing stage, facing the same way and parallel to the kayak.

- The legs are moved from the hips until they are in the kayak.

- The paddler then lies back (your help may be required to lower the paddler until the back is on the ground).

- The paddler then rolls over towards the kayak until face down on the rear deck.

- From this position the roll continues through 360 degrees until the paddler faces upwards.

- The paddler then pulls forward on the cockpit rim, lowering the hips into the seat and bringing the body upright.

- Finally the legs are adjusted in the kayak.

- The exit from the kayak is much the same in reverse. However, this time gravity is not there to help and some assistance may be required.

Sitting without support

The seated position

Much of the advice in this chapter has at its core the need for the person to be seated correctly. Since this need will be referred to several times it is described here for reference.

Support

The person may need support to the back, or to the side or both. Not being secure in the seat makes paddling difficult and the feeling of insecurity can add to anxiety levels.

A basic way to stop people slipping forward is to ensure that the seat is tilted backwards slightly. The seat can also be covered with a thin layer of closed cell foam. This is also a useful strategy to make the seat warmer and more comfortable.

The aim is to make the person secure and stable without compromising their ability to exit the craft in an emergency. However, if the problem is severe and the person needs to be in a seat that replicates the support of their wheelchair it may have straps to keep the spine upright. It is generally not advisable to strap anyone into a craft that could capsize, unless the straps are of a quick release type. There is more information about these straps in the section *"Staying in the kayak"*. If quick release straps are not practical, then two or three canoes, tied together in a catamaran or trimaran, constructs a stable craft that is virtually impossible to capsize.

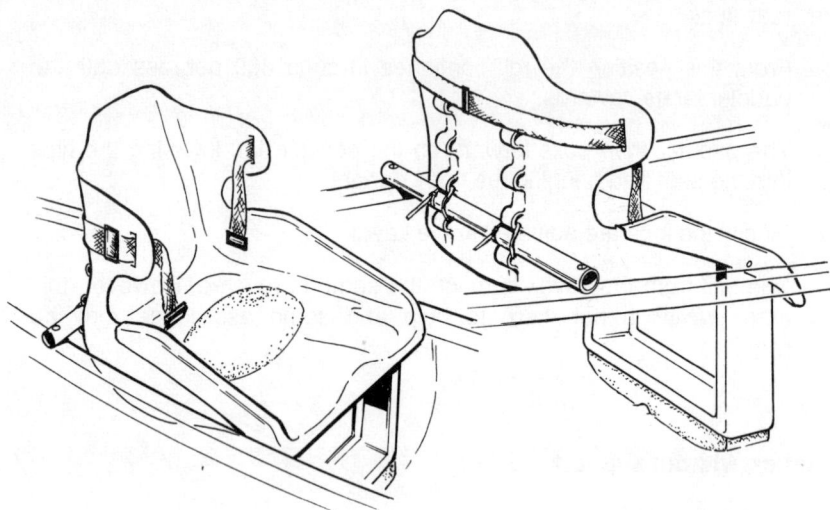

Fig 10:2 *Steve Derwin's backrest*

Steve Derwin, a BCU Senior Instructor with paraplegia, has been assisting with the development of a canoe seat that gives support to someone with spinal damage high in the thoracic region. It does require the person to be strapped in and therefore can only be recommended for use as in the previous paragraph or by someone who is a very competent paddler. Again the use of quick release straps is to be advised.

Backrests - Kayaks

Some kayaks can be supplied with backstraps. However these usually only give minimal support and something longer that reaches further up the back is usually needed.

A backrest comprising of an aluminium frame and webbing straps can be fitted behind the seat on some craft. The Caranoe can be supplied with this. Whilst it gives excellent support, because it is fixed into the kayak it can get in the way when helping someone in who needs to use the rear deck as a staging point for entry or exit.

A moveable backrest made from buoyancy foam is also available from Valley Canoe Products.(*Fig 10:3b*) Although made for the Caranoe I have found that it fits most kayaks with little or no modification. This backrest slides in after the paddler is seated and stays in position by wedging behind the seat and in front of the cockpit.

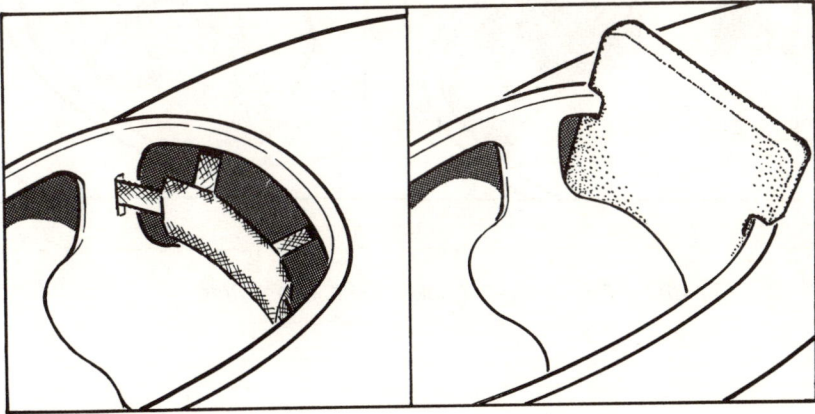

Fig 10:3a *Kayak backstrap*   **Fig 10:3b** *Foam backrest*

In the event of a capsize this backrest will drop out. Therefore, it is advisable to have it secured to the kayak by a short length of line to avoid it floating away or being blown away and lost.

Other styles of backrest are also illustrated, some being as simple as a swimming float.

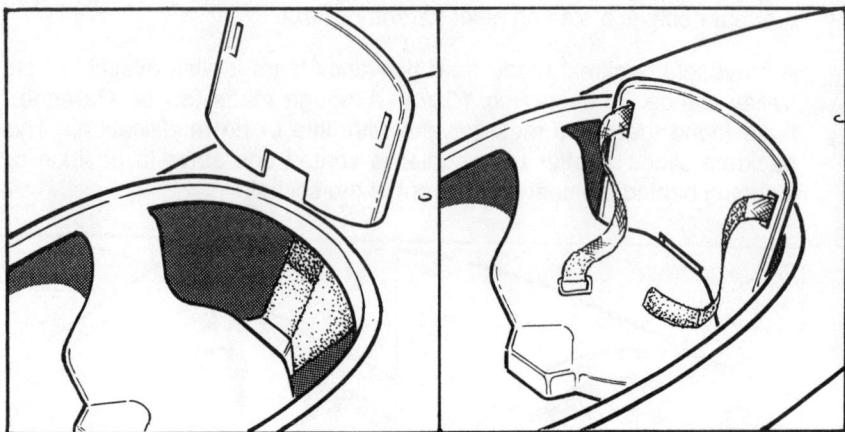

Fig 10:4 a & b *A slip-in backrest with chest strap.*

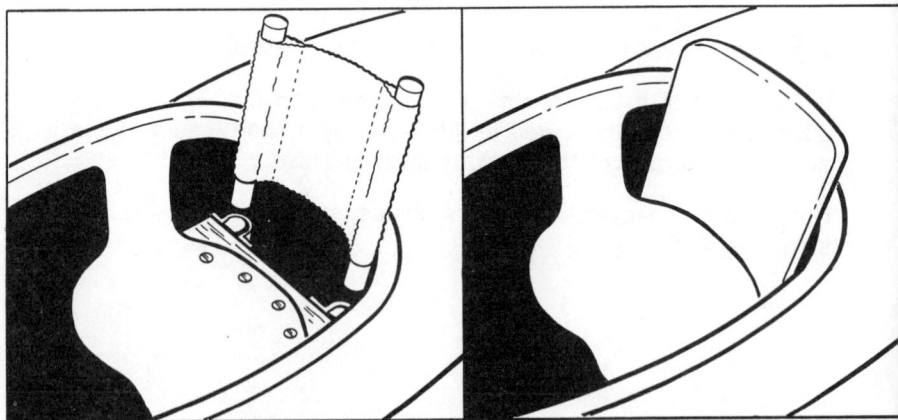

Fig 10:5a *Simple frame backrest* **Fig 10:5b** *Swimming float backrest*

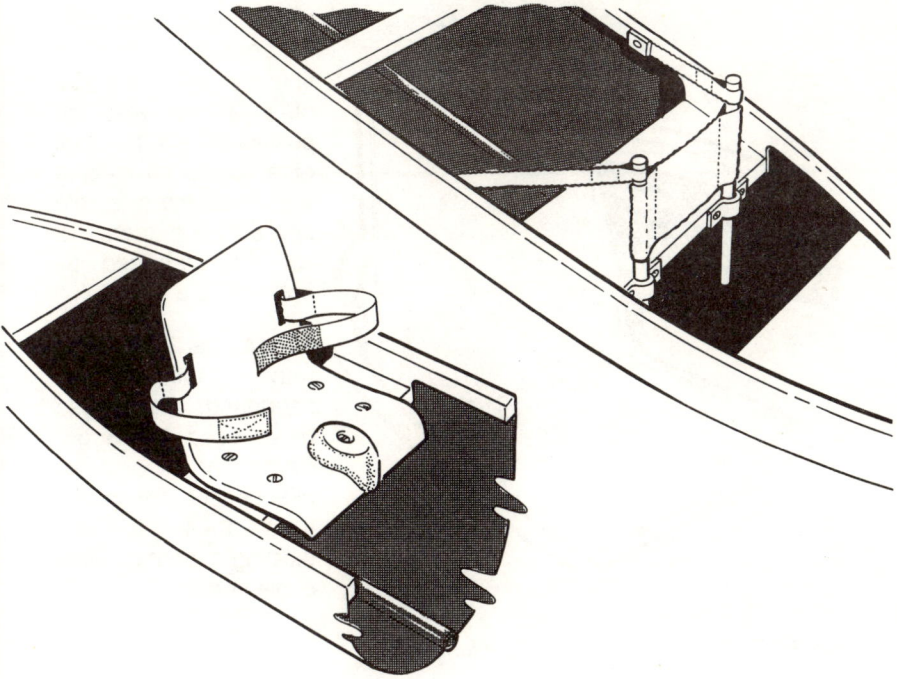

Fig 10:6 a & b *Backrests for open canoes*

<u>Backrests - Canoes</u>

Backrests for canoes are more easily available commercially. One such is made by Coleman to slip onto virtually any canoe seat. Note that this, and similar seats, will not withstand being leaned back into with any weight. To avoid collapse, it may be necessary to position an extra thwart behind the backrest, or add some bracing from the backrest to the gunwale.

Many people use the moulded plastic seat and combined backrest that comes on a metal frame for seating use in institutions such as schools. Removing the metal legs leaves a very serviceable seat and backrest which can easily be bolted to the existing seat of a canoe.

I have also seen this kind of seat modified to fit in a kayak. This type of seat can also be positioned on the hull of a canoe for people who feel more stable lower in the craft. It can be stabilised by bolting it to a thwart.

Plastic garden seats, with the legs shortened, have also been used by Roger Drummond, an experienced coach. He fixes them to the existing seats with cable ties.

Fig 10:7 *The plastic seat adaptation*

Further support can be given by fixing a pommel to any seat, existing or modified. This helps people to stop sliding forward.

Side Support

Support for the person who cannot maintain an upright position can be incorporated in a backrest design by giving it wings that come round the side of the torso. Steve Derwin's design mentioned earlier has this facility. However, such supports should be designed so that they do not interfere with the person's ability to paddle or, if not in a very stable set up, to exit their craft in an emergency.

The garden chairs mentioned previously can give side support if those with arms are used. Padding can also be used to stop people from slipping sideways.

Dynamic position

Further assistance for a good seating position is the placing of a roll of padding under the knees. This helps to create a more dynamic seating position, it puts the back in a stronger position and by flexing the knees helps to keep the legs relaxed.   However this is more effective if the feet can rest against a wide footrest or bulkhead.

<u>Staying in the kayak</u>

Some people with lower body impairments have been able to stay in their kayaks when executing manoeuvres that would otherwise cause them to fall out by strapping themselves in.

The first requirement of using a system of strapping is that the person is able to release the mechanism should they need to exit the kayak. This necessitates both the development of quick release systems and controlled practice of the skill of releasing and exit.

One method is to use a belt that is firmly fixed to the person which is then attached to the kayak. The paddler wears a belt that covers the hips and which has *Velcro* tape attached to it.   Corresponding tape is attached to the sides of the kayak seat. Thus when the person sits in the kayak they become attached to the seat by the *Velcro* contacts.

This method of staying in is secure but does need the person to be able to twist their hips to sheer the *Velcro* contact in order to exit.

A system used more frequently to hold someone into their kayak involves a strap which is firmly fixed to the kayak, or its seat, and then positioned over the person's hips, or chest in the case of a high back rest, and fastened with a quick release buckle.   The position of the strap, and its fixing into the kayak will depend very largely on the needs of the individual and the type of kayak they are paddling. However, for the hips, the belt must be attached as low as possible in the kayak since its objective is to keep the person in the seat whilst upside down. Whilst for the chest, the strap should run parallel to the rib cage. It must also be outside the buoyancy aid, and unable to tangle with any of the fastenings of this.

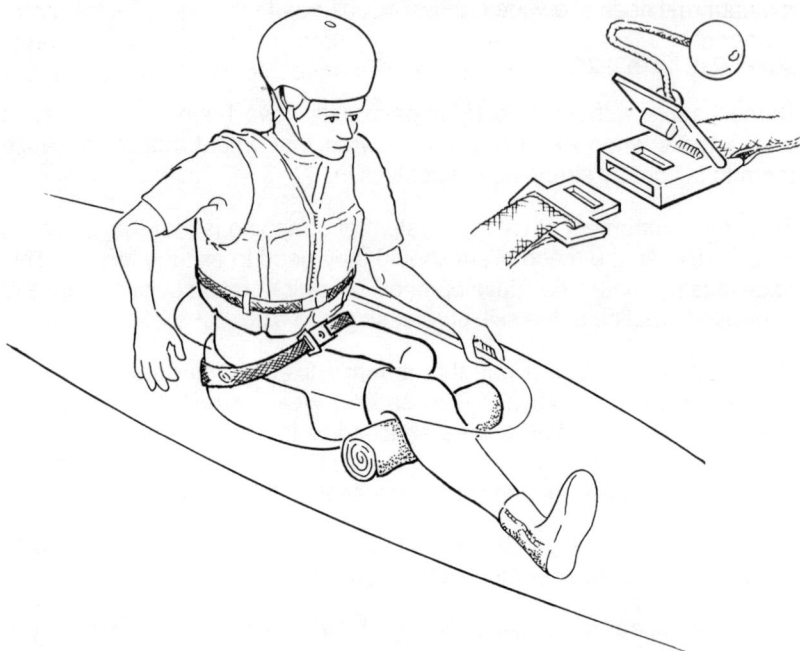

Fig 10:8 *The thigh strap (Note also the support under the knees)*

Quick release car and aircraft safety belts have been used successfully. *Velcro* fastening and the buckles from sub-aqua weights belts have also been used. With all buckles it is important that the person can find the release unseen and often whilst upside-down.   Therefore, any attachment such as loops or cords with balls or knots that enable to the person to find and operate the buckle are invaluable.   This release mechanism should extend to a point outside the spray deck and close to its release strap.   Therefore, when the paddler releases the spray deck the strap buckle is released at the same time.

Belt systems work best when the person adopts the dynamic seating position and other advice regarding the achievement of this should also be studied.

Finally, it cannot be over emphasised, anyone who uses a belt to stay in their kayak must practice safe exit techniques in a safe, and well supported, situation before they put their trust in such devices on open water.   In addition, should a buckle type of quick release be used it is probably advisable to have a secondary fail-safe should this become inoperative. This can be achieved by attaching the straps to the kayak with *Velcro* strips that will sheer when necessary allowing the belt system to pull away from the kayak with the paddler.

Fig 10:9 *An outrigger system*

Maintaining balance

The first requirement of keeping one's balance is to be seated correctly. Therefore, the suggestions regarding seating should be studied first.

The right craft

If there is any difficulty with balance it is sensible to start paddling in a craft that is inherently stable. Virtually all open canoes are suitably stable. For stability, kayaks should have a broad beam and good tracking characteristics. Boats such as the Caranoe, with a specially shaped hull, are very stable. The Kiwi kayaks are also very stable due to their wide beam and flat hull.

Stability modifications

Other kayaks can be made more stable by fixing keels or outriggers to the hull. This is a difficult task and should only be considered if it is not practical to use an alternative kayak. I first saw this strategy used in Italy by paddlers with disabilities who wanted to use fast kayaks for sprint events but also needed to make these kayaks stable. Whilst the fitting of keels and outriggers does affect the speed, such craft are still significantly faster than more inherently stable kayaks.

Fig 10:10 *The Stuart Turnbull stability device*

Stuart Turnbull, whilst a student at Liverpool John Moores University, devised another way of increasing stability. His system uses a series of short wooden bars attached to tapes that are fastened around the hull of the kayak. The arrangement is variable so that the numbers of strips can be reduced as the paddler gains more control and stability.

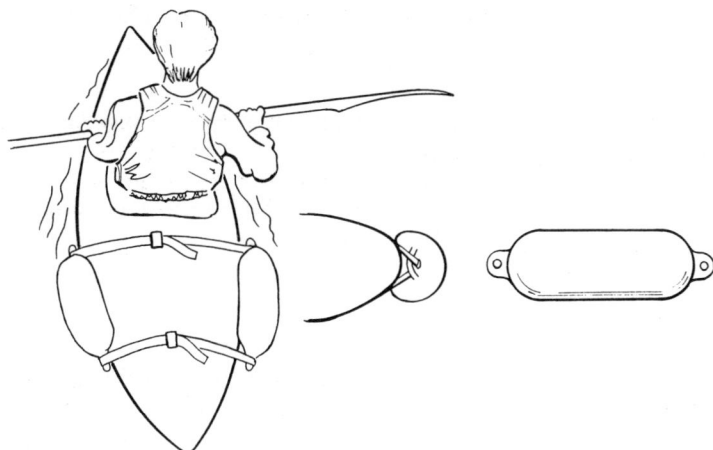

Fig 10:11 *The torpedo fender as a stability aid*

Yann le Carre, who works with paddlers with disabilities in France showed me how he strapped plastic torpedo fenders, from much larger boats, to either side of the sea kayaks he uses, to increase stability. Whilst a suitable strapping arrangement takes some devising, this method works quite well.

The best position seems to be just behind the cockpit, where they do not interfere with paddling too much, and just resting on the water when the craft is level. In this position they present very little drag during paddling yet give reasonable support if the boat should fall to the side.

An eight inch diameter fender, about 15 inches long, is a good compromise between effectiveness whilst not unduly affecting the other characteristics of the kayak.   For some paddlers who need more stability the fenders could be larger, fixed fore and aft of the cockpit, or positioned to be in the water at all times.

Strategies

Other ways to maintain balance are:-

- To sit low in the craft and as close to the hull of the boat as is feasible. This may mean lowering the seat, or taking the seat out completely and sitting on some padding on the hull.

Geoff Smedley   Canoeing for Disabled People

- Stability can also be increased by using a longer paddle and keeping the paddle strokes low.

- Ensuring that the person does not slide about in the seat by;
    covering the seat with neoprene or carrymat to increase friction,
    using padding to the back and sides.

Sometimes the lack of balance is caused by an inability to use the legs for bracing. In a kayak you can use

- a bulkhead footrest (one that completely fills the space where the feet come to),

- a roll of padding to lift the knees,

- a kayak with pillar buoyancy so that the legs go down each side of the boat and cannot both lie on the same side of the centre line.

In a canoe you can ensure that;

- the back and side support is firm,

- the seat tilts backwards slightly into the backrest,

- the lower legs have padded support to prevent them flopping from side to side.

Some people with cerebral palsy may find it easier to balance if they kneel instead of sitting.   This often causes concern to their physiotherapist, as usually the position they adopt is with their bottom resting between their heels. However, whilst this position often means they are very low in their craft, it lowers the centre of gravity which makes them more stable and it facilitates the fact that they also often use hand paddles to propel their craft.

Nevertheless, the adoption of this paddling position should be discussed with the person.   The more mature paddler may reject the potential adverse affect in favour of the benefits they obtain from canoeing. For a younger paddler, whose physiotherapy and the maintenance of good posture is still a fundamental feature for their physical development, this position may not be appropriate.

People with a visual impairment may also have difficulty balancing due to not being able to discern an horizon and thus orientate themselves. Ken Roberts, a disabled paddler himself found that a visually impaired paddler he was coaching found it useful to have a backrest that was fixed to the craft. This gave him an awareness of a vertical plane and any deviation from the vertical was detected by the position of the backrest against his back.

Sometimes one side of a person's lower body is heavier than the other. For these situations in a canoe you can arrange the position of the legs to be off the centre-line sufficient for the centre of balance to be on the centre-line.   This is more difficult to manage in a kayak.   As an alternative, to give equal weight it is possible to use weighted containers (such as BDH bottles) which are fixed in on the lighter side. See also the suggestions for people with leg amputations.

Directional Stability

I am assuming in this section that it is the problem of the solo paddler that is being addressed. Nevertheless, if the person still demonstrates problems when paddling tandem then the same considerations can still be applied.

The reasons for someone not being able to maintain directional stability are usually because:-

- They cannot see where they are going.

    People who are blind or visually impaired will have difficulty paddling on a specific route.   Chapter 11 has a section on Visual Impairment.   This contains useful information to support a coaching programme.

- They are not sitting properly.

- They cannot control the craft.

Not sitting correctly

It is advised that the section on seating is studied carefully and strategies employed to ensure that the person's sitting position is not affecting their ability to paddle in a straight line.

When people have restricted control of their lower body it is possible for them to adopt a sitting position which puts the weight more on one side of the craft than the other. This causes the craft to sit in the water in such a way that the profile of the hull is no longer symmetrical as it was designed to be and this causes the craft to turn continually to one side.

Furthermore, a position where the body may be slewed to one side means that the paddler will not have the same ability on each side to perform paddling strokes. If facing towards the left, paddle strokes will tend to fall behind the line of the hips on the that side, and in front of the line of the hips on the right.

Ensuring that the person is sitting with their weight distributed evenly and with the body in a position that enables equal power to be used on each side, will substantially improve the potential for straight line paddling.

Similarly, study the notes about maintaining balance. A person having difficulty balancing their craft will also have difficulties in maintaining a straight passage.

<u>Lack of control</u>

The reasons why someone cannot control their craft can be because:-

- They are using a craft designed to be very manoeuvrable and have not fully developed the skill to control it.

- They do not have the strength to control the craft they are using.

It is sensible to study the features of the craft and the paddles in the previous chapter to ensure that the person is using appropriate equipment.

Whilst it may be desirable to have a craft that is inherently directionally stable, it is often the case that, because we do not have a large fleet of different craft, we are obliged to use craft that are "general purpose" in their characteristics and a compromise between tracking and manoeuvrability. Aids and modifications to such craft may have to be considered.

<u>Keels</u>

Some canoes and kayak have a strong keel line which helps to keep the boat tracking well. It is not easy to modify the keel line of a craft. Nevertheless, it is possible to fix a keel under the hull of a craft as for a sailing craft.

However, such keels are usually fixed in a way that makes them permanent, thus the boat tend to be dedicated to one person, or, because of the shallow draft of many of the rivers in the U.K. the craft is restricted to the larger and deeper rivers or lakes.

Rudders and skegs

The directional stability of most craft can be improved by the use of a rudder device. Some racing and touring craft have rudders permanently built in to their design.   Fitting a rudder to the stern of a boat is not difficult and some, such as the Kiwi, have a moulded section at the stern that facilitates a rudder fitting.

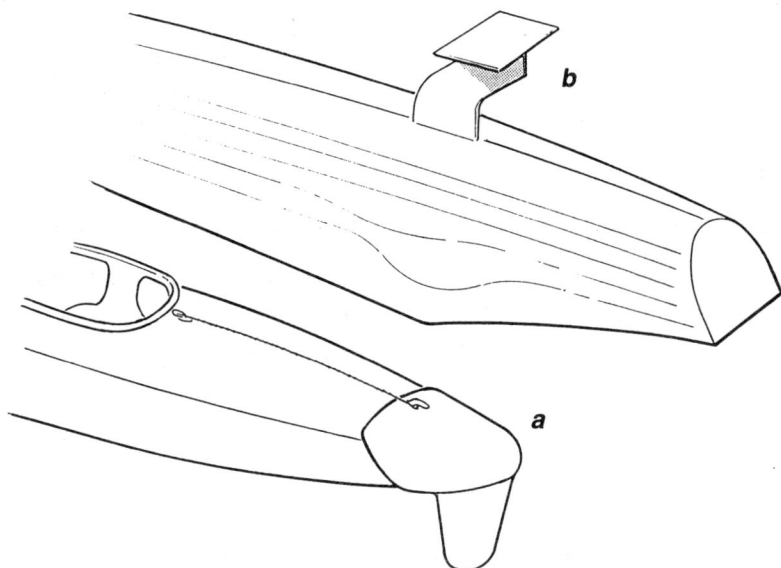

Fig 10:12a *A skeg on the stern*   **Fig 10:12b** *A keel fitted*
of a kayak   *under a kayak*

Other craft can temporarily be given a "skeg" to assist with tracking. A skeg is usually a fixed rudder that can be easily, and quickly, attached to a craft to keep it tracking in a straight line. However, be aware that such devices also make the craft less manoeuvrable and sluggish to turn.

Skegs are available commercially, either specifically designed to fit a particular craft, as in the case of the Rob Roy or Poly Pippin, or designed to adapt easily to a number of different craft. A lightweight skeg with a flexible collar that fits over a variety of different craft can easily be carried by a leader, to use if an individual becomes tired and thus finds difficulty in controlling their craft.

Geoff Smedley   Canoeing for Disabled People

Control acquisition

Teaching the acquisition of skills necessary to paddle in a straight line is part of the repertoire of all instructors and teachers. However, when working with some   people with disabilities there are additional strategies worth consideration.

Encourage the person to use shorter paddle strokes and not allow the paddle to stay in the water behind the line of the hips. Putting power into the forward paddling strokes causes the craft to move from the straight line more quickly that when using gentle strokes. Therefore, gentle strokes, or using a paddle with smaller blades, makes any movement off line occur more slowly, giving the paddler time to react and put in a correction stroke.

Where the individual lacks strength the paddle may be held quite low. This results in the paddle blade describing short arcs through the water on each side, culminating in a passage that tends to make the craft slew from side to side.

By using a lightweight paddle, that enables the person to keep the paddle more vertical, the paddle stroke moves through the water parallel to the craft and is less likely to encourage movement to one side or the other.

Sometimes it is the individual who has one side weaker than the other and is therefore pulling the craft towards the stronger side. Some mechanical evening-out of this strength difference can be valuable. Thus, you could try giving the strong side a smaller blade. or putting guide marks on the paddle so that the hands are slightly off-set towards the weaker side to give it a greater leverage.

Difficulties when capsizing and exiting

For a safe situation, people must be able to exit their craft in the event of a capsize, or, they should be paddling a craft that will not capsize.

A number of strategies to enable a safe stable platform for canoeing have been discussed. By and large, the only really safe situation that can only then be applied to inland waters, is that of rafted canoes or kayaks. All other craft, regardless of how stable they might be, are all liable to capsize.

Therefore, if it is felt that an individual might be at risk during a capsize, the reasons for the concern must be analysed and appropriate action take.

Risk of physical damage

The use of open deck canoes or kayaks or large cockpit kayaks is recommended. However, where the person chooses to paddle a kayak the following may be helpful.

During a capsize there is an increased risk that the paddler will damage the lower body by banging or grazing against the edges of the cockpit. This can be exacerbated if a spray deck is used since this adds another complication to the capsize strategy. Therefore, the use of a spray deck can only be advised when the paddler has demonstrated the ability to remove the deck after a capsize and to exit their kayak safely. Skills to achieve this can be practised in the swimming pool, however, the final assurance that the skill has been mastered can only be given after a practice capsize on open water.

Furthermore, in addition to any padding that the individual might wear, kayaks can be modified so that anyone exiting from them will not be injured in the process.

- Sharp edges, such as cockpit rims, can be padded.

- Footrests that protrude can be removed completely, or replaced with bulkhead footrests.

- The shape of the cockpit can be altered by the removal of knee grips to make the rim as smooth and obstruction free as possible.

- Where support aids such as backrests, side supports or knee rolls have been used to improve comfort or seating position they must not impede the exit.

- To enable the person in the water to maintain contact with their kayak it may be appropriate to have deck-lines to give them something to hold on to. However, the person needs to be aware that the lines are only there for them to keep contact with the kayak with, and pulling on the deck-lines will cause the kayak to swamp.

Difficulty holding a paddle.

This may be caused by:-

- weakness of the grip,
- liability to spasm,
- use restricted to one arm, or an inability to see the angle of the blade.

NOTE: Any adaptation that attaches the paddle to the hand must be easily released in the event of a capsize so that it does not adversely affect the ability of the people to swim. The release of such aids should be practised in a safe situation before venturing onto open water.

Any difficulty with holding the paddle will undoubtedly reduce the ability of the person to paddle and manoeuvre the craft. The solution might be for them to paddle tandem, either in a double kayak or canoe.

However, some people will want to have solo control of their craft. In this situation it may be necessary to explore which is easier for the paddler to control, a kayak or a canoe. Although, on the whole, a kayak is often easier to control for the solo paddler.

They should use a kayak that manoeuvres well yet has good tracking. A craft such as a Kiwi or a Caranoe could be considered. However, if the trips are largely in a straight line, a stable boat with good tracking such as a Poly Pippin could be considered.

<u>Weakness of the grip</u>

Strategies to explore are the ability of the individual to paddle with:-

- A lightweight paddle.
- A paddle with a moulded grip.
- A paddle with a thinner shaft to allow the fingers to encircle it.

If necessary, a wooden shaft can be carved away at the hand grip to make it thinner, or a thinner diameter section can be inserted into an aluminium shaft. This avoids having a thin shaft throughout which might flex too much. However, care must be taken with either method to ensure that the paddle is not weakened too much.

Making the shaft more oval in section to avoid having to bend the fingers too much. This can be achieved by:-

- Gently squeezing the shaft in a vice.

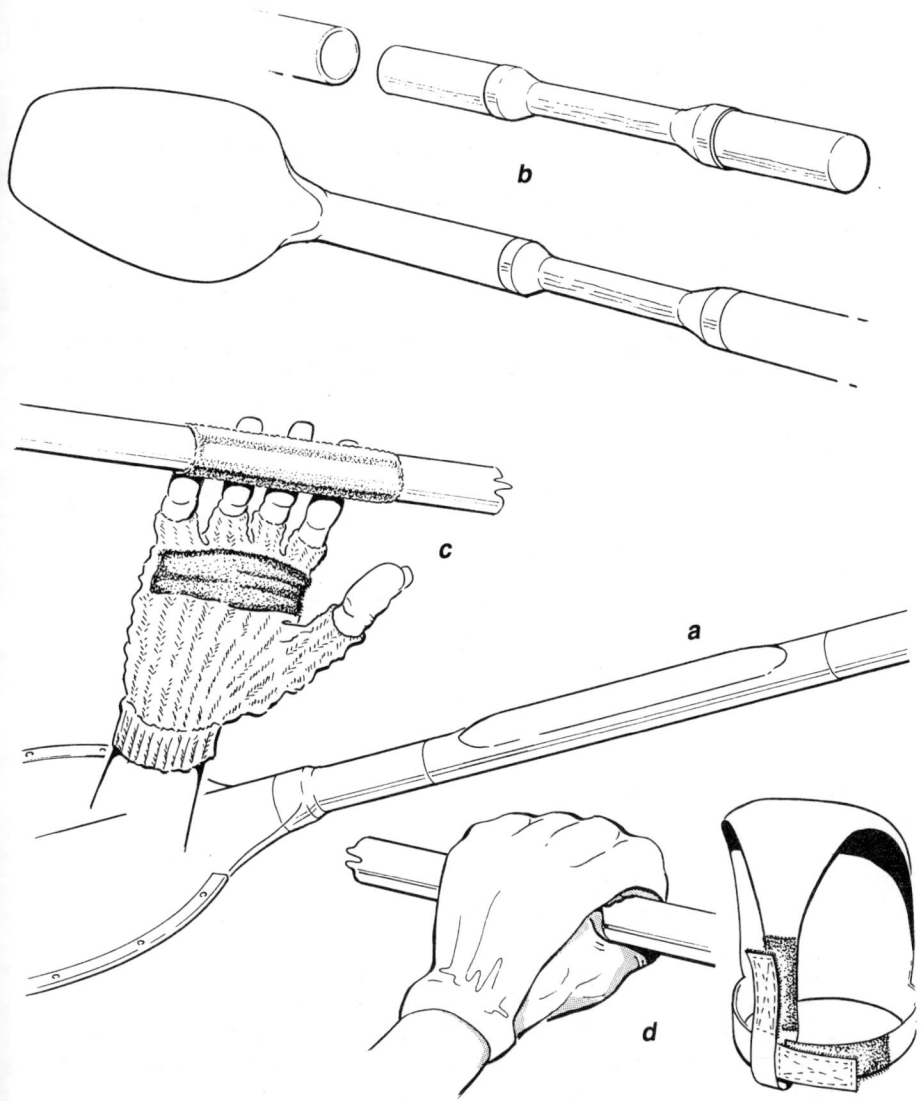

Fig 10:13a Paddle shaft with a moulded grip   *10:13b* Paddle shaft with a thin section inserted   *10:13c* Velcro mitt and paddle shaft   *10:13d* Mitt to hold the hand on the paddle shaft.

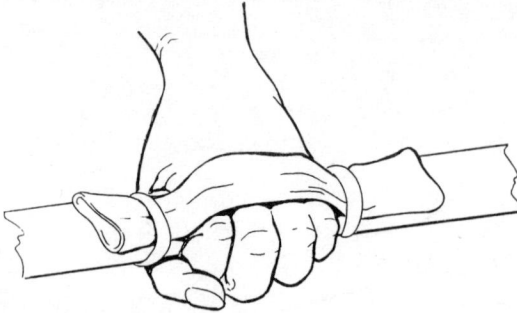

Fig 10:14 *The knuckle grip*

- Using a commercial paddle grip such as those produced by Lendal.
- Taping a piece of wood or plastic to the shaft.
- Using a bicycle grip, it is usually necessary to split the grip to get in onto the shaft and then tape it in place.
- Reducing, or completely removing, the feather on the paddle since this reduces the effort and tension in the muscle required for feathering.

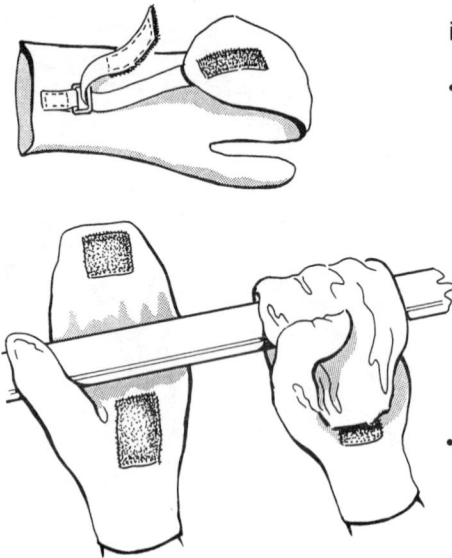

The grip on the paddle can be improved by:-

- Using Velcro patches with the hook side glued, riveted or taped to the shaft and the loop side glued or sewn to a paddle mitt. The positioning of the patches must be accurate if the paddler and the paddle area to be in the correct position for paddling. It may be necessary to use an unfeathered paddle with this adaptation.

- A strap, or section of cycle inner-tube which is taped, or secured with cable ties, to the shaft. The grip is then adjusted so that the fingers can be slid under the strap until the knuckles fit snugly. This type of grip can be taken on and off

Fig 10:15 *Another style of paddle mitt*

quite easily allowing the paddler to use it on whichever paddle is appropriate.

- Using "pogies" or paddle mitts. These have already been mentioned under clothing. Although usually fairly loose in fit, by keeping the hand warm they help the muscles to work efficiently.

- Gloves, or mittens can be fitted with straps that pull the hand around the paddle shaft. It is sometimes necessary to be able to fix the mitten or glove tightly at the wrist to avoid it being pulled of during paddling.

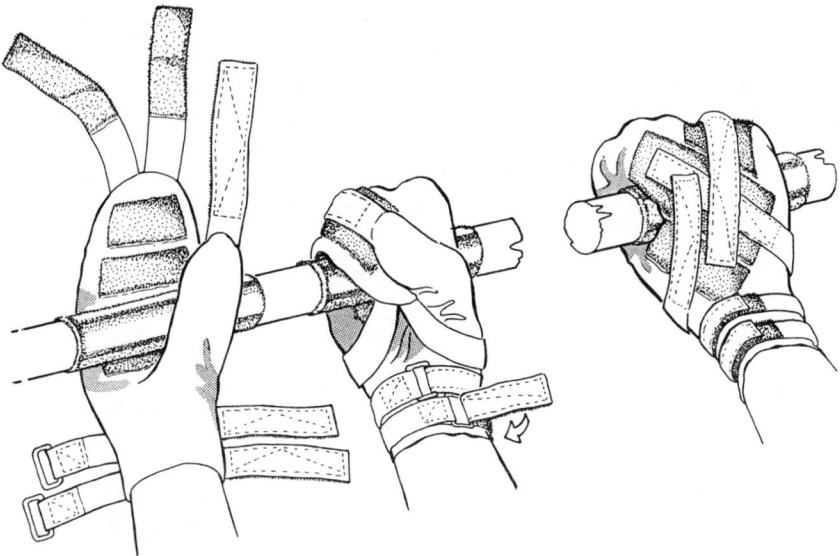

Fig 10:16 *The Velcro paddle mitt made for the Calvert Trust Centre*

The pivoted paddle

In their book *"Kader Informatie Map"* the Dutch SWG describe a device they call a "Peddelsteun". This device has been successfully used by paddlers at the Calvert Trust.

It comprised a stem fixed into the kayak which can pivot in the horizontal plane and, by using a mast joint from a sail-board, can also pivot in the vertical plane. A kayak paddle is fixed to the top of the stem which emerges from the craft in a position where the paddler can hold the paddle shaft.

Since the paddle is fixed all that is required of the paddler is to pull or push the paddle into and through the water.   If necessary, both hands can be used on one side of the paddle for each stroke. The paddle could be feathered if the attachment point allowed the shaft to rotate, although it is probably much easier to operate this device if the paddle is unfeathered.

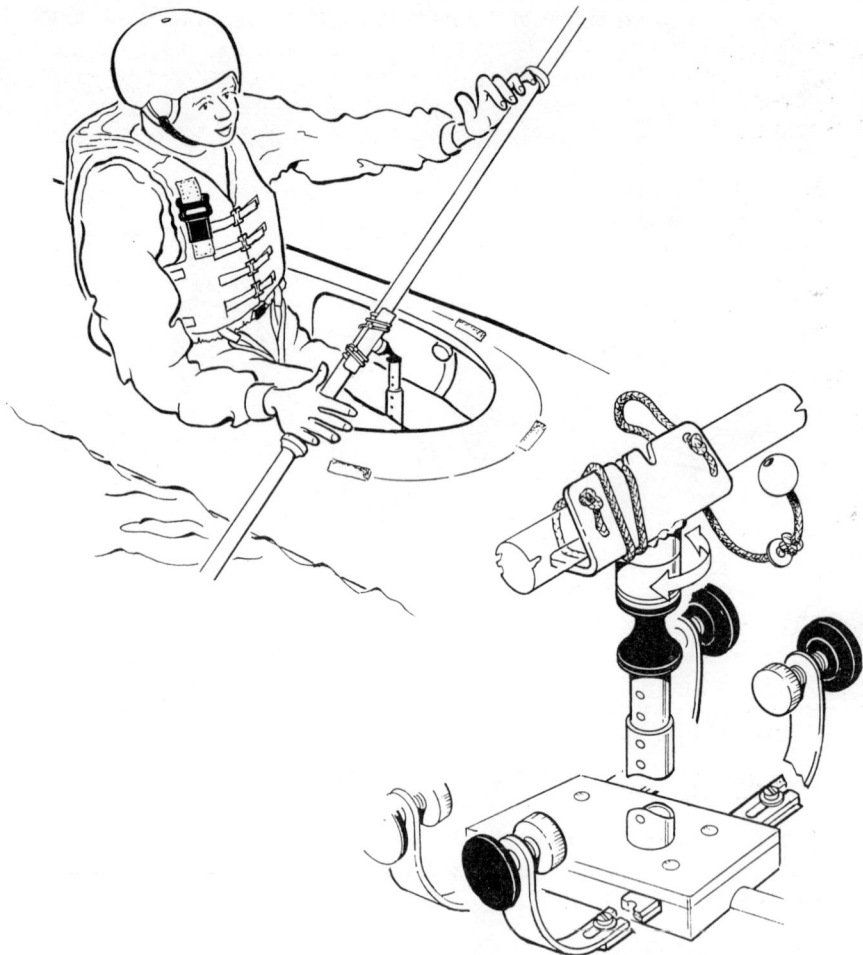

Fig 10:17 *The pivoted paddle device*

This device must be fitted to a very stable craft since it would inhibit any emergency exit. It should also be a craft with good manoeuvrability and tracking characteristics, to avoid excess effort for control. The Calvert Trust have fixed their device to a Caranoe although any stable kayak with a large cockpit would be suitable.

<u>Liability to spasm</u>

There is usually a particular reason why people have spasms. Therefore, it is advisable to consider these and aim to avoid them. Spasms of the lower body will affect balance and stability, whilst spasms of the upper body will also affect the ability to paddle. The following conditions should be addressed.

The craft used must be stable. The open canoe is ideal since it allows plenty of room for movement. This can be important since being restricted can be a cause of spasms. If the person wishes to paddle solo then a stable craft such as the Kiwi, the Caranoe or an open kayak such as the Dimension would be suitable.

A seating position that is comfortable and allows the person to be relaxed is important. See also the sections on *"Sitting without Support"* and *"Maintaining Balance"*.

The individual should be paddling within their strength and mobility levels. Over exertion, over stretching or having to pull or push too hard will exacerbate any tendency to spasm.

Keeping the person warm is important. The effects of cold water especially will trigger a spasm.

Many of the adaptations described for people with a weak grip are applicable to people who lose their grip on the paddle when their hands and arms go into spasm. However, avoid those that put too much tension on the limb, these tend to be counter productive. I have found that using a fibrepile lined pogie seems to work best. It keeps the hands warm, and if the grip is lost the paddle and hand are still retained sufficiently close together by the pogie for the grip to be regained.

<u>Use restricted to one arm</u>

This impairment will affect balance, paddling style and swimming. Since the impairment is also going to reduce the paddling efficiency the individual should consider working in tandem. However, if determined to go solo, initially at least, the craft used should be one that manoeuvres and tracks well without the paddler having to make too much effort. The Kiwi, Caranoe and Dimension fit this category. If the course does not require too much turning, the Poly Pippin is another alternative.

Canoeing

Some people have been able to use a single blade with their functional arm by holding the shaft and tucking the handle under the armpit and braced against the neck. However, this is not an easy position to maintain for long periods and the paddle, or the paddler, needs to be padded at the point of contact to avoid injuries.

Crutch paddle

An alternative system is to use a paddle that has been developed by grafting a paddle blade onto an elbow crutch. A word with your friendly physiotherapist might lead to the acquisition of a damaged crutch, useless for its intended purpose, but suitable for conversion to a paddling device. (*See Fig 9:11*)

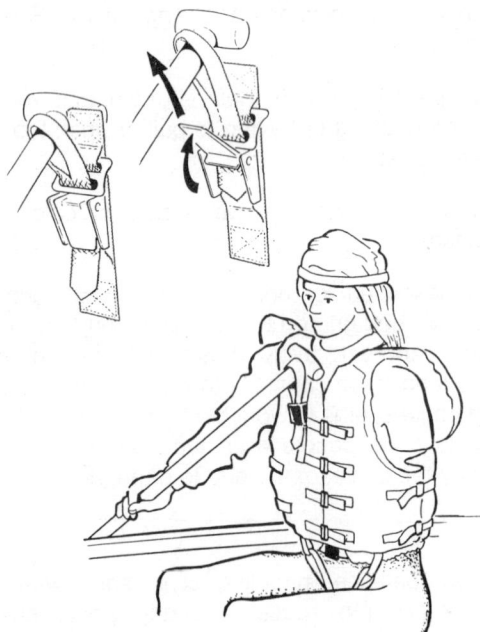

Fig 10:18 A single blade pivot incorporated into the buoyancy aid

The paddle is usable for either position when paddling a double canoe. Adjusting the length of such a paddle is quite critical and realistically each paddler needs to have a paddle of a length suitable for them.

However, this paddle is quite tricky to use if paddling solo, although with practice it can be done. When paddling solo, or when responsible for maintaining direction when paddling tandem, the pitch, or angle, of the blade relative to the hand grip is important for J stroking.   Using an Ainsworth joint allows the paddler to adjust the angle to one that suits them.

<u>Using a pivot</u>

Another system uses a pivot device on the buoyancy aid which accommodates the T piece of the paddle, whilst the paddler controls the paddle with their functional arm.

Note that the pivot device has two safety features.   Firstly, it holds the T piece of the paddle securely, preventing its movement up and towards the face of the paddler.

Secondly, it can be released from the buoyancy aid by one hand in the event of a capsize. Again, the length of the paddle is important.

<u>Single Hand paddle</u>

Finally, although it will not give sufficient power to propel a canoe solo, the hand paddle does allow the individual to participate in the propulsion, and control, when used with another paddler in the craft.

These hand paddles can be made of any material strong enough for the purpose.   For the DIY manufacture marine ply is probably the most easily worked.   Use 5 or 7 ply and smooth all the edges carefully.   A piece of dowel, slit and fixed either side of the part that is gripped helps to make it more comfortable.   Similarly, a piece of padding where the paddle rests against the arm assists comfort. (*See Fig 9:10 in the previous chapter*)

There are commercial versions of these paddles made from plastic or glass reinforced plastic sold as emergency paddles for sailing dinghies.

<u>Arm amputees</u>

Arm amputees, who use an artificial arm, may be able to improvise by replacing the "hand" or "terminal device" with one which can grasp the paddle.

<u>Kayaks</u>

The principle difficulty arises from the need to control a shaft with a blade at each end. If the paddler simply grasps, with one hand, the paddle at the centre point of the shaft it is possible to manoeuvre the paddle.   However, it is rarely possible for an individual to have the strength to do this in such a way that they have control over their craft.

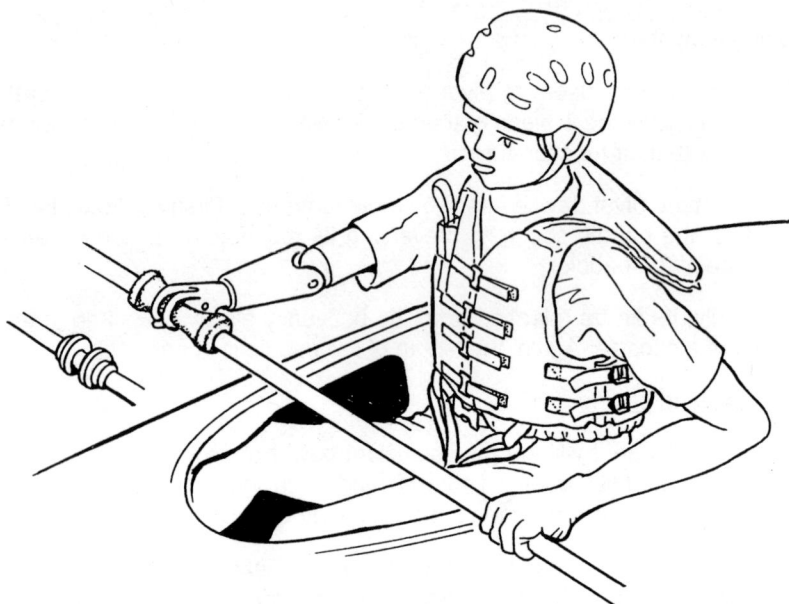

Fig 10:19 *Using a terminal device with an artificial arm*

Vander Molen aid

Devised by Paul Vander Molen, a keen expeditioner who worked enthusiastically with people who had disabilities, the Vander Molen paddle aid assists by transferring the control of the paddle to the whole of the lower arm.

The weight of the device and the paddle need to be kept as low as possible to avoid over fatiguing the user. In this respect the use of closed cell foam and aluminium alloys are recommended.

Systems for attaching the device to the paddlers arm can use Velcro or straps but they must be secure and comfortable. The lever beneath the paddle is the method of releasing the paddle in the event of a capsize.

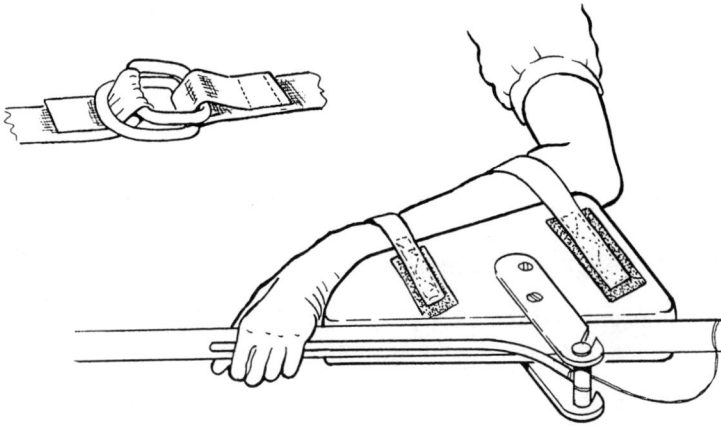

Fig 10:20 *The Vander Molen device*

Inability to see the angle of the blade

The need to know at what angle the paddle blade is, without being able to see it, is very important for efficient paddling.

Geoff Smedley   Canoeing for Disabled People

Ways of giving some form of feedback can be:-

- Making the shaft more oval in section so that the fingers can detect a difference in the width of the paddle should it inadvertently rotate in the hand. This can be achieved by:-

  - Gently squeezing the shaft in a vice.

  - Using a commercial paddle grip such as those produced by Lendal.

  - Taping a piece of wood or plastic to the shaft.

- Using a paddle with a cranked shaft. Many paddle shafts, especially those used for competition, have a crank in them. The purpose is to increase the leverage exerted by the paddle and to lessen the need to twist the wrist for feathering. The mechanics of these designs is quite complex, however, for our purposes it is sufficient to note that cranked shafts demand less strength of wrist to control the paddle, and because of the angle they present to the arm, they enable the paddler to maximise what strength they have in the hands, wrists and arms.

Whilst the Dutch "Pivoted Paddle" would also undoubtedly work since the angle of the blade can be fixed, this system would probably be unnecessary for people for whom seeing the angle of the blade is the only concern.

Lack of strength   - upper body

Firstly, ensure that the paddler is maximising what strength he has by being seated in a comfortable and effective way.

Once again the craft should be one that requires minimal effort for control. Paddlers should either paddle tandem or use a kayak with good tracking characteristics such as the Caranoe, Kiwi, Dimension or Poly Pippin.

The paddle should be kept low whilst paddling, this concentrates the strength into the pulling and pushing. In this respect the Dutch design for a pivoted paddle mentioned earlier would be useful. A further advantage of this design is that it only requires pushing or pulling and to maximise strength both hands can be used on the same side of the pivot point to increase leverage. However, be aware that a low paddle tends to arc through the water which in a craft with poor tracking characteristics makes it slew from side to side.

Encourage the paddler to pull the blade slowly through the water this creates less turbulence and requires less effort.

Try using lightweight paddles, an unfeathered or a cranked paddle also reduces strain enabling maximum use to be made of existing strength. Similarly a smaller paddle blade could be considered.

Lack of strength - lower body

The problems likely to be faced by this person are those of:-

- Getting in and out
- Maintaining a dynamic sitting position
- Difficulties when capsizing and exiting
- Maintaining balance

All these problems have been covered in the earlier sections of this chapter.

Finally

When assessing the needs of the individual paddler and developing an appropriate programme always bear in mind that both needs, skills and aspirations are subject to change.

As people paddle regularly they will develop skills, strength and stamina, enabling them to consider paddling craft that may, in the first instance, have been impossible.   Allow for this process, ensure that modifications and adaptations can be themselves modified or adapted to take account of these potential changes.

Plate 10:a *Making canoeing possible*

Canoeing for Disabled People   Geoff Smedley

CHAPTER ELEVEN

IMPLICATION OF IMPAIRMENTS

This chapter gives some guidelines and awareness of the implications of impairments. It looks at impairments under three main headings:- physical, medical and sensory. Learning disability is considered exclusively in chapter 18.

PHYSICAL

Under this heading will be considered the implications of:-

- **Mobility**

- **Physical Considerations**

- **Communication**

- **Appliances**

- **Wheelchairs**

MEDICAL

Under this heading will be considered the medical conditions of:-

- **Asthma**

- **Diabetes**

- **Epilepsy**

- **Medication side effects**

SENSORY

Finally, under this heading will be considered the implications of:-

- **Visual Impairments.**

- **Deafness**

General considerations

Independence

Always respect the desire of people for independence. It is often more effective if you focus the major part of your support on ensuring that access, and the removal of handicapping situations, is such that people can get about independently.

With young people and children you may feel sometimes that it would be easier, perhaps even kinder, to help them rather than stand by and watch their slower, often awkward progress.   However, you must respect the desire for independence and also recognise that for young people and children much of what they do is part of the learning progress; as they practice so they will become more proficient, quicker and less awkward.

Generally speaking people know when they need help. When they need your assistance they will usually ask for it; although this can be facilitated if you make it known that you are willing to help if they should need it.

If you should be asked to help, bear in mind that people with disabilities are the ones who will know best what they are able to do themselves and what you can do to enable them to achieve the more difficult tasks. If someone asks for your help, don't rush in, ask the person what you can do to be of the most assistance.

Perhaps the most valuable thing you can give a person who wishes to be independent is time.

Dignity

Sometimes you may find yourself assisting a person with a disability to go to the toilet or to get changed. At these times be very clear about the amount of assistance the individual requires. Both of these exercises leave the individual vulnerable to embarrassment. Often you can assist to the stage when it might become embarrassing and then let the individual take over.

Bear in mind that the toilets and changing rooms of most canoe clubs are likely to be more spartan in appearance and function than those at home. Ways to improve comfort and access are outlined in chapter 19.

Communication

People learn and develop through relationships. A close reciprocal relationship can add significantly to the individual's perceptions of self esteem and value. Feeling valued helps people to feel good about themselves. You can contribute to this process by treating people with respect and valuing them as individuals; recognising the distinct contribution they have to make. How you talk about, and how you talk to people with disabilities can convey respect for them and give a good example to others.

It happens frequently that questions are directed, not to the disabled person, but to their parent or carer. The vast majority of people can speak for themselves and even if they are communicating through an interpreter, you should always direct your conversation to the partner in the conversation.

Some people have communication difficulties. They know what they want to say but the speech organs cannot articulate the words easily. Be patient and listen carefully. Even if you do not understand first time you will eventually be able to understand if you keep trying.

Do not be afraid to ask people to repeat what they have said. This is better than guessing and perhaps getting it wrong. However, if you think you have understood what has been said you can always seek confirmation from the speaker. They can say "yes" or "no" in reply to your query.

Carers and parents are often more experienced at understanding. Use this knowledge to establish communication, but again, remember to speak to the person not their interpreter.

PHYSICAL IMPAIRMENTS

Mobility

The British Sports Association for the Disabled suggests three broad categories of mobility that can be applied to people with disabilities.

<u>Non Ambulant</u>

These are people who spend most of the time in a wheelchair. However, it is possible that some may be able to stand, or even walk a few paces.

Ambulant

These are people who are able to walk but some may require support through the use of sticks, crutches or walking frames; or even callipers or artificial limbs.

Slippery surfaces must be taken into consideration and some assistance may then be required.

Visually Impaired

These people do not usually have physical impairments of mobility but they will need support in certain circumstances.   Refer to the section on Visual Impairment later in this chapter.

Physical Considerations

Dressing and undressing

Acknowledgements   Steve Devlin

Give the person advance notice of the need, and the reasons, for changing, the type of clothes to wear and the facilities available.   This often enables them to select those clothes which make this operation easier, such as loose fitting clothing, the minimum of fastenings and the use of Velcro.

A number of techniques are suggested in this section, not all of them will be effective for some individuals.   Each individual will usually know which techniques work best for them and therefore you should discuss this with them and take their advice.   To be safe, always ask, do not assume anything.   Sometimes it is necessary to make these enquiries of parents or carers.

One of the most difficult operations is that of getting clothes over people's hips. If the person is lying down they can assist the helper by lifting the buttocks, either by pushing down with the feet or by lifting on the hands. If this is not possible then rotation of the body from side to side often allows clothes to be moved down over the hips one side at a time. Again this is easier if the person is lying down.

Observe the head position of the person when they are moving since this often gives an indication of their stability and the likely direction for them to overbalance.

Some people use certain strategies to help them dress and undress. Ideally the head should be kept in a neutral position during this process.

It is easier to remove clothing over the shoulders and head if the head is kept well forward.

It helps some people to turn their head to the hemiplegic side, then the muscle tone is reduced and it is easier to put clothes with sleeves on over the head.

People who have increased muscle tone are helped in the changing process by a number of factors.   A warm environment, a relaxed unhurried approach, confidence in their helper and a stable sitting or lying position.

It is generally helpful when helping a person to get a limb in the right position, to start from the trunk and work outwards towards the extremities.

You can help to relax increased muscle tone by gently shaking or vibrating the limb. This often allows a few minutes of relaxation that will allow the limb to be moved or clothes to be moved over that limb.

Once a limb is relaxed, the control of the limb can sometimes be encouraged to stay relaxed by keeping the thumb clear of the palm and the big toe bent gently upwards.

Stomas

If the person has a stoma you must take extra care when changing. Dragging on the bag can cause it to become disconnected, and although this is not usually painful it can be quite distressing.   Whilst changing might be a good time for the person to empty any bags.   See also the section on Stomas in the next chapter.

Skin Care

Many impairments have associated with them poor circulation of the blood. This, in turn, leads to reduced, or no, sensation of the skin.

Regardless of the impairment, the problems of poor circulation and the lack of skin sensation always give cause for concern.   It is relatively easy for individuals to bruise themselves without realising it.

Therefore, care must be taken when getting into or out of the craft, especially if closed cockpit kayaks are used.

It is also important to note that, when the skin damages easily, the healing process is often impaired and so the recovery from the injury can be slower.

After getting wet the skin must be carefully dried. A poor blood supply increases the susceptibility to chilblains and skin ulcers, especially so when the skin is cold and wet.

Warm, protective clothing is essential. Area of special vulnerability such as the bottom, the heels and knees should be padded, either directly or by applying padding to the craft.

Great care should also be taken when supporting, transferring, lifting or carrying someone with poor skin sensation. Unfortunately, even with this process it is all too easy to damage the skin without realising it. For this reason the helpers should ensure that they do not have watches, rings or other jewellery exposed, and that there are no sharp buckles or catches on their clothes that could damage the skin of the person they are helping. They should also check that when positioning the person in the craft or in their wheelchair that their clothing is not bunched or creased in such a way that it could put pressure on a particular point.

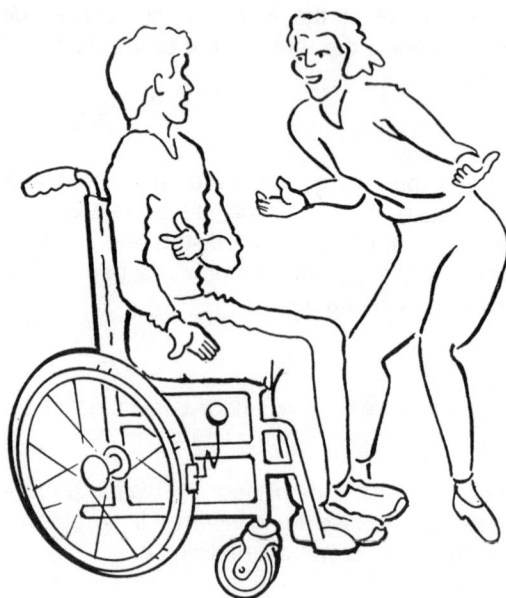

When talking to someone in a wheelchair you should establish eye contact, preferably at the same level. This can be achieved by getting a chair and sitting in front of and slightly to the side of the person you are talking to. Doing this avoids the appearance of "talking down" and also avoids the necessity for the person in the wheelchair to be looking up continually straining the neck.

Fig 11:1 *Talking to someone in a wheelchair*

If you cannot sit next to them, move away from the person until you can establish eye contact without you looking down, or them looking up, at an acute angle.

It is not good practice to stoop down, squat or crouch to talk to people in wheelchairs.   They often find this patronising.   Furthermore, these positions are difficult to maintain for any length of time before the blood circulation is cut off, the legs then go "dead" and you fall over!

Talk to people in wheelchairs as you would talk to anyone else. Do not be afraid to use words like walk or stand. They are used to mean the same things by people in wheelchairs; as in "are you coming for a walk?" or "they left me standing in the rush for the bar."

Communication Systems

Some people with speech impairments may use alternative methods of communication. It may be a signing system such as the British Sign Language (BSL) or a simpler signing version called Makaton. The first system is most commonly used by deaf people, the second where the person may have a learning disability.   Later in this chapter are some BSL signs that have been especially developed for canoeists.

Talk to the person and ask them to teach you some of the basic signs that will be helpful whilst you are together. This will help both of you to establish a fundamental level of communication.

Makaton

The illustrations on the next two pages show a few of the signs that are useful. Always use the signs with the spoken word and not instead of. Whilst the signs are fairly self explanatory it is always valuable to get someone experienced in their use to show you how to perform the signs correctly.

Be patient with unclear signs; if you persist you will gradually be able to understand better. If you do not understand ask a carer to assist. Some people with learning disability are not very accurate in their signs and some have a totally individual approach.

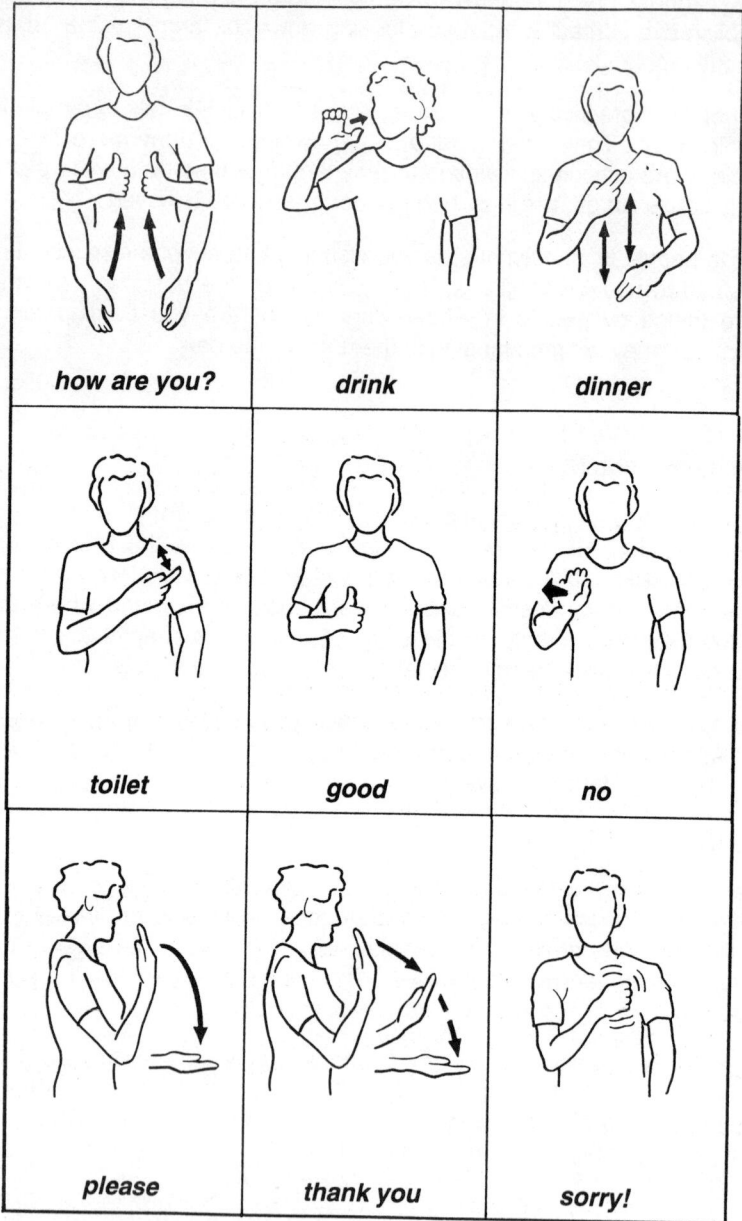

how are you?	drink	dinner
toilet	good	no
please	thank you	sorry!

Fig 11:2 (and facing page) Some useful Makaton Signs

Canoeing for Disabled People   Geoff Smedley

hot	**cold**	**boat**
name	**to stop**	**to help**
listen	**good-bye**	**to hear**

THE DEAF-BLIND MANUAL ALPHABET

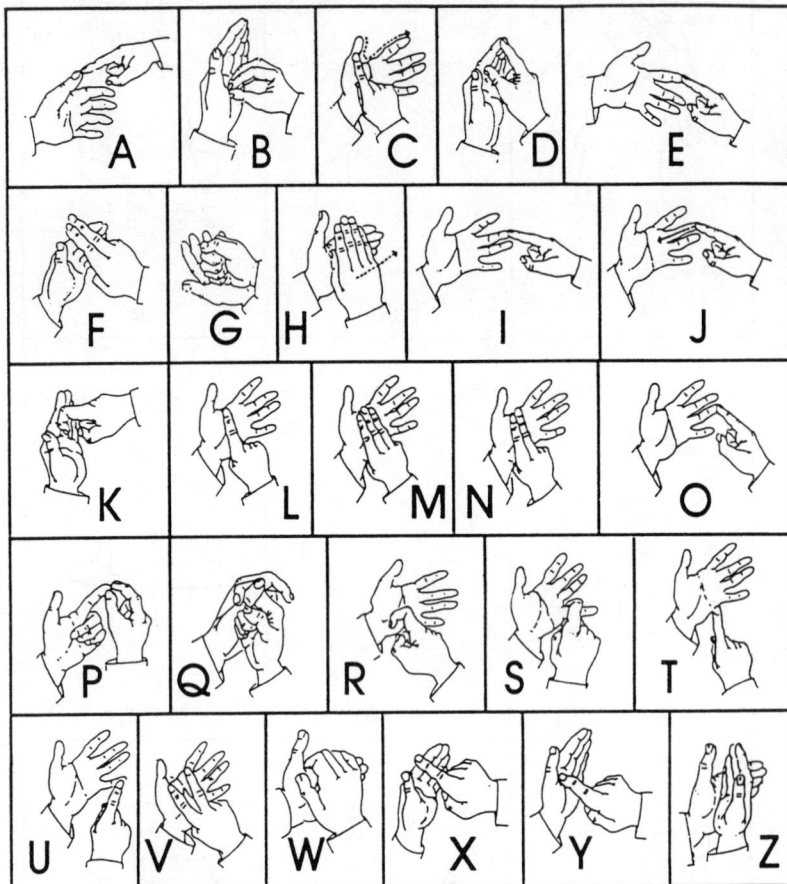

The eyes and ears of
deaf-blind people

Sense
The National Deaf-Blind and
Rubella Association

For further information please contact
the Appeals Department at
Sense
311 Gray's Inn Road
London WC1X 8PT
Tel: 01-278 1005

Fig 11:3 The deafblind manual alphabet

British Sign Language

For deaf people, who use this system, it is a total communication system and takes a lot of constant practice and use to become proficient.   However, it can be learned by non deaf people to enable communication.   Courses are run at a number of centres throughout the country.

To find out more you should send a stamped addressed A4 envelope to:-

> British Deaf Association
> Into-Sign
> 38 Victoria Place
> CARLISLE CA1 1HU

There are some signs on pages 147 and 148 specifically designed for paddle sport by Simon Scandrett and Keith Ripley.

Deaf Blind Manual Alphabet

For people who are both deaf and blind you can use the *Deaf Blind Manual Alphabet* (See opposite)

To find out more you should sent a stamped addressed A4 envelope to:-

> SENSE
> 11-13 Clifton Terrace
> Finsbury Park
> LONDON N4 3SR

Symbols and boards

Some methods of communication use boards on which certain key words, or symbols to represent the words have been drawn.   The user will point to the words on the board to establish communication.   If they do not have a board that contains the vocabulary for canoeing you can work on this with them and produce a special board, preferably waterproof, that can be taken out on the canoeing sessions.

Some tips when using boards are to try to avoid too many words that only require Yes or No for answers and establish how the user indicates, this may be by:-

- finger pointing,

- gross hand movements,

- head pointing or

- using a pointer attached to the head,

- or by pointing with the foot.

- For someone who has difficulty in accurate pointing they may indicate an area for you to scan with your finger and then tell you when to stop. Scan down the rows until the person tells you to stop and then along the row until told to stop.

- Always support the use of a board with speech.

- Avoid asking negative questions such as "you don't want a drink do you?"

- If you do not understand try again.   Establish eye contact for confirmation that you are finding the correct word or symbol.

- Only ask one question at a time.

Technology

With modern technology other communication devices are also to be seen.   Operating like small computers these devices can be used to spell words out letter by letter. They can also be programmed so that a single key press will print whole words or complete sentences on a small screen. Some devices are capable of speaking the words through a speaker using an artificial voice.   However, as yet these devices are not waterproof and so they must be kept away from the water.

If you are attempting conversation with someone in a wheelchair who gesticulates towards the back of their chair, it is probably to indicate that they have a communication board or device in their wheelchair bag, and want you to get it for them as an aid to communication.

Other devices that support communication on the water are described in Chapter Sixteen.

Appliances

Splints or callipers

Splints and callipers are metal, leather or plastic supports for the limbs or body that are worn to give extra support where there is a weakness or deformity.

They can be quite small and unobtrusive, such as those worn to support the wrist or ankle. They can also be quite large and cover the whole of the torso from the hips to the neck.

The splint or calliper can be secured either by leather, or nylon, straps and buckles or Velcro.

Implications

Great care must be taken of splints and callipers, and whilst the support they give can give considerable advantage to the individual when in a boat, some are easily damaged by water, or by unusual use for canoeing or kayaking. Furthermore, if worn in a kayak they could impede the person's ability to exit in the event of a capsize, and also their ability to swim.

Each individual will know when they can remove their splints or callipers for swimming or sitting without seriously impairing their mobility. However, they may need to take advice about the appropriateness of removing the splint or calliper for canoeing or kayaking.

Discuss the potential for damage with the individual. It may be that they can substitute the leather and metal appliance for a plastic or nylon one. This may be a type they already have and use when resting. However, it will not give as much support, but, because of its construction, it will not be damaged by water.

Whichever type is worn, when the person adopts a position that they do not usually assume, such as that for canoeing or kayaking, care must be taken to see that the splint or calliper does not chafe or cause sores.

If going away on an expedition it is a good idea to advise the wearer that the appliance is given a thorough overhaul to minimise the risk of failing. They should also take a spare, or spare straps or padding in case the appliance should become damaged.

Artificial Limbs

These may be worn because of a deformity from birth or as the result of losing a limb in an accident or through a post disease disability.

Some artificial limbs may have mechanical or electronic parts that enable the user to simulate natural functioning. These types of limbs should not be worn for canoeing or kayaking.

Implications

As for splints and callipers you should discuss with the wearer the pros and cons of wearing the artificial limb for canoeing or kayaking.

If contemplating an expedition ensure that artificial limbs have had a thorough overhaul to minimise the risk of them failing. Taking spares is also to be recommended.

Wheelchairs

Some people with physical impairments use wheelchairs. This enables them to be mobile and in many cases, because they can propel their wheelchair themselves, they can also be independent. However, this is not always the case since some people are unable to propel their wheelchair.

Self propelling wheelchairs may be either manual, where the person uses a rim attached to the wheel, or they may be powered by electric motors. There are a few that are propelled by a hand cranking system, either large levers that are pushed forward and backwards or by a system not unlike bicycle pedals operated by hand.

Be aware that this latter type, and electric wheelchairs, are usually very heavy. If the canoeing programme you are planning involves moving over rough ground, steps or negotiating small gaps you should advise the wheelchair users accordingly. They will then be able to make a decision about the type of wheelchair they will use since many users of electric wheelchairs also have a manual wheelchair.

This type of information must be very thorough to enable sensible decisions to be made. Some people who use wheelchairs also have other vehicles such as motorcycles, tricycles, quads and scooters that are specifically designed for rough terrain.

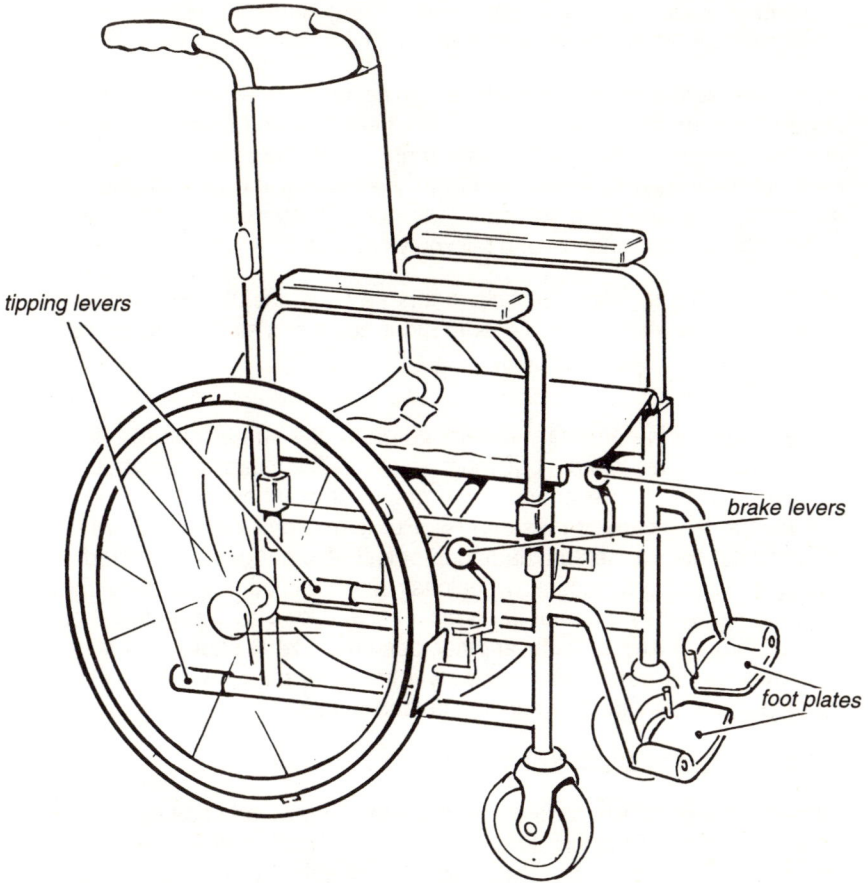

tipping levers

brake levers

foot plates

Fig 11:4 *Key parts of the wheelchair*

Don't touch!

For someone who uses a wheelchair, the chair becomes as important to the person as legs are to someone who walks. For this reason the wheelchair should be given the same respect as a person's legs would be.   Therefore, the first rule is don't touch.

When talking to someone in a wheelchair, do not lean on it or sit on the arms. Do not even rest your hand on it, unless you have established a relationship with the person that would make it permissible for you to put your hand on their shoulder during a conversation.

Geoff Smedley   Canoeing for Disabled People

A cardinal sin is to use someone's wheelchair as a coat stand or equipment rack.   I have seen people hang items of clothing on a wheelchair whilst the owner was sitting in it!

If you see someone in a wheelchair going up a steep slope or at the edge of a curb or step, don't grab the wheelchair and push.   This can give the person in the wheelchair a fright; apart from the fact that they may not want your assistance.   Go to the front of the person and ask them if there is any thing you can do to help.   They may say no, or they may welcome your support and tell you what to do.

If you are going to offer your help in this way it is useful to know how to push, or pull, a wheelchair.   To learn more about this study Chapter 16.

<u>Look after the bits!</u>

Occasionally, it is necessary to remove parts of a wheelchair to enable the person to get in and out more easily.   The usual parts that are removed are the footrests and the armrests.   If you help someone to do this please take care of these parts.   Put them somewhere safe where they will not get trodden on, damaged or lost.   Do not get them mixed up with the parts from another wheelchair since although the parts may look the same they may not fit correctly.   Think of it as you getting your size 6 shoes mixed up with another person's size 6 shoes.   Although they may be the same colour and style the other shoes will not feel the same as your own shoes when you put them on.

<u>Folding, unfolding and carrying</u>

One of the easiest ways I know to injure the fingers, and sometimes the ego, is to try to fold or unfold a wheelchair for the first time.   However, folding wheelchairs is often a necessary exercise if there are several wheelchair users in one place.   Once the person has left the wheelchair and got into their craft it can be useful to fold the wheelchair to give more space. The technique for most chairs is quite simple.

To fold the wheelchair (fig 11:5a):-

• Remove the seat cushion and put it down safely.

• Fold the foot plates up.

• Hold the fabric of the seat along the centre line at the front and back and lift.

• The chair will then close up with a scissor action.

To open the wheelchair (fig 11:5b):-

- Put your hands between the armrests and locate the side supports of the seat.

- Using the heel of the palm, and with the fingers pointing into the centre of the seat, push down to open the wheelchair out fully.

- Lower the foot plates.

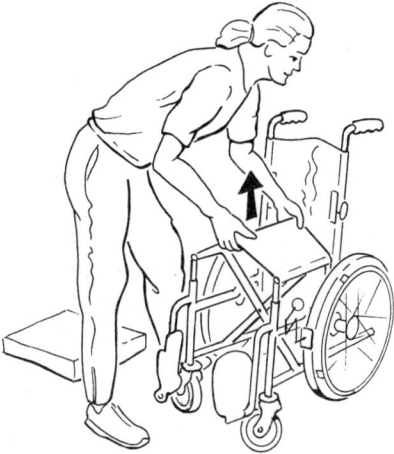

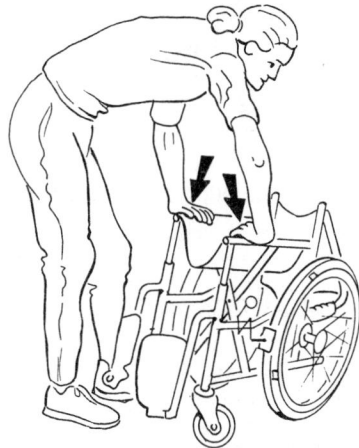

Fig 11:5a *Folding a wheelchair*   **Fig 11:5b** *Unfolding a wheelchair*

The majority of wheelchairs operate in this way. It is a good idea to check this system with the owner if the chair looks unfamiliar to you.

Wheelchairs can be folded even smaller for transporting or storing by folding the footrests back and by lowering the back, but you should consult with the owner regarding the strategies for this.

When you move or carry a wheelchair always do so by holding the frame of the wheelchair. Do not use armrests, footrests or wheels since all of these can move causing the wheelchair to swing. This may make you drop, and damage, the wheelchair; or could cause it to hit and injure you or anyone nearby.

Maintenance

If you are going to be away from base for any time, such as on a trip or an expedition, and are taking wheelchairs with you, it would be wise to have a wheelchair maintenance kit with you also.

Note that not all wheelchairs are the same, so if taking more than one make sure that the maintenance kit is large enough for the numbers and contains all the appropriate spanners, screwdrivers and axles.

A kit should contain:-
• tyre pump,
• puncture repair outfit, ("Tyre weld")
• suitable spanners, screwdrivers,
• strong needles and thread.
• You should also consider taking a spare axle.

Always pack spares where you can find them easily, and wrap parts to protect them and also give them some buoyancy in the event of a capsize.   Sleeping mat foam can be useful for both of these purposes.

MEDICAL CONDITIONS

General Considerations

These notes are intended to give some awareness of the medical conditions that may give rise to special considerations or needs.

They are not comprehensive, but give an overview of some of the difficulties encountered by people with ASTHMA, DIABETES and EPILEPSY, and the implications for canoeing of some forms of medication.   They should be used to enhance opportunity and not restrict the participation of any individual.

Involvement in an activity for the first time often means unforeseen changes in the daily routine which can affect medication and meal times.   An extra level of exercise or anxiety can affect the manner in which effective and balanced medical regimes usually control the individual's condition.

For these reasons it is advisable to be aware of the potential implication of such changes and discuss them with the individual concerned.   In some cases you may also need to talk to parents, friends and carers.

It is hoped that these notes will be useful for the instructor or leader who has not had a person with these conditions in a group before.

A better understanding of asthma, diabetes, epilepsy and medication, and a knowledge of simple precautions and treatments means that no-one need be excluded from an activity or exercise programme because of their condition.   The leader or instructor should:

- be aware of any medications that are being taken and the times at which they should be taken,

- have clear emergency procedures,

- know who to contact if you have difficulties,

- consult the National Body for the impairment for specific advice,

- nominate a "buddy" who will be aware of the person's needs and, if necessary be prepared to support them if they should become incapacitated or distressed.

ASTHMA

Acknowledgements

The National Asthma Campaign.

What is Asthma?

This is the most common chronic disease in the western world but it is a treatable condition.   The four main symptoms of asthma are: coughing, wheezing, shortness of breath and a feeling of tightness in the chest. Asthma attacks can be triggered by many different things, including:-

- allergies (dust, furry or feathered animals, pollen and certain foods),
- changes in air temperature,
- stress,
- 'flu or colds,
- pollution (such as traffic fumes or cigarette smoke), or exercise.

However, modern medicines do help people with asthma considerably.

Implications

Make sure that people with asthma have their relief medication with them all the time. Many asthmatics have relief inhalers, such as Ventolin or Bricanyl, which can alleviate the attack once taken.

Asthma attacks can appear quite frightening. You must try to stay calm because if you panic you will only make the situation worse for the person having the attack.

If you can try to avoid the things which you know are triggers for the person with asthma, e.g. dust, pollen, cigarette smoke etc.

Note: for dealing with an attack consult; "Take control of asthma" or the advice given in the National Asthma Campaign's *"School Pack"*.

Asthma and Exercise.

Everyone gets breathless after exercise, but only those with asthma can develop a cough and wheezing.   However, exercise is good for everyone, including those with asthma, so it should not be avoided by people with the condition.

If exercise does bring on asthma symptoms, the answer is to modify the type of activity that is undertaken.

People with asthma should not exercise outdoors on cold days, and should avoid long spells of exercise. If necessary, they should take two puffs from a relief inhaler before starting an activity.

For more advice see *"Exercise and Asthma"* (National Asthma Campaign) If there is any doubt about the suitability of a particular activity, suggest that the individual consults their GP, or calls the National Asthma Campaign Help line, on 0345 010203 (9.00am - 9.00pm)

Useful Publications

"Exercise and Asthma"

"Take Control of Asthma" "Secondary School Pack"

All from the National Asthma Campaign

DIABETES

Acknowledgements

The British Diabetic Association and Brian Hunter of the International Diabetic Athletes Association.

What is Diabetes?

This condition is caused by a lack of the hormone insulin in the body. Lack of insulin causes sugar levels in the body to rise. People of all ages can have diabetes and are treated with regular injections of insulin combined with a prescribed eating pattern. Some older people who have low insulin levels may have the condition controlled by taking tablets or just with dietary changes.

Implications

High blood sugar levels can lead to tiredness, thirst and lethargy in the short term (a few days) and in the long term (a number of years) lead to complications involving the eyes, kidneys and nerves.

Of more immediate importance is the condition of hypoglycaemia. This is when there is too little sugar in the blood. This can be a side effect of insulin treatment and some tablets for diabetes. Symptoms which can occur are confusion, trembling and hunger. The overall effect may appear as drunkenness or hypothermia.

The restoration of the blood sugar level with sweets, glucose tablets, or sugary drinks takes only a few minutes and then needs to be followed with either a meal or snack such as a sandwich or a few pieces of fruit.

However, if the blood sugars are extremely low and kept low for a period, convulsions or unconsciousness may result. In this case do not attempt to give sugar or glucose but obtain medical help immediately.

A Strategy for Regular Exercise

(With acknowledgement to "The Benefits of Exercise" Brian Hunter, NURSING March 8-21 1990 vol. 4; no. 6)

For many people regular participation in the programmes described in this book is not always possible. However, when the activity can be made regular, exercising at the same time each day or each week is to be advised.

With this in mind the following advice is offered to the person who has diabetes. The same rules apply to any fitness programmes:-

- Have a medical check-up and approval from your consultant before you start an activity programme.

- Request some guidance on the most suitable type of exercise.

- Make a slow start, for example 10-15 minutes daily

- Try to exercise at the same time each day. Just as insulin and diet are taken at specific times, so should activity.

- Wear well fitting shoes and cotton socks.

- Learn how to take your pulse

- Take blood sugar checks before, during and after exercise.

- Do not exercise if your blood sugar is below 5 mmol/l or above 10 mmol/l.

- Be aware of low blood sugar and carry fast-acting glucose, such as "Hypostop" or "Lucozade".

- Be aware of the dangers of over-compensating to a hypoglycaemic state.

- Maintain hydration by drinking sugar-free liquids before, during and after exercise.

- Talk to an exercise psychologist or someone involved in sports medicine about your programme.

- Do not take an excessive intake of glucose or carbohydrate before activity, in an attempt to prevent a hypoglycaemic attack. Excessive intake of glucose or carbohydrate at the onset of hypoglycaemia is also to be discouraged.

- 10g carbohydrate is sufficient.   As a rough guide, one digestive biscuit weighs 10 grammes.

Guidelines for the Coach

- Ensure medication is taken as prescribed

- Ensure that meals are taken at regular times following the prescribed dietary needs.

- Approved snacks should be regularly available especially before, during and after exercise.

- Keep sugar/glucose tablets/sweet fizzy drinks to hand.

Useful Publications

"The Benefits of Exercise" Brian Hunter, NURSING March 8-21 1990 vol. 4; no. 6   "Diabetes"
                        "Diabetes and Hypoglycaemia"

Published by the British Diabetic Association

Especially recommended

"A Diabetics Guide to Health and Fitness", Professor Kris E Berg. Human Kinetics

EPILEPSY

Acknowledgements

The British Epilepsy Association

What is Epilepsy?

It is a tendency to have recurrent seizures (also known as fits). The seizure may take many forms, differing from one person to another, but the reason for it is always the same. It is due to an altered state within the brain.

Who has Epilepsy?

- At least 1 in 200 of the population.

- It can affect anyone, at any age, but most commonly develops before the age of 20.

N.B.

- Many people will have their epilepsy controlled by medication.

- It is not a mental illness or psychiatric disorder.

- It is not infectious.

What causes Epilepsy?

Some people will develop epilepsy because of brain damage brought on by injury, infection (e.g. encephalitis or meningitis), hormonal problems, circulatory problems or tumours (Symptomatic Epilepsy).

However, for most the cause remains a mystery (Idiopathic Epilepsy). It appears that those who develop epilepsy have a lower resistance to seizures than most of the population.

What Triggers Epilepsy?

Some people with epilepsy may identify factors which bring on seizures. These could include stress, hormonal changes or illness.

A small percentage (3-5%) of people with epilepsy have seizures which are triggered by flashing or flickering lights or patterns, such as strobe lights, television, computer games, (Photo-Sensitive Epilepsy).

Types of seizures

There are many types of seizures and a person may have more than one type. No two people will have the same symptoms. The type of seizure depends upon which part of the brain is affected. If the whole brain is affected then the fit is known as generalised and there is a loss of consciousness, however brief. If only one part of the brain is affected, then it is known as partial and consciousness, though affected, may not necessarily be lost.

Just as people's seizures vary, so do recovery times. This can vary from seconds to minutes. Some people may need to rest or sleep for a while. It is not usually necessary to call a doctor or an ambulance.

Medical help should be sought if:-

- a seizure shows no signs of stopping after a few minutes,

- a series of seizures takes place without the person properly regaining consciousness in between,

- there is physical injury during the seizure.

How to recognise a seizure and what to do.

Generalised Absence (previously called Petit Mal)

The person looks blank and stares. They may have slight twitching or blinking. This will last for a few seconds, then normal activity will continue.

<u>What to do</u>

- Be reassuring.

- Go over everything which may have been missed. The person may be unaware of the seizure.

<u>Generalised Tonic-clonic (previously called Grand Mal)</u>

A common sequence would be; staring, stiffening of the body, possible blue colour round the mouth, convulsions (jerky movements of the body).

As breathing recovers, normal colouring returns. There may be incontinence. These seizures last for only a few minutes.

<u>What to do</u>

- Protect the person from injury, cushion the head.

- Do not restrict the person's movements or put anything into their mouth.

- After the seizure help them to breath by turning them onto their side.

- Stay with them until they have fully recovered.

<u>Complex Partial (affecting a specific area of the brain)</u>

May start with an "Aura" or warning. The person will appear confused and distracted. They may repeat a series of movements, e.g. plucking at their clothes.

<u>What to do</u>

- Do not try to stop the seizure.

- Remove harmful objects and guide the person away from danger.

- Talk quietly to reassure them.

Useful Publications

> *"Epilepsy - Sport and Leisure"* and *"Living with Epilepsy"*
> *Both from the British Epilepsy Association*

For details regarding the management of activities see also Chapter 17. For the implications of Epilepsy and Diabetes for members of the Coaching Scheme see also Chapter 14.

The addresses for further information about all these conditions may be found in Chapter 21.

THE SIDE EFFECTS OF SOME MEDICATIONS

Many medications have side effects, and whilst not all side effects are sufficiently significant to cause concern, it is advisable to discuss the possible side effects with anyone who takes medication, whether regularly or temporarily.

Temporary Medication

Often, because a condition and its medical treatment are temporary, the person does not always consider the implications and inform the leader.

However, some drugs taken to relieve temporary situations such as colds, coughs or hay-fever can make the individual drowsy.   This potential, seen alongside the possibility of becoming fatigued by the activity, should be considered seriously if a trip is being planned.

Be aware also of drugs that may affect the digestive system such as aspirin or ibuprofen.

Psychotropic medicines

Many psychotropic medicines cause the body to dehydrate, sometimes quite severely. A person on this medication must replenish fluid loss frequently to avoid going into shock.

Increased sensitivity to sunlight

A number of medicines including psychotropic medicines and Tetracycline give the person hypersensitivity to sunlight which means they burn more easily. People should be aware of the effect that their medication has upon their sensitivity to sunlight and will probably be prepared. However, they may not be fully aware that being on the water greatly increases the effects of the sun, and that on the water it is possible to burn in sunlight that off the water would not be a problem.

Using a sun block, or a sun lotion with a high sunscreen factor on all exposed skin is advisable.   In addition, people at risk should always wear a light coloured hat with a brim, and light coloured clothes that cover up as much of the skin as possible.

Any sunscreen should be reapplied regularly if the person is getting wet.

VISUAL IMPAIRMENT

Acknowledgements

I am grateful for the advice and support of Gina Southey with this section.

People with visual impairments have visual abilities that range from no sight at all to vision that is only mildly affected. It is a fact that most people who are registered as being blind do, in truth, have some form of vision.

It is sometimes useful to know at what age a person became visually impaired.   The person who was born with a visual impairment will usually be very competent in strategies that help them to maximise their abilities and in reducing the disabling effect of their impairment.   The person who developed a visual impairment will probably still recall vision and therefore have a mental picture even if they do not have a visual one.

However, the conditions of the environment we are in affect the ability of all of us to see.   No-one sees particularly well when it is dark, or very bright, or when there is a mist or haze.   Equally, we all find it difficult to see when there are extremes of light contrast such as trying to determine someone's features when they are stood in front of a brightly lit window.

The quality of natural light also tends to vary according to the season, and day by day according to the weather.   It also tends to vary during the day; improving after dawn and deteriorating towards dusk.

Indoors the quality of the light can vary according to what natural, and what artificial light there is, and which direction it is coming from.   At times it is not just a question of how much light but what type it is, direct or diffused, bright or subdued, or white or coloured?   In this respect the colours of the surroundings are also important. Sometimes everything is of a similar colour or tone and, therefore, blending together.   In other settings there may be contrasts of colour and tones between the walls and the furniture.

Of course, these latter conditions do not just apply to artificial environments such as buildings; the natural environment can equally be one of little or no contrasts or can present startling variations of colour and tone, light and shade.

Therefore, the key question to ask of anyone that you will be canoeing with is:-

"What can you see; here; and now?"

Do not be anxious about asking this question. By doing so you will be able to determine whether the individual has a perception of colour, shape, or movement. The person may also be able to distinguish contrasts such as light and dark, or one colour against another. Some people have a spatial awareness whereby they can distinguish between large objects and small objects.

Other people have visual impairments that distort what they see. The most frequently occurring visual impairments are the ones which follow.

Cataracts This impairment is like looking through frosted glass. Therefore, large movements can be seen better than small movements. Bright colours and clear contrasts are more easily seen.

Glaucoma This and other eye conditions can lead to tunnel vision. The view is that of seeing only what is at the centre of the vision. As if looking through a small hole cleared in the centre of a misted window. To see around them, people with this impairment need to scan the area they wish to see, not by moving the eyes, but by moving the whole head.

Macular Degeneration This impairment gives the viewer the opposite effect to that of tunnel vision. The vision is clearer at the periphery of the visual field. It is still necessary for people with this impairment to scan by turning the head, as for tunnel vision, in-order to see through the usual range of vision.

Diabetic Retinopathy This impairment is caused by the fragmentation of the retina, usually as a result of diabetes. The vision is that of a partially blurred jigsaw. No one part of the visual field is complete, as if looking into a mirror in which the glass has been shattered. It is worth asking people with this condition

"How is your vision today?"

Double Vision The effect of this impairment is fairly self explanatory. It is caused by a number of conditions including multiple sclerosis.

Implications

People with visual impairments often have an increased awareness of their environment and can use strategies that draw upon their other senses. For this reason you should consider carefully the following.

- Give people accurate information about their surroundings.

- Tell them where doors, furniture, equipment are, and especially where the water's edge is.

- Have easily seen contrasting blocks of colour that identify where edges of steps or landing stages are.

- Establish clear, safe walk-ways, and let everyone know where they are and why you have established them.   Keep walkways clear of obstacles.   This is not just those things that are on the floor, but also anything that overhangs a walk-way, especially anything at face level.

- Do not leave doors partially open and take care with windows that project across walk-ways when they are open.

- Establish tidy habits. Discourage people from leaving equipment and boats across walk-ways.

When talking to people with visual impairments:-

- Remember that you cannot "catch someone's eye" or use the usual body language in initiating, or terminating a conversation.

- Precede all conversation with the person's name. Then they will know that you are talking to them.

- When you are leaving a person, tell them that you are going so that they will not assume you are still there.

- Never touch someone who has a visual impairment. To attract their attention, first say "hello", tell them your name, and then touch them lightly on the arm to let them know you are addressing them.

- In conversation, don't be afraid to use terms like "nice to see you", visually impaired people use this, and similar phrases also.

- Always talk directly to the person, not to the person guiding them or their companion.

- Position yourself facing the light, so that those people will some vision can see you more clearly.

- Always look at the person you are talking to. Although they may not be able to see you they will know from the sound of your voice when you are facing away from them.

- If you are going to give out notes, determine the best way to do this. You could put them onto audio tape, or have them enlarged on a photocopier. Discuss the most appropriate format with the person involved. Some visually impaired people can have reading material brailled. This is worth doing if it is something that is used often.

- Study chapter 19 which looks at Access.

Coaching

Use hands-on coaching to explain to the individual what the stroke looks like and how to perform it. Use verbal descriptions at the same time so that later when you are analysing the skill you both have a common terminology for the process.

Because there is little, or no, visual feedback to give clues about orientation, some people with visual impairments have difficulties when balancing their canoe or kayak. Ken Roberts discovered that by using a simple backrest, some people with visual impairments have a sense of what is vertical that assists them with their balance. He found that something as simple as a swim float, wedged between the paddler and the boat was sufficient for this purpose.

Once on the water the need to know which direction to go can be supported by a number of strategies.

The obvious strategy is for the person with a visual impairment to be paired with a sighted paddler in a K2 or canoe. A number of visually impaired paddlers compete very successfully using this technique.

For those people who wish to paddle solo, directions need to be given.

The first method is to utilise what vision the person has. If they can see colours or can determine contrasts, then these visual clues can be built into the rear view of a "buddy" who will then always paddle conscious of the fact that they are leading the way for a buddy who has a visual impairment.

Another method is to use a radio system that enables two people to communicate without shouting instructions across the water. Details of these systems may be found in chapter 9 on Equipment.

Utilising the abilities of the visually impaired person to hear is also possible. Mechanical aids such as sound beacons, whistles, and radios carried by a sighted buddy, and even non stop conversation or singing, have all been used to give directional clues. However, in using such strategies there is also a tendency to drown out any natural sounds of the environment which, to the more practised ear, can themselves give clues to the whereabouts of the individual.

Leading

There are times when it may be necessary to lead someone who is visually impaired; in the busy swimming pool or at the naturally hazardous water's edge this may be advisable.

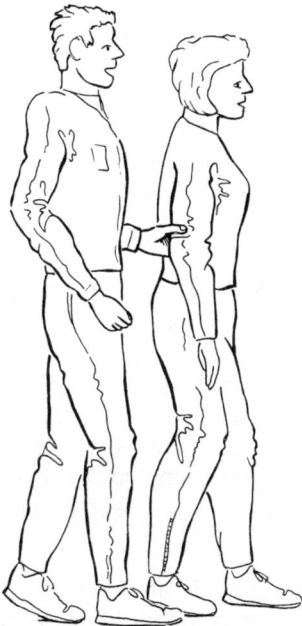

Some people with visual impairments are "touch sensitive". When you cannot see it can be quite disturbing to be touched. Therefore, you should always ask before touching, and if you are going to lead seek advice on how the person would like you to do this.

The general method used to lead confidently is to place the person's hand on your forearm just above the elbow. Keep your guiding arm straight with the fingers pointing to the ground, with contact like this you will naturally be about half a pace in front. Your partner's contact with your arm will give them clues about the direction you are going, when you are turning, and when you are going up or down steps or slopes. Before you set off make sure that you are both facing in the same direction.

Fig 11:6 Leading a blind person

You should always supplement leading with verbal information about where you are going and when you are going up and down steps. Always tell the person how many steps if you can, but certainly warn them when they come to the last step. You can use phrases such as "step up" or "step down" for each step.

Some people with visual impairments will want to stop and feel for the edge of the step with their foot before proceeding. Give them time to do this.

Be especially careful when going through doorways or through other narrow openings, remember that you are two people wide. At these times it helps to be in single file. To do this, move your guiding arm to the centre of your back, still keeping it straight. Your partner will then move to a position behind you and extend their own arm to avoid walking on your heels.

HEARING IMPAIRED

Acknowledgements

I am grateful to Simon Scandrett, who was the first deaf Instructor in the B.C.U., for his advice and personal input when preparing this section. There is an address for Simon in Chapter 21.

My thanks also to Tricia Harris of the Royal National Institute for Deaf People, for her advice.

Terminology

Tricia Harris tells me she is aware that some deaf people are not keen on the term hearing impairment. This is, she believes, a cultural issue, in that profoundly deaf people do not wish to be known by a term that implies they lack something. They feel that they cannot lack something they never had and that they are as complete as someone who has hearing.

Therefore, I have decided to use the phrase "deaf" to cover, deaf, deafened and hard of hearing to avoid having to repeat these terms in every reference.

Introduction

A deaf person is the same as you and I, it is just that their hearing is different and their means of understanding and communicating may be different.   There is no obvious disability to give any notice to other people that a person may have problems with hearing, until conversation is attempted.

If the hearing loss is severe, and has been so since birth, then the person often has difficulties with speech and their tonal quality may make it difficult for others to understand what they are saying.

People who go deaf after being able to hear still retain speech but because they cannot hear their own voice the tonal quality of their speech is also impaired to a lesser degree.

Deaf does not mean dumb, in either sense of the word. Neither does deaf mean daft.

Do not refer to deaf people as deaf and dumb.

Implications

Hearing aids are not always as useful as they appear to be.

They are no more than mechanical amplifiers and they cannot differentiate between sounds from different sources. Therefore, increasing the amplification in order to hear a person speaking against a background noise does not always work since the background noise is also amplified.

Furthermore, some hearing impaired people have nerve damage which means that what they hear is often just a cacophony of sounds that are unintelligible as speech.   These people wear a hearing aid, not to hear speech but to be aware that there are sounds about them that may mean someone is trying to attract their attention or there may be machinery or traffic present.

However, used correctly, hearing aids are useful. Be cautious about people wearing them on the water since they are very expensive and could be damaged if they got wet.   However, if a deaf paddler finds a hearing aid useful when on the water, and paddles sufficiently to warrant it, there is a waterproof hearing aid available.   (See *Lotos* Chapter 21) "Lotos"

Some conditions of partial hearing results from a hearing loss in a particular frequency range.   Therefore, the individual may be able to hear sounds that are pitched high, for example.   Knowing this you may be able to pitch your voice higher to enable a person with such a loss to tune into you. Or you may decide to ask a female instructor to give the information since the female voice is generally higher in pitch than the male.

Damage to the inner ear may result in a person's balance being affected. Such a person may not be able to determine what is up and what is down when they cannot see an horizon line. The implications for this are obvious during a capsize or on water that varies in height or swell such as river rapids or on the sea.

Communication

- Determine which ear, if either, has the better hearing.

- Do not shout. This distorts the quality of the speech and when communicating to young people even the politest of remarks can appear like angry ones when shouted.

- Cut out as much background noise as possible.

- Establish what you want to say and give all your instructions before a deaf person moves away. Remember that you cannot recall that person to give additional instructions.

- Have someone, who can hear you, paddle in front of a deaf person so that they can relay messages from you.

- If in doubt write things down. A pencil and a piece of white "Formica" works very well even when wet.

- Attracting attention can often be affected by tapping the canoe of a deaf person since vibrations can be felt if not heard.

- Some simple instructions can be conveyed by signal even over a distance. e.g. Patting the head means "come to me", an arm sweeping across the body to point means "go that way".

- You can also get the person you are coaching to teach you some basic communication signs.

- Although they cannot replace the hearing aid, there is the *Commlink* radio transmitter and waterproof receivers that allow communication between an instructor and a deaf person. The quality of such devices varies and are very dependent upon the hearing ability of the individual user. Nevertheless, for a number of people with partial hearing they have proved to be quite successful. "Commlink" (See Chapter 21 for *Commlink*)

If the person lip reads:-

- Keep the light behind them so that they can see your face clearly.

- Face them on the same level (especially important for people in wheelchairs or children).

- Speak carefully and clearly, but not too slowly or with undue emphasis. Lip reading relies on pace and intonation.

- Do not smoke, eat or do anything else that involves putting your hand to your mouth. Lip readers must be able to see your mouth.

- Use plain language. Many words look the same to a lip reader. The more common the word the better.

- Use facial expression and your hands to clarify or emphasise what you are saying. Many hands movements are natural and universal. e.g. "Do you want a drink?"

- If you are not immediately understood, repeat what you said. If there still appears to be doubts, try re-phrasing.

On the whole, deaf people use visual contact, facial expressions, writing, lip-reading, gesture, body language and speech for communication.

Finally, if the person is communicating with you via an interpreter, always address your conversation to the deaf person not to their interpreter.

The BSL signs on the next two pages are reproduced by kind permission of Keith Ripley and Simon Scandrett from their book "Signs for Canoeists".

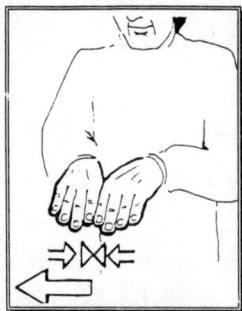

Raft up   Flat hands are tapped together, then moved to the left and tapping is repeated.

Roll Hand forward, index finger pointing up, rotate finger fully to mimic going down and back up.

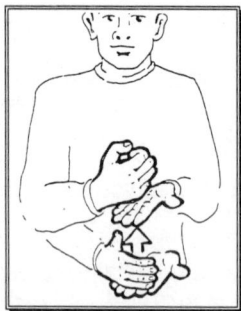

Rescue Blade of right hand on open palm, hands moved backwards, right hand closed.

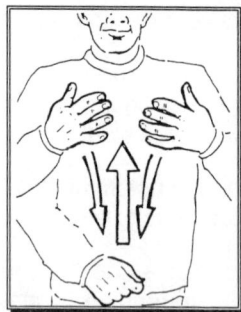

Buoyancy Aid   Mimic pulling buoyancy aid over shoulders and pulling zip up.

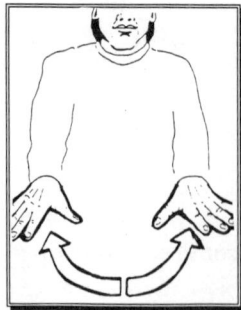

Spraydeck   Open hands start together in front of body, and move sideways and backwards.

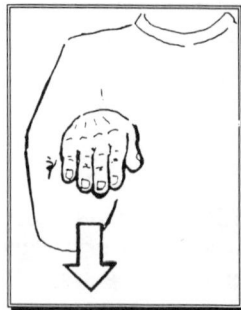

Canoe Palm down, mimic boat moving forwards.

Canoeing for Disabled People   Geoff Smedley

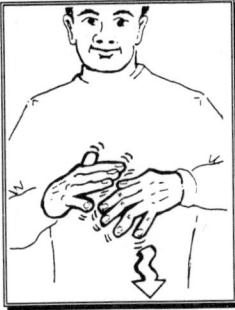

Rapids Open hands, fingers slightly bent, R hand over L. L hand moves forward and down, mimicking rapid.

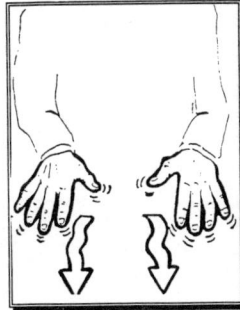

Weir Open hands, fingers slightly bent, mimic movement of boiling water going forwards and down.

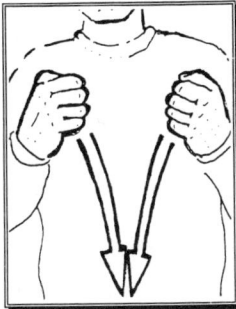

Cagoul Mime pulling cagoul over body

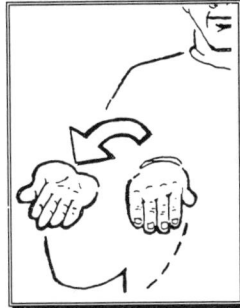

Capsize Palm down, mimic boat turning over

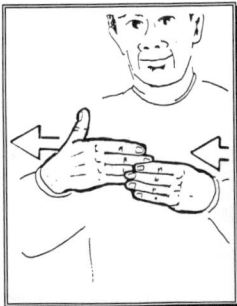

Leader Flat hands, backs forward, L hand holds fingers of R. R thumb held up. Hands are moved to R.

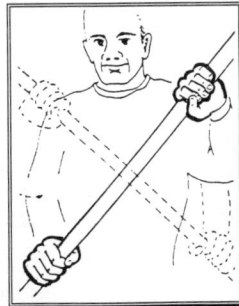

Paddle Mimic paddling action

Fig 11:7 BSL for Canoeists

Geoff Smedley

Canoeing for Disabled People

CHAPTER TWELVE

IMPAIRMENTS EXPLAINED

Contents

- Amputee

- Arthrogryphosis

- Arthritis

- Brittle Bones

- Cerebral palsy

- Clumsiness

- Congenital Heart Disease

- Cystic Fibrosis

- Down's Syndrome

- Friedreich's Ataxia

- Haemophilia Incontinence

- Mental Illness

- Multiple Sclerosis

- Muscular Dystrophy

- Parkinson's Disease

- Poliomyelitis

- Spina Bifida

- Spinal Cord Paralysis

- Stomas

- Stroke

- Impaired Behaviour

General Considerations

These notes are not comprehensive, they cover the major impairments only and contain no prescription for automatic success.   Since the emphasis of this book has been to focus on the abilities of the individual, these notes only refer to those implications that need significant attention to ensure that the participant is safe and comfortable in the chosen activity.

These notes should be used to enhance opportunity and not restrict participation.

As a coach you should look to each person as an individual with individual abilities and aspirations.

In determining these abilities and aspirations do not make assumptions; you should talk to the individual. (In some cases you may also need to talk to the person's parents or carers.)

In addition you should:-

•   have clear emergency procedures,

•   know who to contact if you have difficulties,

•   consult a medical adviser if in doubt.

NOTE

Some impairments have specific implications for the delivery of coaching programmes. Therefore, information about :-

• Hearing and Vision, and the medical conditions of

• Asthma, Diabetes and Epilepsy may be found in Chapter 11.

• Notes for Learning Disability may be found in Chapter 18.

Amputee

Limbs are amputated as a result of injury or disease. The amputation may be of arms or legs and may be partial or complete.

Implications

Mobility for amputees is often made possible by the use of artificial limbs or other aids, such as crutches or wheelchairs. Either can be difficult to control where the surface is wet or slippery.

Amputees who have lost limbs can sometimes experience a "phantom limb" sensation. This causes them to feel that the limb is still there. Sometimes the person may then rely on the missing limb for support with the result that they overbalance or fall.

In canoeing the problems arise, in the main, from not being able to hold a paddle conventionally, or to sit steadily in the craft. If there is a loss of only one arm or leg then the person may have difficulties with balance.

Some amputees have artificial limbs that would assist them if they were worn for canoeing. However, you must check to see if the limb is suitable for this use. Many limbs are very expensive and could be damaged by using in this way or even by contact with water.

There is more information about artificial limbs in Chapter 11.

Arthrogryphosis

This is a congenital impairment that affects some or all of the joints. The symptoms are stiffness of the joint and a weakness of the muscles. People with this condition may have a restricted range of movement in their joints. However, most people with this condition do not have any impairment of speech or learning capacity.

Implications

Exercise is usually recommended since this helps to increase and maintain flexibility in the joints. Your programme will need to take account of the limitations in the range of movement. This can affect the type of craft the person paddles related to the amount of flexibility there is in the legs. Be aware that if joints are stiff then staying in the same position, either sitting or kneeling, could cause the person to stiffen to an extent when they need assistance to move. This must be born in mind if closed deck kayaks are to be considered.

Stroke development will also need to take account of the degree of stiffness and the range of mobility of the upper body joints.

As always take your lead from the individual about what kinds of exercise are most appropriate and which strokes are best to develop. The aim must be to use the exercise to develop and maintain flexibility but not if it causes excessive discomfort or pain.

Arthritis

With acknowledgements to the Arthritis and Rheumatism Council.

Arthritis means disease of, or damage to the joints. Rheumatism is a more general term used to cover any pain in the bones, muscles, joints or the tissues surrounding the joints. The term "rheumatism diseases" is used to refer to all types of arthritis and rheumatism.

There are about 200 different types of rheumatism disease. Fortunately many of them are rare, but generally they fall into four main types:

Back Pain

This may be due to mechanical stress on the spine, degeneration and prolapse of the discs, inflammation of the ligaments and in the joints of the spine and pelvis, degeneration and bony outgrowths with entrapment of nerves and diseases of bones. Sometimes there is no obvious physical cause for back pain.

Soft-Tissue Rheumatism

This is pain in the structures around the joints often related to minor injury or over-use, they are usually short-lasting spells of pain, for example, "tennis elbow".

Inflammation of the Joint Lining

This condition can cause extensive damage to the joints, such as in Rheumatoid Athritis.

Damage to the Surface of the Joints

A common example of this condition is Osteoarthritis.

It is these last two types of arthritis, Rheumatoid Athritis and Osteoarthritis that are the most disabling.

Implications

Changes in the weather can affect the feelings of pain and stiffness.

Gentle exercise is to be encouraged since this eases the joints and keeps them mobile. However, rest is equally important. Therefore, some balance between rest and exercise is advisable. It is recommended that the person with arthritis consults their physiotherapist regarding the suitability of any exercise.

The amount of exercise possible for any individual will vary, however a little and often is better than prolonged continuous exercise. If a particular activity causes a lot of pain, lasting for over an hour, it is wise to avoid it.

People with Arthritis are sensitive to cold. They should not over exert themselves. Movement is often slow and the drugs used frequently create depressive moods. Therefore, to avoid over-stressing the individual, the instructor needs to be understanding and sensitive to the special needs of the person with Arthritis when organising a programme.

Brittle-Bones

These people are often weak usually with a small build and often have limbs that are deformed as a result of frequent fractures. The bone defect almost always causes some form of deafness also. As children with brittle bones grow older they tend to become stronger, this is because their bones stop growing in adolescence.

Implications

People with brittle bones have a not unnatural fear of falling or being pushed over. Handling, lifting and carrying should be performed with great care. Canoeing should take place where there is easy access and egress and there is no danger of the person being knocked or of falling.

An open canoe with an experienced paddler may well be the most successful craft. All sharp or hard edges should be padded.

Cerebral palsy

With acknowledgements to Howard Bailey of SCOPE (previously the Spastics Society) and Steve Devlin.

Cerebral palsy (CP) is not a disease nor is it an illness. It is the description of physical impairment that affects movement and muscle tone (stiffness). The movement problems vary from barely noticeable to extremely severe. No two people with cerebral palsy are the same - it is as individual as the people themselves.

Some people with cerebral palsy have higher than average intelligence. Others have moderate or severe learning difficulties. Most people with CP are of average intelligence, although it is often assumed, wrongly, that people who are unable to control their facial expressions are intellectually impaired.

Cerebral palsy describes a variety of conditions. There are three main types, corresponding to the different areas of the brain which may be affected.

Spastic cerebral palsy

For people with spastic cerebral palsy, there is an increased muscle tone (stiffness), especially with effort affecting control over movements. A quick stretch of the muscle produces a contraction. This may occur in any part of the muscle range. Occasionally there are tremors or shudders in a limb. There can be a change in the muscle tone and posture with excitement, fear or anxiety. Sudden, as opposed to slow, movements and contact with cold water can also increase muscle tone. The position of the head and neck is also very important.

Spasticity should not be confused with paralysis; there is voluntary movement, but it is not the smooth, co-ordinated pattern of movement observed in someone with normal motor skills.

Athetoid cerebral palsy

People with athetoid cerebral palsy have excessive jerking or writhing and loss of control of their posture, caused by loss of brain programmes for the control of movement. These involuntary movements can be increased by excitement, insecurity and the effort to make voluntary movements. They are decreased if the attention is deeply held, but they can also be decreased by fatigue or drowsiness. With voluntary movements there is sometimes an initial delay before movement begins and a lack of fine movements.

Some people with athetoid cerebral palsy find that the effects of the conflicting reflexes causes difficulties when weight bearing, their feet withdraw upwards. There is often an associated hearing impairment in the high frequency range.

Ataxic cerebral palsy

For people with ataxic cerebral palsy there is a disturbance of balance with a poor ability to fix the head, trunk, shoulder and pelvic girdle. Voluntary movements are often clumsy and uncoordinated. People with this condition can either under or over reach. There may also be shaky hand movements and jerky speech.

The distribution of limb impairments

Depending upon which parts of the body are most affected the terms used are:-

Quadriplegia   Both upper and lower limbs,

Hemiplegia   Mostly affecting one side,

Diplegia   Mostly affecting both lower limbs.

Reflexes and Spasms.

Although not present in everyone with cerebral palsy there are reflex conditions of the neck and head that are worth noting. When they are present it is important to ensure that the head is in a neutral position, and that the person is relaxed when dressing, eating or being lifted.

TNR (Tonic Neck Reflex) refers to the influence of the head position backwards and forwards. In the forward position there will be a tendency to extend the upper limbs and flex the lower limbs. When the head is back the reverse applies.

ATNR (Asymmetric Tonic Neck Reflex) refers to the head position turned left or right. When turned to the left, the left arm, leg and trunk, will tend to be extended and the right side will tend towards flexion. When the head is turned to the right the opposite may be observed.

On the whole a calm, unhurried approach to movement is best, whether in using canoeing skills or in the changing room.

Implications

Athetosis can lead to a sudden loss of balance. Muscle spasm can inhibit the ability to expel water should a person with spasticity inhale it. Be cautious of over exertion, this can lead to stiffness especially when the weather conditions, or the sports environment is cold.

Because some people with cerebral palsy have difficulties with speech you may have to give particular consideration to communication. Whilst it is possible to understand the speech of many people with cerebral palsy you do need time to "tune in". Therefore, initially, at least, you may need to enlist the help of family or carers.

Even if the person appears to be able to move quite easily, control of the muscles is not particularly efficient and requires effort. Movements may for this reason be tiring. Whilst the instructor should be aware of this, giving due consideration to the speed at which people with cerebral palsy may move, exercise is to be encouraged.

It is also probably that as young people come to adolescence their mobility decreases and they have a tendency to stiffen up. This effect can cause anxiety since it is often more apparent when people are active. The instructor will need to be sensitive to this possibility.

Sometimes other parts of the brain are impaired, leading to sight, hearing, perception and learning difficulties. Between a quarter and a third of children and adolescents and a tenth of adults with cerebral palsy are also affected by epilepsy.

See also the notes in the previous chapter on skin care.

This explanation is only brief and for any individual will need to be expanded upon by discussion with the individual, parent or carer, a physio-therapist or medical practitioner.

Clumsiness (Mild Motor Impairment)

When we perform even the most apparently simple action a very complex series of messages is transmitted from the brain, through the nerves, to the muscles. We are usually unaware of the complexity of these messages and take for granted that by thinking about what to do the body will follow naturally. Occasionally this system fails and we make a clumsy response.

Temporary clumsiness

All of us have experienced this for reasons of:-

- tiredness,
- illness or injury,
- the influence of drugs or alcohol,
- anxiety or stress,
- excitement.

The clumsy condition

For some people clumsiness is more frequent because the patterns of control are impaired. This may be due to:-

- some form of brain damage either at birth, from an

   accident or through infection,

   diseases or injuries to muscles or nerves,

   a physical or visual impairment,

- lack of experience, maturation or poor concentration, as in young children.

Implications

The worse reaction is to be impatient and assume that the clumsiness is carelessness or even deliberate.

If the condition of clumsiness is recognised as an impairment, and given the same sensitivity and sympathy as any other impairment then the instructor will develop appropriate strategies to minimise the disabling effect.

By giving such recognition, instructors and helpers are more likely to be patient and understanding, and pressure is taken from the clumsy person.

Being clumsy is no reflection upon the learning ability of the person. Clumsy people can be intelligent, however, the intelligent clumsy person may become frustrated because he cannot keep up with his thoughts and intentions.

Allow time to practice skills. Break them down into small sections. Consider some of the chaining skills as described in Chapter 8.

Congenital Heart Disease

About 1 in 250 people are born with a defective heart. Most of these people are given corrective surgery.

Some people with congenital heart disease also have other impairments. For example, German Measles in pregnancy may cause a child to be born with congenital heart disease, learning disability, deafness or cataracts. About 1 in 4 of people who have Down's Syndrome also have congenital heart disease.

Problems associated with Congenital Heart Disease.

Breathlessness   Many people with congenital heart disease are breathless all the time. This can be exacerbated by exercise.

Tiredness   People with congenital heart disease get tired more easily and more quickly that most people.

Cyanosis   This is a blueness that indicates that the blood is not being oxygenated properly. It is more noticeable in the beds of the fingernails and the lips. Sudden worsening of the blueness is serious and medical assistance should be sought.

Infections   If bacteria get into the blood stream and to the heart this can cause a serious illness. Great care must be taken with hygiene. Whilst on open water care should be taken to prevent excessive contact with the water. Afterwards people should wash thoroughly.   If a person with congenital heart disease becomes unaccountably ill they should be referred to their doctor quickly.

Chest infections are more likely for people with congenital heart disease than for most others.

Nose bleeds   Some people with severe congenital heart disease are prone to nose bleeds. These usually respond well to simple first aid. However, if the bleed lasts for more than 15 minutes then this should be treated as an emergency.

Sudden death   In some rare instances, people with Aortic Stenosis may die suddenly if they exert themselves excessively.

Implications

Many people with congenital heart disease can participate fully in canoeing programmes. However, it is wise to check the following points with them first.

Exercise

How much exercise should the individual take?   Some people with congenital heart disease simply cannot over exert themselves. Others may require advice on activities to ensure that they do not become excessively breathless or tired.

This must all be taken into account when planning trips. It is very distressing for people to have to abandon a journey or expedition when only part way through.

Antibiotics

Some people with congenital heart disease need to take antibiotics if they get an infection. If you are planning an expedition you should have clear guidelines from the participants, or their medical adviser, regarding the circumstance which might necessitate the use of antibiotics.

Cystic Fibrosis

With acknowledgement to the Cystic Fibrosis Trust.

Cystic Fibrosis is an inherited disease. It is the UK's most common genetic disease. It affects the glands which secrete body fluids, damaging many organs including the lungs, the pancreas and the digestive tract. The disease causes thick sticky mucus to be produced which clogs the bronchial tubes and also prevents the body's natural enzymes from digesting food. It means that people with cystic fibrosis are prone to constant chest infections and malnutrition.

Implications

A combination of constant vigorous exercise, drugs, enzymes, physiotherapy and attention to diet help people with cystic fibrosis to control their symptoms.

Physiotherapy is vital to prevent build-up of mucus in the lungs. Children are encouraged to take responsibility for their own physiotherapy and daily breathing exercises.

Regular exercise is valuable in maintaining fitness. It should be possible for people with cystic fibrosis to participate in most activities, but consultation with them, or their carers, will be essential in order to devise the most suitable provision.

Inhaled drugs and antibiotics are crucial for controlling recurring chest infections.   People with cystic fibrosis need high energy foods, frequently supplemented by enzyme tablets.

Down's Syndrome

With acknowledgements to MENCAP and the Down's Syndrome Association

You might think that Down's Syndrome sounds technical. It is, but it is the correct term to use.   You should never use the term Mongol, it is incorrect and offensive.

1 in 4 people with Down's Syndrome also have congenital heart disease.

Implications

Down's Syndrome creates a susceptibility to respiratory infections such as coughs and colds. This, in turn, creates chestiness and occasionally partial deafness. An enlarged tongue and deformed palate can similarly cause speech problems. Therefore, be aware that with some people with Down's Syndrome the ideas are there but the speech organs may not co-operate to express them.

Some people have heart defects and these need to be investigated fully to determine the amount and extent of exercise that can be undertaken. Some people have poor muscle tone and so exercise is to be encouraged.   For others, with a congenital heart defect, steady moderate exercise is best, with careful monitoring to ensure that they do not become distressed.

Take care, especially when outdoors, to protect from the cold since some people with Down's Syndrome have poor temperature regulation. This would, of course, be exacerbated by any immersion in the water.

Atlanto-Axial Instability

Some people with Down's syndrome can have a weakness in the upper vertebrae of the spine. However, it is believed that the very few sporting injuries recorded by people with Down's syndrome which have been caused by atlanto axial instability "atlanto axial instability"would have been just as likely to occur in an ordinary person as the result of a similar fall or accident.

Different doctors have different views about the risks of atlanto-axial instability and will give different advice.   If clarification of the situation is required the following booklet may be useful.

"Atlanto-Axial Instability among People with Down's Syndrome"
The Down's Syndrome Association

Freidreich's Ataxia

This is a neurological disease that progressively affects the control and co-ordination of the muscles.   The symptoms are poor balance and a lack of co-ordination particularly in the limbs and trunk.   The condition does deteriorate.

People with this condition have varying disabilities when walking.   Their walking is clumsy and awkward with the legs moving out wide.

Implications

Because the condition gets progressively worse it is important to monitor activities and consult regularly with the individual.

A canoeing programme that is developed as appropriate to the abilities of the individual may need to be modified over time to take account of the changes in their abilities.

The wise range of opportunities that canoe sport offers is a distinct advantage when determining what is an appropriate programme. This is particularly important when looking for ways to continue participation whilst recognising the reduction in the ability of the individual to develop skills.

Haemophilia

This is an inherited condition, occurring in males.   For a person with haemophilia there is an absence of one of the factors required to clot their blood.

Bleeding may occur from quite minor injuries, and people with severe haemophilia may bleed spontaneously.   It takes a long time for the blood to form a clot. Even when it does so the clot is soft, liable to be dislodged and does not stem the flow of blood completely.

Internal bleeding to the joints is quite common especially to the knee joints. Minor injury causes excessive bruising and the joints swell and go stiff. Bleeding into muscles can put pressure onto nerves causing numbness or pain. It is necessary to recognise the symptoms early since treatment is required to avoid damage to joints and tissues. Repeated bleeding into joints causes arthritis

Implications

Due to the strict level of care that people with haemophilia need, it is necessary for very careful consideration to be given to the potential canoeing programme. However, as long as care is taken canoeing and kayaking are appropriate activities.

Care should be taken to ensure that people do not get unnecessarily bumped or put at undue risk of falling. All cuts respond in the usual way to pressure, they should then be treated with sticking plaster or bandage to stop the flow. If the bleeding does not stop within a minute or two the person must go to hospital, immediately, by ambulance.

Deeper bleeding with stiffness or pain will need treating with injections of factor VIII. Some people with haemophilia will carry these injections with them and will be able to inject themselves. A joint subjected to internal bleeding must be rested.

Particular attention must be given to head injuries. If the person loses consciousness or becomes drowsy or vomits they should be referred for medical help.

The person with haemophilia must carry their haemophilia card with them at all times. This has details of the factor he requires and the address of the haemophiliac centre that he usually attends.

N.B. Not all hospitals have the resources to deal with haemophilia and it is advisable to check with the hospital local to the activity before you go canoeing. Aspirin or any drug containing aspirin must not be given for pain relief since this drug prolongs the bleeding time.

Incontinence

This is the inability to control the actions of the bowel or the bladder. It may derive from pre-natal defect, or an infection or it may be a side effect of a fit such as that experienced in epileptic seizure. It may also be as a result of over-excitement either through fear or an uncontrollable response.

Implications

Someone who is incontinent may face problems associated with anxiety, guilt or ridicule and this can lead to behaviour disorders, depression and isolation, either voluntary or peer enforced.

It is tactful to discuss the problem with the person concerned, or their carers, to determine the arrangements usually made. A sympathetic approach to the problem, and reasonable precautions can negate any of the serious effects.

If on an expedition, ensure that the toilet is easy to find and well illuminated at night and gives privacy to the individual, and that going to the toilet is not an embarrassing or unnecessarily uncomfortable experience.

Mental Health Difficulties

Mental health difficulties may affect such conditions as the individual's personality and reasoning ability. Generally, however, it is a condition that will improve, the person with mental health difficulties often gets better. Whilst people who have mental health difficulties are under treatment they may require professional support. Liaising with this professional will be imperative to any instructor contemplating a canoeing programme for people with mental health difficulties.

Be careful that you, or your helpers, do not confuse mental health issues with Learning Disability since this condition is still sometimes referred to as a Mental Handicap.

Implications

With appropriate help and support a canoeing programme could be used as successful therapy as well as for the sport itself.

Your programme needs to be well structured with clearly defined specific objectives explained to the participants.

Routine is very important. By setting out clear guidelines, procedures, timetables and rules you will help to channel some potentially unacceptable behaviours into healthy activity.

The instruction should be calm, patient and diplomatic. Praise helps to build confidence. The instructor should show an interest in the person and their activity without getting into an emotional involvement.

Some people are "touch sensitive". They are very reluctant to have any physical contact with other people. You need to be aware of this and discuss strategies with their carers.

You may also need the assistance of carers if there are any demonstrations of bizarre behaviour since they will know best how to deal with this.

Multiple Sclerosis

Multiple Sclerosis or as it is more commonly known MS, is a progressively degenerative condition. Isolated plaques of degeneration occur throughout the nervous system, producing a variety of signs and symptoms. As the paralysis worsens the limbs become tight or spastic. Many people with this condition become incontinent.

Speech and balance can be affected, as can vision, sometimes the condition leads to total loss of vision.

People with MS often get periods of remission when they appear to be in better health.

Implications

Depending upon the degree of spasticity, and whether or not the individual is in remission, the capability for canoeing is quite variable.

See also the notes in the previous chapter on skin care.

When in remission people with MS can tire easily. At these time care must be taken to ensure that the programme does not over exert the individual.

Some people with MS have a tremor of the hands, whilst others might find it difficult to use their arms.

It may be necessary to consider the implications of deteriorating vision and Chapter 11 should be consulted for appropriate information.

Muscular Dystrophy

This is a progressive disease of the muscles. It starts in childhood and is most prevalent in boys. The muscles lose their tone and become flaccid as they become replaced by fibrous tissue. Eventually the respiratory muscles are also affected. As the condition progresses the person becomes weaker and usually becomes confined to a wheelchair.

Implications

The muscle flaccidity makes it quite difficult for the individual to move effectively. It also makes it difficult for the carer or helper to support or transfer them. However, the intellectual functioning is not affected.

There is a strong possibility that, due to the enforced inactivity, the individual will put on weight. This increases the difficulties in moving and also for the person giving support or assisting in transfers.

See also the notes in the previous chapter on skin care.

Eventually, it is possible that the person with muscular dystrophy will become too weak to paddle. Moving from an active to a passive participant can be acceptable to some people. They will still continue to enjoy other aspects of the sport such as the outdoor experience and the company. However, for all people with muscular dystrophy it is important to recognise the possibility of them becoming less active and discuss potential alternatives with the individual concerned.

Parkinson's Disease

This is a disease of the nervous system which inhibits the passing of messages from the brain to the muscles. The symptoms are tremors in the muscles, slow movements and stiffness.

Because all muscles are affected then many movements of the limbs are affected. Additionally, other movements such as speech are affected.

The capacity to think is not affected and therefore this condition can also be very frustrating since the individual knows what to do or say, its just that the muscles appear to be uncooperative or too slow to respond.

Implications

People with Parkinson's disease do canoe and kayak. Determining the right programme and the corresponding craft and equipment may take a period of development.

Movements are sometimes difficult to start and at times once started are difficult to stop, furthermore, balance is often affected. In addressing this there is a need to give people time, patience and understanding, so that they can achieve at a speed which is appropriate for them.

However, since this is a condition that usually affects people later in life, some people who have Parkinson's disease may have been active as canoeists or kayaks prior to them contracting it. In these circumstances you will be able to discuss more fully with the participant their abilities and the suitability of the programme.

Whilst there may be a certain amount of frustration as the individual tries to recover some of the skills lost with the onset of the disease, the motivation to succeed is often very high.

If the person has an excessive tremor that makes it difficult to control the paddle, try putting weights into a tight fitting cuff, or using a heavier paddle. However, both of these methods also make paddling harder work.

Poliomyelitis

This is a viral infection that affects the cells of the nerves supplying information between the spinal cord and the muscles. This results in a paralysis of the muscles. These weak, or floppy, muscles may be isolated in a shoulder or a foot, for example, or they may be widespread throughout a whole limb. In addition, the person may be affected by a deformity of the limb due to the muscle wasting and the tendon contracting.

Implications

Special consideration needs to be given to the protection of severely affected limbs. See also the notes about skin care in the previous chapter

People with post polio disabilities have found canoeing to be a beneficial sport because the movements and strength requirements are often within the capabilities of those limb functions that they have.

Some people with post polio disabilities will wear callipers or splints on their legs. The section referring to these appliances is in Chapter 11.

Spina Bifida

This is caused by a failure of the spine to develop properly when in the womb which results in the spine being divided by a cleft. This means in the spinal nerve is not fully protected by the spine, thus leaving it susceptible to damage.

The resultant effect is a weakness and wasting of the muscles in the legs and feet with perhaps a Club Foot or Hydrocephalus (fluid on the brain). To relieve this latter condition a plastic valve is sometimes inserted under the skin at the side of the neck to relieve the fluid retention.

There may also be a paralysis of the nerve supply to the bladder and bowel. This causes incontinence. Some people have an opening in the abdominal wall so that the internal organs can be connected to an external bag to collect the body's waste. For more information about this see the section on Stomas.

Implications

See the section on skin care in the previous chapter.

Because the limbs are so floppy they are easily twisted and so great care must be taken when supporting, transferring, lifting or carrying someone with Spina Bifida.

A blockage in the fluid drain valve is serious and needs immediate medical help. The symptoms that indicate that this has happened are a headache and sleepiness or lethargy.

Hydrocephalus can also cause learning problems. Although the individual may be apparently quite able to learn, this condition does create difficulties in spatial awareness and perception which in turn affects hand and eye co-ordination.

A high temperate may be an indication that there in an urinary infection. This happens quite often in children who are incontinent.

See the section on Stomas for the implications of these.

Some people with Spina Bifida will wear callipers or splints on their legs. The section referring to these appliances is in Chapter 11.

Spinal Cord Paralysis

This occurs when disease or injury damages the spinal cord or a part of the brain that controls the limbs.

Depending upon which parts of the body are most affected the terms used are:-

Quadriplegia   Both upper and lower limbs,

Hemiplegia   Mostly affecting one side,

Diplegia   Mostly affecting both lower limbs.

The limbs below the point of the damage will be paralysed. This paralysis may be flaccid (floppy), or spastic (tight).

Implications

The point at which the injury occurs, and whether the damage or lesion is complete or incomplete determines the degree of impairment.

A complete lesion results in no sensation or movement below the point of damage.   An incomplete lesion gives varying degrees of sensation or motion.

The spinal column

The vertebrae in the spine are divided into sections and given numbers. From the head down they are:-

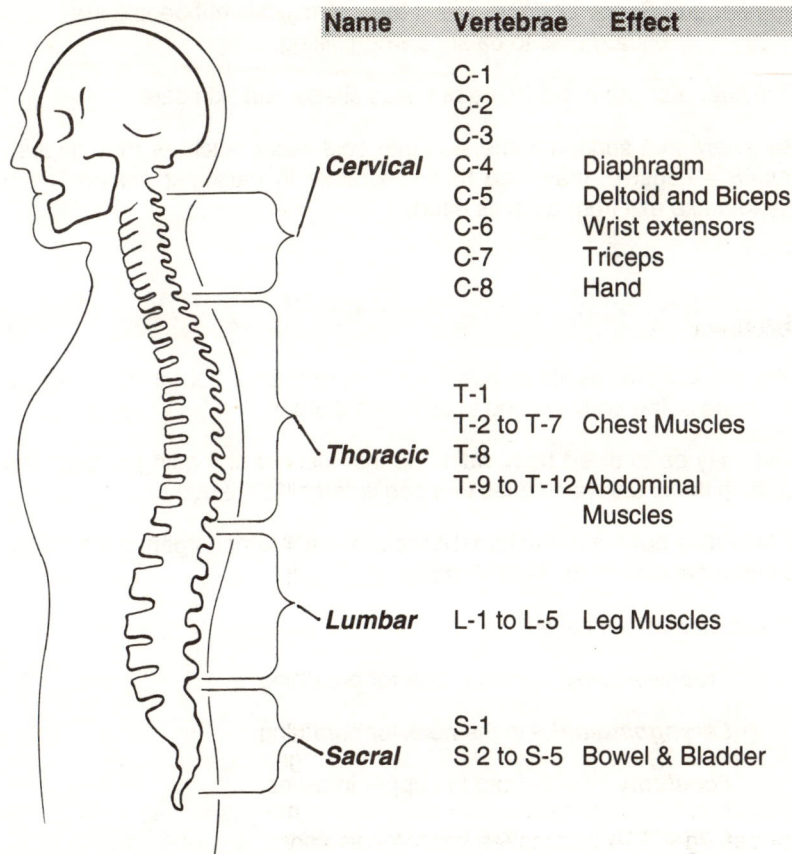

Name	Vertebrae	Effect
	C-1	
	C-2	
	C-3	
Cervical	C-4	Diaphragm
	C-5	Deltoid and Biceps
	C-6	Wrist extensors
	C-7	Triceps
	C-8	Hand
	T-1	
	T-2 to T-7	Chest Muscles
Thoracic	T-8	
	T-9 to T-12	Abdominal Muscles
Lumbar	L-1 to L-5	Leg Muscles
	S-1	
Sacral	S 2 to S-5	Bowel & Bladder

Fig 12:1 The spinal column

From the point below the lesion the following will probably apply.

C-6 to C-8 the hand and lower arm are affected and some people will not have full hand movement but may be able to hold a paddle.

T-6 all muscles below a line drawn across the nipples will be affected

Geoff Smedley   Canoeing for Disabled People

T-8   the person will probably be unable to balance when sitting

T-9 to T-12 possible loss of balance, unable to rotate trunk or bend
              backwards and forward.

Lumbar and Sacral Lesions   affect the leg muscles but people are
              usually able to balance when sitting.

Consider also the notes in the previous chapter on skin care.

Be aware that sudden immersion into cold water, such as may happen
during a capsize, may lead to an increase in muscular spasm which
could make exit from a kayak difficult.

Stomas

Stomas are the results of surgery which makes a hole in the external
structure of the body leading to an internal organ.

This may be to divert body waste so that instead of it going through the
body in the usual way it goes to a bag external to the body.

It may also be to allow external access to an internal organ, such as the
need to get air into the body directly.

These stomas are called:-

> **Tracheostomy**   - in the neck for breathing
>
> **Laryngostomy**   - in the neck for breathing
>
> **Ileostomy**   - from the upper intestine
>
> **Colostomy**   - from the lower intestine
>
> **Urostomy**   - from the bladder

Implications

Clothing needs to be loose enough to avoid pressure or obstruction to
the stoma and in the case of a bag to allow easy access for emptying.
Problems are sometime experienced with the tightness of canoeing gear
such as buoyancy aids and spray decks as well as the tight fit of some
kayaks.

Where the stoma is in the neck, great care must be taken to avoid the person getting wet in this area.

Stoma bags do need to be emptied and for this the individual will need access to a toilet and some privacy. It is very important that care is taken with hygiene and some people will need to be very careful about what they eat and the quality of the fluids, especially water, that they drink.

Stroke

A stroke is the result of the blood supply being cut off to part of the brain. This reduces the supply of oxygen which damages the brain cells. The affected area of the body is controlled by the opposite side of the brain. A stroke to the left side of the brain affects the right side of the body. Hemiplegic paralysis, ranging from mild to severe affects the person.

Whilst a stroke to the right side of the brain affects the left side of the body, a stroke on this side also affects speech and communication. It is this latter effect that distinguishes the two strokes, sometimes quite significantly.

Implications

Depending on which side was affected you will need to consider either the physical condition alone, or the physical condition and communication.

You should also be aware of when the stroke occurred. With physiotherapy many people who have had strokes make quite significant recoveries. You should discuss any programmes of physiotherapy that the person is following and consult with them, and their physiotherapist, to develop suitable activities.

If speech and communication is affected then giving and receiving information may be difficult. Keep all your instructions short and simple and be patient with any response since it may be garbled and use the wrong words. Be patient and try to imagine what the person is trying to say. Correct the words that people use since by doing so you are helping them to retrain their memory.

If the paralysis is severe then attention must be given to the notes on skin care in the previous chapter.

Impaired Behaviour

This is an area of impairment that is constantly being discussed on Disability Awareness Training courses. Many people see the need to address this as an impairment particularly as sports such as canoeing are being seen as appropriate sports to address some of the needs of behaviour impaired people.

Some of the sub objectives for this group that were referred to in Chapter 7 are, giving people a sense of achievement, raising self esteem and taking responsibility for the care and well being of others.

The impairment

Remember that even people with severely impaired behaviour do not see themselves as always behaving badly. They still need to feel that they can be liked and respected for themselves although recognising that sometimes they upset people. Without this they will have a very low opinion of themselves, little confidence and a feeling of low esteem. If you come across these people your main objective is to restore their belief in themselves and demonstrate that you like and respect them.

Other kinds of behaviour exhibited may be:-

• distractible,
• over active,
• aggressive,
• withdrawn,
• immature.

In addition the individual might have physical problems of co-ordination and deficiencies in perceptual awareness.

The programme

The focus is on the programme, rather than particular strategies, since a properly prepared programme will do much to minimise the effects of impaired behaviour.

Plan your programme, with any other helpers or assistants you have with you. Agree on the activities and how you will deal with any totally disruptive behaviour. After the session you should review it and learn from the good and bad parts of it to plan for the next one.

Throughout you should aim to have a relaxed manner, even when you are not feeling relaxed, since this helps to relax the people in the group and reduces their levels of anxiety.

Exercise

Regular exercise has proved to be beneficial and have a positive influence on disruptive behaviour.   Therefore, you should begin all sessions with warm up exercises. This helps to settle the group and to warm up muscles. Furthermore, it is also good coaching practice.

With your skill training look for activities that help to:-

- condition the body,
- encourage good balance,
- extend the range of movements,
- assist in the co-ordination between hand and eye.

Patterns of behaviour

You should be an active member of the group not a bystander or observer. By joining in you are able to demonstrate how people should behave more directly.

It is very important that this involvement is complete. It should start from the moment of arrival, through the periods of changing, getting boats out, and later putting them away, showering and perhaps refreshments. This imposes quite a responsibility upon the instructors and helpers but if you choose to work with people with impaired behaviour you should accept the demands that doing so appropriately makes.

Your respect for the people in your group, their activities and opinions should be a good example for the members of the group.   The often heard saying, *"do what I say and not what I do"* is inappropriate. Good social behaviour and response to others is also very important.

Generally speaking, shouting or losing your temper are counter productive. Where ever possible you should focus on the appropriate behaviour of the members of the group and praise this, rather than criticise inappropriate behaviour. This latter type of behaviour should be ignored as much as possible although this cannot be done if it impairs the safety of the group.   Expressing you disappointment in the behaviour of an individual, whilst still confirming that you like them, can be effective.

Whatever you do, avoid confrontation. If a situation appears to be getting to a confrontation always offer the individual some way of getting out of this without them appearing to lose face. Use suggestions such as *"would you like to go somewhere else for a moment to think about this?"*; or, if you can, get another leader to take the main group away leaving you with the individual to resolve the situation. If you can return to the main group as friends so much the better.

You can help to avoid confrontation if clear limits of what is and is not acceptable behaviour have been set. This is even more effective if those limits are set by the whole group.

If two people are displaying inappropriate behaviour towards each other you should intervene as soon as possible.

If behaviour becomes very disruptive, the best plan is to separate the individual from the group. If this is done quickly the person can do something with one of your assistants, away from the main group but related to the group activity. If this is not seen to be a punishment there is more likelihood of the person coming back into the group successfully.

If you use this strategy to separate two antagonists do not imply that one is more to blame than the other unless this is obviously so. The apparent injustice of some strategies will cause resentment and even more disruption. If you believe they are equally to blame, say so, then ask them to decide who goes with which instructor or helper. If they cannot agree, split the time out so they do equal amounts.

Threatening to withdraw disruptive people from your programme totally is usually non-productive and may suggest to other members of the group that you dislike them or do not fully value them.

At times the group will get excited about the activity. This not a bad thing but you must make sure that you have calmed them down before you go on to another activity and especially before you end the session.

Severely Impaired Behaviour

Some people will demonstrate quite extreme behaviour. This might be:-

* total non co-operation,
* running away,
* extreme aggression to anyone near,
* crying, screaming or shouting,
* head banging or body rocking.

In these circumstances the control of these people is likely to impair your management of a group on the water and safety might be in question. You should insist that they only participate in a one to one situation in an open canoe with an instructor and a parent or carer who will either control the behaviour or withdraw them from the group.

Games

Games form an important part of any programme.   You need to think about games in a particular way if they are to be beneficial to your group. Consider games that: are-

- non-competitive,
- co-operative,
- have few or simple rules,
- require only the skills that the group have mastered,
- do not have any body, paddle or boat contact with other people in the group.

If they have an element of competition try to ensure that they also require the co-operation of people for success,

Reflective time

Throughout the session, and especially at the end, encourage people to talk positively about their experiences. Awards can be given for achievements, you should ensure that you can say something positive about everyone, even if it is only their resolve to do better next time. During this time the participants can suggest what they consider to be behaviour worthy of an award.

Note that the awards need not necessarily be tangible. For some people sweets might be appropriate but for others just knowing that something they did has received positive recognition is sufficient.

Plate 12:a *Disability is no bar to success*

Canoeing for Disabled People   Geoff Smedley

CHAPTER THIRTEEN

PADDLE-ABILITY

(previously known as HANDYKAYAK)

Introduction

It is B.C.U. policy to promote canoeing for people of all abilities. However, as we are aware, there are numerous activities currently, and especially in the competition field that are difficult either to access, or to find equality of opportunity, if the paddler has a disability. It has always been the intention of the B.C.U. to address this issue and establish competitions that redress this imbalance of opportunities.

In addressing the needs of paddlers with disabilities, the B.C.U. saw as its first responsibility the raising of awareness for members of the coaching scheme and establishing good "grass-roots" practice. In so prioritising, the question of competition was not addressed until 1992. In the meantime, the Italian Federation, F.I.C.K., had firmly addressed the question of competition at a national level.

Therefore, it seemed sensible to give serious consideration to their proposals rather than going our own way independently. Visits to Italy, to study their programme, led me to believe that we could join them at an international level for *"HANDYKAYAK"* competition.

There are three reservations that, whilst they will not inhibit our collaboration, will need addressing ultimately.

- **Firstly, the use of the term** *"Handykayak"*.

In this country we are moving away from the use of handicap and towards the use of the term disability. Furthermore, we would prefer to use the term ability as in the adoption of the word *"Paddle-ability"* to describe our current programme.

- **Secondly, is the limitation of Paddle-ability events to people with physical disabilities that, largely, affect their mobility.**

We would wish to involve more people with disabilities (physical, sensory and learning) than this group, although there are precedents to this limitation of ability as seen in Wheelchair Basketball for example, in order to establish an activity.

- **Finally, there is the limitation to specific competition types.**

There are established events within Sprint Racing, in addition, many Marathon Races now have classes for people with disabilities.   In the near future it is expected that there will be opportunities within Slalom.

Once again we would wish to extend opportunities to other styles of craft and competition to match the extensive opportunities that exist within the B.C.U.   To be aware of these concerns is important, although it is equally important that we also grasp the opportunity to join an international arena and bring to this our own thoughts for future developments and expansion of opportunity.

International Opportunities

At this time the only opportunities for International Competitions are for Sprint Racing Paddlers.   However, it is worth a close study of the development and functioning of this since it will give guidelines and ideas for the development of other International events in other disciplines.

Developed in Italy, by their Federation F.I.C.K., Handykayak is the term used which, as well as reflecting a policy towards provision for canoeists with disabilities and their access into the sport of canoeing or kayaking, is also a class of competition, initially for people with physical disabilities comprising:-

- metre sprint events for:
    - men and women
    - K1 and K2
    - in two disability categories

N.B. When reading the rest of the information please bear in mind that, at this time, the sport is still in its developmental stages.

The Kayaks

Discussions have taken place between ourselves and the Italians regarding both the styles of kayak and classification systems. However, nothing has been fully decided as yet.

Nevertheless, the paddlers themselves are making decisions upon the style of craft that reflects their ability. In this respect, additions to the kayak in terms of keels and even outriggers have been used where necessary.

As yet, people in classification A have paddled the more stable kayak, whilst paddlers in classification B have been paddling a range of craft including stable K1 racing craft and full I.C.F. specification Sprint craft.

Classification

The Italian Federation have defined a Classification system based on both medical and functional ability. Based on discussions in Ferrara in 1992 and my own observations at their National Championships in 1991, the disability classifications as adopted in the U.K. are as follows:

CLASS A

- These paddlers will be able to use their arms to propel the kayak forward, but are unlikely to be able to control a full specification racing craft.

- They will have great difficulty in walking and will probably use a wheelchair for mobility.

- They will have limited balance when sitting.

- They have no muscle that controls their hips to give a stable balance.

- They cannot use their legs to assist their stability in the kayak.

- These paddlers will generally need a backrest for support.

- Amputees will have lost both legs without visible stumps.

CLASS B

- They will be able to use their arms to propel the kayak forward, and will possibly be able to control a full specification racing craft.

- These paddlers have difficulty in walking and, whilst they may need some support, sticks or crutches, will not use a wheelchair except where mobility is very difficult.

- They can balance when sitting.

- They have limited use of their legs to assist their stability in the kayak.

- Amputees will have lost both legs with visible stumps (one above the knee) or one leg without visible stump.

The B.C.U. Proposals for the Development of Paddle-ability Sprint Racing

These come in three parts but are under the guidance of the Sprint and Racing Committee and may change:

- A National Championship with competitors invited to an open meeting to take part within a BCU recognised Sprint Regatta.

- The establishing of a National Training Squad for Paddle-ability.

- Participation in International Paddle-ability Regattas.

Selection for International Events will, in the first instance be paddlers drawn from the National Training Squad.

The National Championships

It is hoped that each club will encourage and facilitate any of their membership who have disabilities and are eligible for the National Championships.

From the national event, appropriate paddlers will be encouraged to join the National Training Squad.

International Events

The team to represent the BCU will be drawn from the National Training Squad. The Team Manager will consult with the coach responsible for the Training Squad and they will determine representation and the composition of the support team as appropriate to the venue of the Regatta.

National Training Squad

In liaison with National Coaches, the Training Squad organiser will arrange regular squad coaching sessions with properly devised coaching programmes.

All paddlers with a disability, especially those within the classification groups described, will be encouraged to attend these sessions.

CHAPTER FOURTEEN

PERSONAL TESTS AND AWARDS

The Policy Statement

The BCU supports the promotion of canoeing for people with disabilities and encourages them to take the Award Scheme Tests. The Union's policy is to avoid a separate system.

Tests of Personal Ability

Where a specific disability prevents a candidate from completing a particular part of a test the examiner may still give the award, as long as she believes that the candidate has received appropriate coaching and is, therefore, performing to the best of his ability. In addition the candidate should show that even though he cannot perform the skill he understands the technique and its purpose.

Approaching this way, awards help give all canoeists confidence and improve self esteem, and most important, credit for what they have achieved.

Implementation

Whilst most coaching scheme members are aware of the above policy there are some who are not and there will be many who are unsure of its implementation. Hopefully the following guidelines will enlighten all with regard to both policy and implementation.

1. Candidates who cannot perform a part of the test.

There are many reason why the above might apply. A blind paddler will have some difficulty in directional paddling. A paddler with a physical impairment may not have the strength or balance to perform support strokes, and so on.

The objective for the examiner must always be for him to establish to his satisfaction, that a candidate can perform all parts of the award. Where it is apparent that an impairment; physical, sensory or intellectual, is going to limit the candidate's ability to perform a part, or parts, of the award, then the examiner needs to be satisfied that the candidate, even after proper and appropriate coaching, is unable to complete a specific part of the test or award. Nevertheless, knows how the skill is performed and for what purpose.

The candidate's involvement in an appropriate coaching programme before an exception to a part of a test or award is essential if the BCU policy is to have credibility.

2. Candidates who can achieve the test or award but need special resources.

There may be a number of reason for the above.

A. Certain impairments have not necessarily disabled the participant when adaptations have been made to the craft or equipment, the use of modified seats and backrests for example.   In some cases paddlers have used different styles of craft such as the Rob-Roy or the Caranoe. Such craft do not perform in the recognised way. For example a capsize in a Rob-Roy does not allow the paddler to perform the usual exit drill.

B. Some paddlers find the use of hand paddles beneficial and better than the conventional shafted blades. Quite obviously the rules for paddle presentation for some strokes cannot apply to the use of hand paddles.

In these circumstances, the examiner needs to be confident that whilst using such equipment the paddler is performing to the best of her ability subject to the appropriate coaching.

3. The Certificate

It has been decided by the BCU Coaching Committee, that the certificate for a test or award, that is given to some-one who has been unable to perform a part, or parts, of the conditions for the test or ward, will not have any comments or other statements on the certificate to indicate this.

However, examiners should instruct candidates in their responsibility to:

• Not tackle any activity that their certificate might indicate they are capable of, but which they know their disability might impede.

• Tell any activity leader of their disability if they believe the disability might impede their ability to take part in the activity appropriately and safely.

4. Responsibility.

The Leader

In some instances it is apparent that the holder of an award has an impairment. In this case the leader of the activity in which this person is involved, is advised to discuss with that person the implications of their impairment for the activity.

The Paddler

Some impairments, which may, or may not, have prevented the paddler from performing parts of the test or award, are often not apparent to the observer. These may be medical conditions such as Asthma, Diabetes or Epilepsy. It is the responsibility of the individual paddler to disclose to the leader the implications of their impairment relative to the activity they are undertaking.

5. Candidates with Learning Disability.

Some paddlers with learning disability may be able to perform the parts of a test or award within, or shortly after the coaching session. However, it is possible that they might lose the skill, either because they have been learning a new skill, or because in the period of time since learning the skill they have forgotten it.

For these reasons it is acceptable for them to be examined for a test or award on a "modular" basis. That is, they may be tested after coaching each part of the award. It is advisable for the examiner to keep some form of record that registers this. Once all parts of the test have been completed and tested, the certificate is awarded as usual.

In these circumstance the section on "Responsibilities" should be studied and the paddler, or if appropriate their parent or carer, should assume the responsibility to inform the activity leader as necessary.

6. Coaching Awards - Disability Awareness Training

It is recommended that members of the coaching scheme who coach people with disabilities enrol on one of the B.C.U. Disability Awareness Training courses designed to give skills for this purpose.

The syllabus for this course can be found in Chapter 15.

Details of courses are published in the BCU "Year-Book".

Statement of Physical Competence

Candidates who sign an application form for a course leading to a BCU qualification have agreed to the following.

"I understand that in law I have a 'duty of care' to others, and this duty of care is enhanced with regard to my responsibility to those whom I reach because of the training and any qualifications which I may receive.

I declare that to the best of my knowledge and belief I am physically fit, and do not have any condition* which may impair my ability to be responsible for the overall safety of canoeists in my charge.

I do not have diabetes* or epilepsy*, and understand that in the event of any change to my fitness to be responsible for the safety of others I must declare the fact to the Director of Coaching of the BCU."

*The declaring of an impairment does not necessarily debar a person from holding a coaching qualification. The BCU does its utmost to ensure that only common sense conditions are placed on those who are unable to fulfil all the requirements, stated and implicit, for the holding of a coaching qualification. The following policy statements apply.

Awarding Coaching Qualifications to Persons with Diabetes

In the situation where individuals wish to enter the coaching scheme and have a history of Diabetes the following criteria must be met:

1. That they undergo regular medical reviews, at least once a year, by a specialist medical consultant.

2. That the individual's diabetic condition is stabilised through diet, oral medicine or insulin.

3. That the individual will request their GP or Consultant to confirm the status of their condition.

4. That any changes in medication which, in the opinion of their medical adviser, could affect the stability of their condition, should lead to a supported coaching situation or a break in coaching for six months or until the medical adviser confirms that their condition is once more stabilised.

5. Similarly, any changes in circumstances, such as an operation or

major injury or illness, which causes instability in the individual's diabetic condition, then the same recommendations as at '4' apply.

6. That the individual's coaching award is limited to three years to coincide with the return of a completed questionnaire updating the status of their condition, whereupon the coaching office, in the event of a nil change, can arrange for a re-issue for a further three years; or seek advice in the event of a changed condition and make alternative arrangements, such as:- to reduce the period of the award, or suspend the award.

7. That it remains the individual's responsibility to notify the BCU of any change in their circumstance.

In the event of an existing coaching scheme member who develops diabetes, then they are obliged to notify the BCU coaching office. They may be requires to move to a supported coaching, or 'frozen' status situation, subject to the previously stated criteria coming into effect.

In the event of an individual not meeting any of the criteria, but who could offer skills to the coaching scheme, then the case will be considered individually and relevant support given to enable the individual to participate in the coaching scheme. Examples of special requirements are:-

• To work only in the presence of another appropriately experienced member of the coaching scheme, or

• To work only from the bank as a Competition Trainer or Coach.

Awarding Coaching Qualifications to Persons with Epilepsy

In the situation where individuals wish to enter the coaching scheme and have a history of epilepsy the following criteria must be met:

1. That the person with a history or diagnosis of epilepsy has been free of epileptic seizures during the period of two years immediately preceding the date of application; or in the case of an individual who has had such attacks whilst asleep, then they should not have had any day-time attacks for a period of at least three years prior to the application.

2. That they undergo regular medical reviews, at least once a year, by a specialist medical consultant.

3. That the individual's condition is stabilised with the use of medicine.

4. That the individual will request their GP or Consultant to confirm the status of their condition.

5. That any changes in medication which, in the opinion of their medical adviser, could affect the stability of their condition, should lead to a supported coaching situation or a break in coaching for six months or until the medical adviser confirms that their condition is once more stabilised.

6. In the event of a seizure occurring within this six month period then the individual will need to move to a supported system, or 'frozen' status, or await the two year seizure free period again to qualify.

7. Similarly, any changes in circumstances, such as an operation or major injury or illness, which causes instability in the individual's epilepsy, then the same recommendations as at '6' should apply.

8. That the individual's coaching award is limited to three years to coincide with the return of a completed questionnaire updating the status of their condition, whereupon the coaching office, in the event of a nil change, can arrange for a re-issue for a further three years; or, seek advice in the event of a changed condition and make alternative arrangements such as:- to reduce the period of the award, or suspend the award.

9. That it remains the individual's responsibility to notify the BCU of any change in their circumstance.

In the event of an existing coaching scheme member who develops epilepsy, then they are obliged to notify the BCU coaching office. They may be requires to move to a supported coaching, or 'frozen' status situation, subject to the previously stated criteria coming into effect.

In the event of an individual not meeting any of the criteria, but who could offer skills to the coaching scheme, then the case will be considered individually and relevant support given to enable the individual to participate in the coaching scheme. Examples of special requirements are:

• To work only in the presence of another appropriately experienced member of the coaching scheme, or

• To work only from the bank as a Competition Trainer or Coach

CHAPTER FIFTEEN

Course leading to the British Canoe Union

DISABILITY AWARENESS TRAINING for CANOE SPORT

Purpose

To give participants an awareness of the needs of people with disabilities and the relationships between disabilities and canoeing. To give them knowledge and skills to enable them to widen the scope of their existing leader qualifications so that they may feel capable of introducing people with disabilities to canoeing.

Pre-Requisites

Either

- Hold a coaching award to the standard of either, Placid Water Teacher, Trainee instructor, Instructor, Senior Instructor or Coach of the B.C.U.

- At the discretion of the course leader, people over the age of 16 years without the pre-requisite qualifications, but who wish to become "helpers", may also attend the course.

Recommendations

Participants should hold the B.C.U. Canoe Life Saving Award (Co.C.L.G. Canoe Safety Test) or R.L.S.S. Life Saving Skill 3 or equivalent award.

It is also recommended that participants hold a recognised certificate in basic first aid. (British Red Cross, St. John's Ambulance or equivalent.)

"Canoeing with Disabled People" is the main text for this course and participants are advised to read this.

QUALIFICATION

There is no formal assessment. Leaders, on successful completion of the course, and who pay a registration fee to the B.C.U. will be given a Certificate to confirm their satisfactory attendance.

Certificates will state that the holder is aware of the needs of people with disabilities with particular respect to their participation in canoeing.

The Certificate is not a qualification in itself.

The Certificate will not permit a leader to teach or coach in any situation other than the one for which he or she is qualified.

Candidates may be refused the Certificate if they prove to be unsuitable. E.g. they have unacceptable attitudes to disability or are unsympathetic to the needs of people with disabilities.

Syllabus

Aims

To enable more people with disabilities to participate safely in the sport of canoeing.

To train leaders and helpers to be aware of the needs of people with disabilities so that they might be able to instruct and assist them safely and effectively.

Objectives

To impart basic knowledge on aspects of teaching and aiding persons with disabilities.

Theory

- To discuss attitudes to disability.

- To understand the implications of disability

- To develop coaching programmes under the general headings of :-

> **Preparation**
> **Education**
> **Participation**

Preparation

- Access to the site and resources

- Resources - transport, equipment, helpers, social needs, toilet and changing facilities.

- "Risk" factors and safety

Education

- The disabled person in society

- Relationships with other canoeists

- Parents, teachers and care staff.

- Assistant instructors and helpers.

Participation

- Styles of Programmes

- Introducing People with Disabilities to canoeing

- The issues of Integration and Segregation

Knowledge

- Canoeing considerations and provision

- Clothing, buoyancy aids and life-jackets.

- Paddles, canoes, kayaks and other paddle-craft.

- Special adaptations and modifications.

- Programmes of instruction.

    - swimming and water activities

    - paddling skills

- capsizes and rescues

- courses and expeditions

- competition

Clinical Background

- Disabilities and their implications -   physical
                                          intellectual
                                          sensory

- communication skills

- personal profiles

- emergency procedures

Lifting and carrying people will be studied although it will not be possible to do other than explain the principles. Course members are advised to seek appropriate training from qualified physio-therapists.

Practical Sessions

All aspects of safety and rescues in particular will be studied, discussed and practised - sometimes in simulated emergency situations.

Various craft, canoes, kayaks, leisure-craft and rafts, some designed or adapted specifically for use by people with disabilities will be paddled, not just as a "try-a-boat" session but as a matter of course.

To assist them when developing appropriate coaching strategies, participants will take part in practical activities , relevant to paddle sport, with simulated disabilities. They may spend time in a wheelchair or be temporarily incapacitated to simulate the effects of physical and sensory (seeing and hearing) disabilities both off and on the water.

In addition to any who may be participants on the course, people with disabilities will attend for parts of the course. Their presence will be an opportunity for the participants to discuss the implications of disability at first hand, to explore these with people with disabilities and put into practice some of the practical skills they will learn on the course.

CHAPTER SIXTEEN

GIVING SUPPORT TO PEOPLE WITH DISABILITIES

A Note of Caution

In giving assistance to people with disabilities it is often necessary to consider the appropriateness of transferring, supporting, lifting or carrying the individual.   A European Community Health and Safety Directive (1993) on this subject states that employers should:-

"... so far as is reasonably practicable, avoid the need for employees to undertake any manual handling operations at work which involve a risk of injury."

Manual Handling Operations Regulations 1992 SI No. 2793

The Sports Council's view is that:-

"... it is the responsibility of the Governing body to undertake a risk assessment on all lifting and handling tasks that their staff undertake. In the case of any lifting which cannot be eliminated either by not doing it or mechanisation, there should be a clear identification of the risks involved in the task.   Appropriate procedures should be drawn up for undertaking such tasks accompanied by training where appropriate."

The Royal Life-Saving Society UK, for whom lifting was an assessed feature of many of their life-saving examinations, in the light of the EEC Directive, came to the following conclusions.

Whilst the regulations applied to employees in the work-place, the term employee need not imply that the person is being paid. Therefore a volunteer working on a regular basis is bound as much by the principles of the Health and Safety at Work Act as is the professional.

Subsequently, unassisted lifts are no longer part of the skills required in any life-saving award.   Furthermore, the R.L.S.S. instruct that all candidates for training and assessment are warned that:

"The society does not support the use of unassisted lifting during training and assessment. You should take note that all casualty lifting carries with it and element of risk."

At the time of writing there are no specific guidelines regarding lifting and handling from the B.C.U.

I can give no advice other than to emphasise the statement that lifting a person carries an element of risk. Anyone considering working with people who are disabled physically, who will require lifting or handling, is advised to acquire appropriate professionally delivered training.

Nevertheless, it is necessary to consider that there are people who enjoy canoeing who would not be able to continue to do so if they were unable to be lifted or supported by their colleagues or instructors.   If, in consultation with the individual you consider giving your assistance, whilst the following guidelines are no substitute for training, they may be useful as an aide memoir on the completion of such training.

Lifting and Supporting

The following guidelines are broadly based upon the Manual Handling Operations Regulations 1992 SI No. 2793

- Avoid manual lifting and handling if possible.

    There are notes about mechanical ways to reduce the strain of lifting further into this chapter.

- Make an assessment of the situation and if you must proceed study the Regulations and Advice given.

- Reduce any risk to the lowest level reasonably practical

- Seek appropriate information - talk to the person to be lifted or supported to unsure their co-operation and advice.

Preparation

Warm up

- Lifting is an exercise, much like the rest of your sport. Therefore, you should always warm up and loosen the muscles appropriately before you start.

Clothing

- Take off any exposed jewellery or watches etc.

- You should wear flat shoes with a non slip sole

- Clothing should be comfortable and allow easy movement.

  The implications of this advice for canoeists needs special consideration.

- If you are wearing a wet suit will it allow you full movement?

- Do your canoeing shoes support your ankles, and are they non slip?

- Is your buoyancy aid free of buckles, catches or even exposed Velcro tape?

Clearing the way

- Is the person to be moved as close to the final destination as possible? Move the chair to the kayak if possible. Or, consider moving the kayak to the chair, helping the person in, and then sliding the kayak to the water.

- Is the pathway for the transfer free of boats, paddles and discarded equipment?

- Can the person being supported assist in any way?

- Is there any other assistance than can be sought, human or mechanical, such as slings, transfer boards or hoists?

Walking support - Some people will be able to walk short distances with your support.

Double forearm support - Face the person offering both of your forearms for them to grasp. You hold your forearms steady and level and walk backwards as they walk forwards.

Trunk Support - Stand beside the person face slightly towards them. Put one arm round their waist and the other hand holds their upper arm.

Hand and Elbow support - Stand slightly towards the person and support them by holding them at the elbow and wrist of the same arm.

Lifting Process

- Make sure that you have enough space to move in, don't forget to allow for any turns you may need to make.

- Never lift at arms length, keep the person you are assisting close to you so that your centre of gravity is close to theirs.

- Maintain your back in a natural position, do not keep it rigid.

- Bend your knees, not your back, and use your thigh muscles to lift. Aim to get down to the lift and as you lift raise your head to straighten up and bring the load with you.

- To maintain stability you need a wide base.   Have your feet a shoulder width apart, keep your heels in contact with the ground and point your feet in a direction that will allow you to move without twisting your spine.

- Avoid bending from the hips

- Do not hold the lift. Always make the lift and lower as close together as possible.

- Make all move smooth and do not jerk.

- Never do alone what you can get help with.

- If there are two or more people appoint a leader.

- The leader should check that everyone is ready to lift give the commands to make the lift or to lower from the lift.

- If during the lift or transfer the person you are assisting falls, do not try to catch them but try to guide him to the floor.

Notes for particular attention

- Never lift if you have doubts about your ability to manage. You must always consider your own safety.

- Always consult with the person your are lifting and if necessary consult with a physiotherapist about the best way to lift.

- It is a good idea to practise lifts or transfers, especially those involving getting into craft and on difficult water's edges, with someone who is not disabled, before you lift or transfer a person who is.

Holds

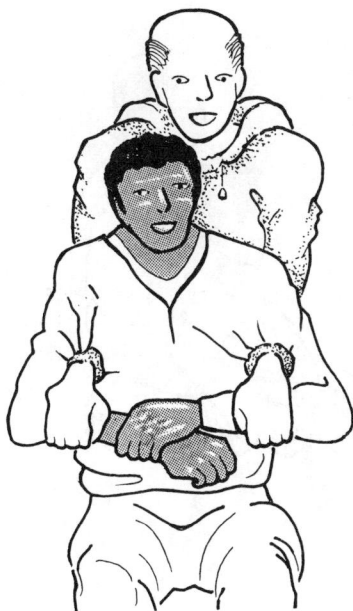

The way you hold people is very important to avoid hurting them. Always take your hold on a person from underneath the limb or part you are holding.

"Top and Tail Lift   (To work with a partner) - Put your arms though the person's arms as far as you can, then bring your arms back to the person's forearms and hold both arms together with the whole of your palm. keep the thumb on the same side as the fingers to avoid pinching.

In this way you can support the upper body of the person whilst a partner, or partners, supports the legs.

Fig 16:1 *Holding the arms*

Carrying with a partner

By standing side-by-side and linking arms with a partner you can make a human seat to carry someone.

To reach round the person to be lifted hold your partner's wrists.   If carrying small people hold your partner's forearms.

However, using a lifting sling may be safer and more comfortable that any hand holds. (see later in this chapter)

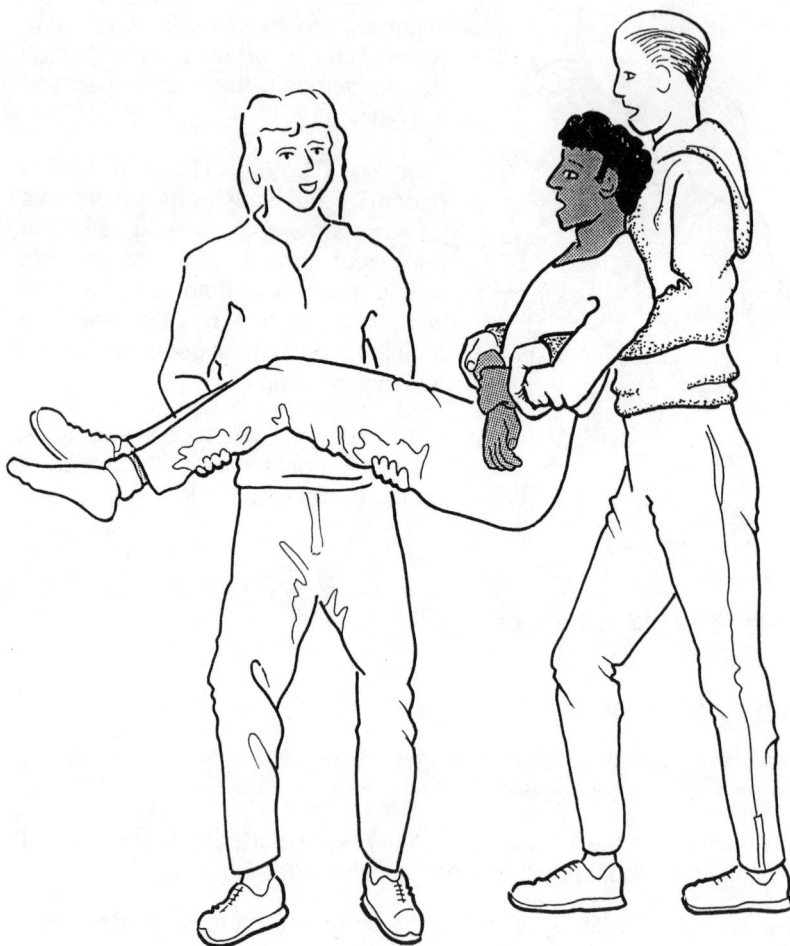

Fig 16:2 *The 'Top and Tail' carry*

Canoeing for Disabled People   Geoff Smedley

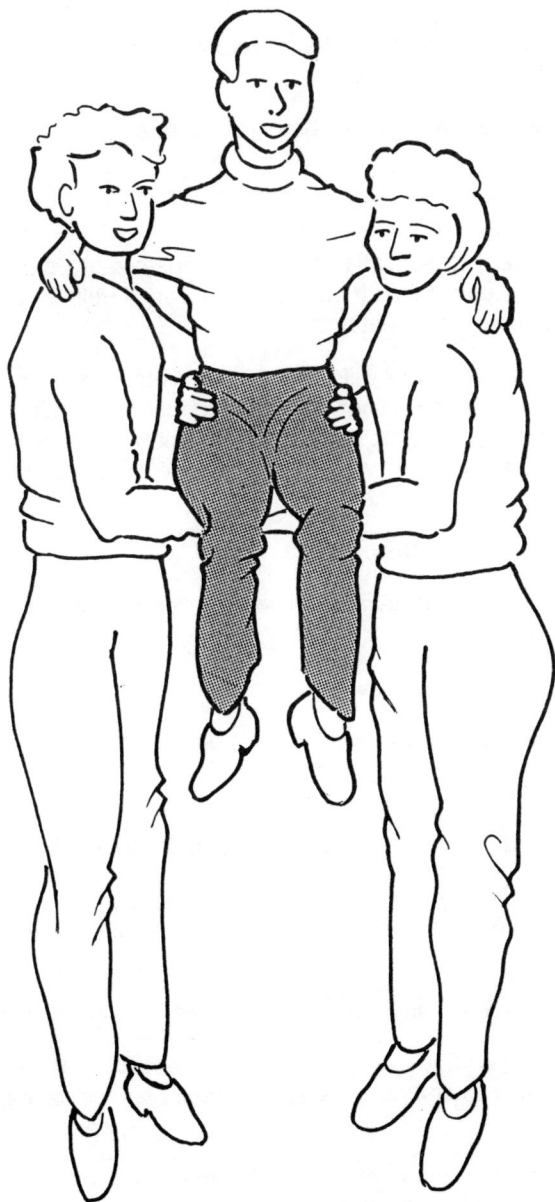

Fig 16:3 *The 'Orthodox' carry*

Geoff Smedley   Canoeing for Disabled People

Wheelchairs

There is a section in Chapter 11 that covers wheelchairs, looking at their use, construction and maintenance.

In this chapter we will look at how you can assist someone in a wheelchair.

- **Talk first!**

  It is a primary essential to determine whether the person in the wheelchair needs help. If they do, what kind of help they need and how should you give that help.

  People in wheelchairs will tell you how disconcerting it can be to have some "well meaning" individual suddenly pounce upon them from behind and whisk them away, possibly to somewhere they didn't want to go anyway, and if they did they would have preferred to have got there themselves.

Learn about the wheelchair.

- Learn how it folds and unfolds, without hurting yourself or damaging the chair. (See chapter 11)

- Know how the footrests move.

- Find the brakes and which way the lever operates for on and off.

- Locate the tipping levers.

To push a person in a wheelchair - suggested guidelines.

- Check the position of the person in the wheelchair, are they sitting comfortably, are arms and legs safe and especially are fingers clear of the wheels?

- If the person uses any safety straps, make sure that they are fastened.

- Check that any cushions, straps, blankets or shoe laces are not trailing

- Use both hands on the pushing handles to ensure that you have full control and should a wheel hit an obstacle you can keep the chair balanced.

- If the chair seems stuck, do not force it to move. Check to see what is causing it to be stuck - it may be the brakes or it may be the person's hand in the wheel!

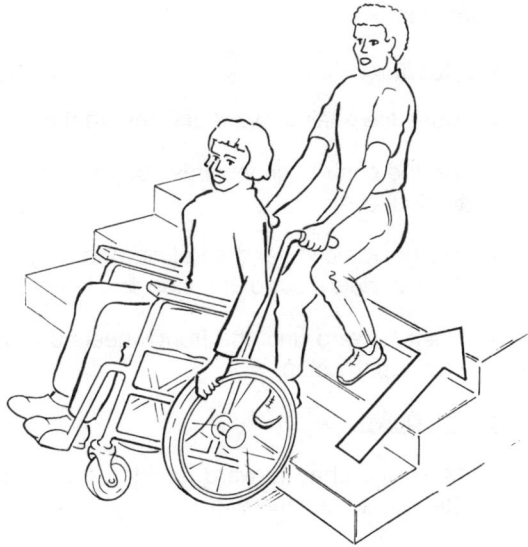

Fig 16:4b *Going up steps*

Fig 16:4a *Going down steps*

Geoff Smedley   Canoeing for Disabled People

Steps

You should always try to use ramps, these are much easier to negotiate than steps.   However, if you need to go up or down a step tell the person in the chair what you are going to do at each stage of the operation.

<u>Going Up.</u>

• Move the chair forward until the front wheels reach the step.

• Tip the chair back towards you, use the handles and one foot on the tipping lever.

• Tip back slowly and carefully and only far enough to get the small front wheels clear of the step and keeping the chair balanced.

• Push forward until the front wheels are on the step and then lift the chair up the step.

<u>Going Down</u>

• Move the chair forward until the front wheels reach the edge of the step, and are square to it.

• Tip the chair back towards you, use the handles and one foot on the tipping lever.

• Tip back slowly and carefully and only far enough to get the small front wheels clear of the step and keeping the chair balanced.

• Lower the rear wheels down the step supporting some of the chair's weight against yourself.

• Make sure that both of the wheels touch the ground together and lower the chair onto all four wheels gently.

• You can ask the person in the chair to help by pushing on the handrims or holding them to steady the chair.

Ramps

• When you are going down a ramp you may find the person in the chair would prefer you to tip the chair back so that they are not leaning forward.

- On steep slopes, and large steps, or when pushing a heavy person, it is probably better to walk the chair down backwards.

- If the slope is steep, beware of the chair running away. Get the person it the chair to help by using the hand rims or gently applying the brakes.

Brakes

- Always apply the brakes when:

  - Leaving the person unattended
  - Resting or waiting
  - Helping the person to get in or out of the wheelchair.

- NEVER push the chair out into traffic. Use a crossing or wait until the road is clear.

- Push the chair smoothly and steadily. Avoid sudden movements, rough handling or sharp turns.

- Practise with an empty wheelchair first.

Stairs

Taking people in wheelchairs up and down a series of steps or stairs is very hazardous for person and pusher. You should look for a lift or ramp first, even if it means a much longer walk. Never attempt stairs until you have had some specific instruction in the strategy and always try to get someone to help you.

Getting in and out

Although many people in wheelchairs can transfer themselves out of, or into, their wheelchair, it is sometimes necessary to give wheelchair users some assistance.

If you are going to offer such assistance consider the following.

- Ask the person to advise you on the best way to help you and to describe to you how much they can do for themselves.

- Always get someone to help you if it is possible.

<u>Preparation for the process of helping.</u>

- Move the person and the wheelchair close to the position that they will be transferring to.

- Always apply the brakes, and if it is an electric wheelchair, make sure that it is switched off. (Catching the control lever accidentally can send you and the person in the wheelchair on an unexpected and potentially dangerous trip.)

- Put the wheelchair against a solid object such as a wall, or have someone else stood behind it.

- Check that it is at the best angle to enable the transfer to be made without over twisting yourself or the person in the wheelchair.

- Make sure that you have sufficient space for all the manoeuvres.

- Lift or detach the footrests so that they are out of the way.

- Sometimes, such as when the person is moving sideways, it is a good idea to remove the arm rests.

- Position your feet firmly and either side of the other person's feet.

- You can use your knees outside theirs to help maintain stability.

- Remember all that you have read previously about using your legs.

<u>The Action</u>

- Ask the person to slide forward in the chair until they are sitting on the edge of the seat.   If they have difficulty with this, put your arms behind them and help them to rock gently from side to side whilst they slide slowly forwards.

- In preparation for the lift, they put their arms over your shoulders with the fingers interlocked. If you have any concerns that the person may pull on your neck as you lift them, get them to put both of their arms over the same shoulder.

- At an agreed signal you lean backwards, to counterpoise their weight, and use your legs to lift.   The person in the wheelchair also applies whatever strength they might have in their arms or legs to assist you.

- Use your feet and knees to provide support and stability.

- Move together smoothly avoiding any sudden or jerky movements.

- When the person is in the right position reverse the process, again using your legs, to lower them.

- The person in the wheelchair may have reduced skin sensitivity so take care that they are not knocked during the process. Also ensure that their clothes are not rucked up when they are seated again.

Lifting Aids - Slings

Helping someone, who cannot walk, by carrying them over even quite short distances is considerably assisted if the carriers use aids such as a sling or a carry seat.

Slings can be soft and made of nylon or canvas, or they can be made of a moulded strong but flexible plastic.

They have carrying handles at each end and are used by two people. The sling is placed under the thighs of the person to be lifted, who places her arms around the shoulders of the lifters, they grasp the handles on the sling and lift.   Slings are easy to place in position and slide out again when the transfer is complete.

Canoeing clothes are often made of woven nylon cloth and so it is important to check that the sling does not slip against such surfaces. If they are prone to slipping, place a towel between the two surfaces.

On occasions two slings can be used, one under the thighs and the other round the back.   This system can be used by two or four helpers if necessary.

These devices will usually cost less than £10 making them a cheap resource to have around any canoe club where there may be people needing assistance with transfers.

Lifting Aids - Carry Seats

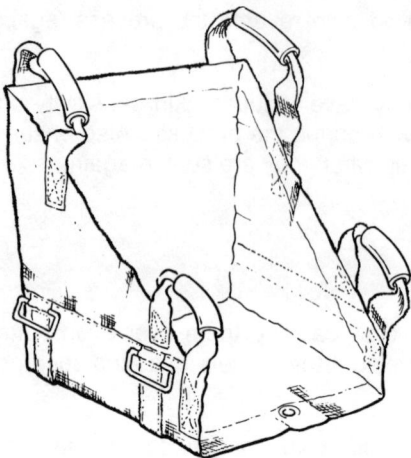

When two or more people are available it is often easier, and safer to use a carry seat. The *Trans-sit* seat is made from nylon with a reinforced and padded backrest. It also has four carry handles covered by polythene tubes to make it comfortable to hold for the carriers. For additional safety it also has a waist belt for the occupant.

Two, three or four people can assist with the comfortable carrying of a person in this seat making it particularly valuable when crossing rough country or when the carry is a long one

.*Fig 16:5 Trans sit carry seat*

Since it is easily washed and does not suffer by getting wet, it can be used to transfer someone into a canoe or kayak and they can remain sitting in it until needing to be lifted out again.

The Trans-sit costs less than £40 which makes it a relatively cheap resource. Since it also folds up quite small it could be considered for expedition use where longer transfers over rough terrain are often necessary.

Lifting Aids - Hoists

Where the activity is centred around a single base then hoists are often a practical solution to lifting people with mobility difficulties into and out of boats. Hoists are generally similar to those quite frequently seen in swimming pools.   I know of clubs who have installed hoists, often obtaining them quite cheaply as manually operated hoists from establishments who are changing to electrical or hydraulic systems.

Used in conjunction with a Trans-sit, as mentioned previously, or a similar seat or sling, hoists enable a person, once seated within the seat or sling, to be lifted from the wheelchair and lowered into the boat. Likewise they can be lifted from the boat and returned to the wheelchair. The seat or sling used should be comfortable because it is often more convenient if the person can remain sitting in it whilst canoeing.

Fig 16:6 *A lifting hoist in use on a jetty*

Hoists employ a variety of mechanical systems to lift and lower. Some use a manual winch, others an hydraulic or electrical system. Whatever system you decide upon, or acquire, you should seek technical advice regarding the suitability for the task and especially for the installation of a suitable anchor point.

Users should be fully conversant with the manufacturers' recommended weight and range limits and the approved practice for its use.

Assessing suitability

Even a second hand hoist can be quite a financial investment and you should assess the functioning of the hoist to see if it is suitable for the purpose you have in mind.

Generally speaking mobile hoists are not suitable since they require the base to extend under the person to be lifted. Used to put a person into a canoe would mean that this base would extend over the water. However, if you are considering building a docking jetty (see Chapter 19) you may be able to use a mobile hoist.

With a fixed hoist look for the following.

- Can you fix a suitable socket for it to fit into?

- Does it have a wide arc of swing to go from the landing stage and over the craft in the water?

- If it has electric motors can you arrange a suitable safe supply.?

- It there sufficient space to manoeuvre the wheelchair under it and then remove the wheelchair whilst you swing the hoist over the canoe or kayak.

The use and siting of a hoist is closely associated with *landing stages* and *docking bays*.   Further information about these may be found in Chapter 19.

Transfer Boards

(Sometimes called sliding boards)

Sometimes it is possible to assist a person who can sit on the ground to get into their boat by using a "transfer board". This is no more than a plank, strong enough to withstand the combined weights of the person and a helper. It should have a smooth surface and be tapered or rounded at its edges.

It is used when the level of the bank and the craft on the water are similar since a difference of a few inches makes its use difficult. It is also necessary that the boat to be entered has a cockpit sufficiently large for the person to enter from the board.

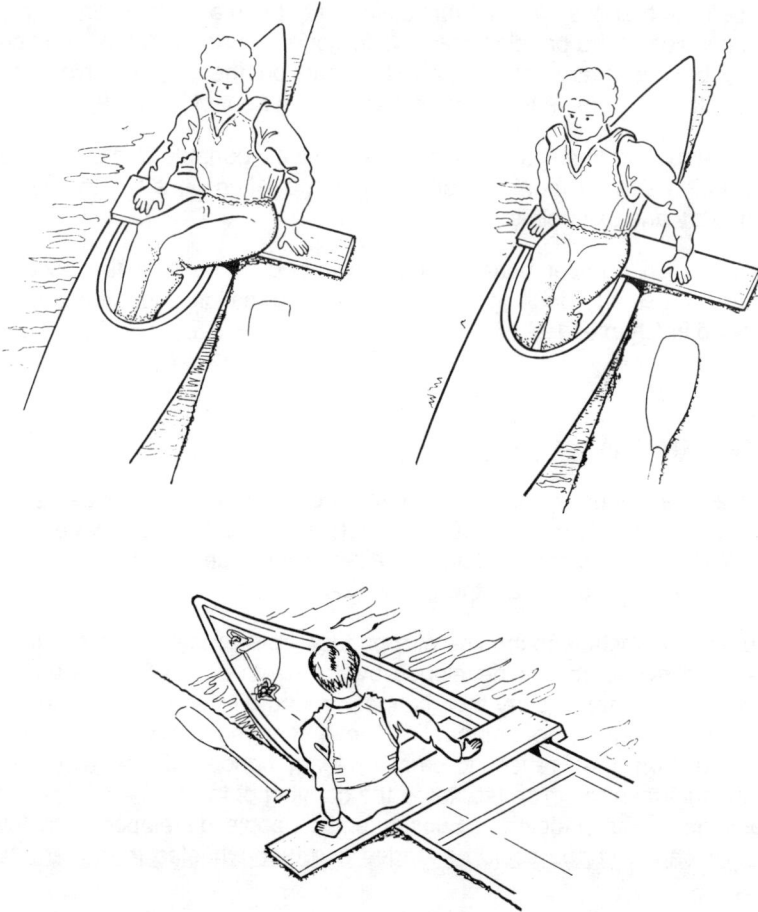

Fig 16:7 *Transfer boards in use*

As can be seen from the diagram the process is relatively simple. Once seated on the floor the person transfers to the transfer board. Then,

Geoff Smedley   Canoeing for Disabled People

with support as appropriate they gradually transfer themselves along the board until they can lower themselves from it into their boat.

Throughout the operation care needs to be taken to ensure that neither the board or the boat moves. In this respect it is often desirable to have a craft and paddler in the water along side the boat to be entered to give some support and stability.

Please note that it is considerably easier to get into a craft, when gravity is on the side of the paddler, than it is to get out. For this latter exercise it may be necessary for a helper to stand on the board behind the paddler to give some support when lifting up and out of the craft.

An advantage of this system is that it is relatively portable and subject to there being suitable bank conditions, may be taken on a trip to use at other entry and exit points.

The use of a transfer board can be extended as seen in the section *landing stages* and *docking bays*. Further information about these may be found in Chapter 19.

Portage Trolleys

I have mentioned earlier that many people with disabilities seek independence. To carry a canoe or kayak to and from the water can sometimes present too difficult a challenge for a person who may not have the required physical strength or mobility.

In these circumstances the use of a portage trolley may offer a solution. These trolleys were first developed by the users of open canoes who found it necessary to carry their canoes around difficult river sections or from one waterway to another. These manoeuvres were called a *"portage"* from the French "to carry". Many canoes still have a yoke across their centre which facilitated the carrying of the canoe across the shoulders of the paddler. Subsequently, people developed a trolley onto which the canoe could be loaded and then wheeled from place to place.

Such trolleys enable many people to wheel their canoes or kayaks to and from the water. Ferrara Canoe Club in Italy has a large number of members with disabilities. This organisation reserves all the lower level storage racks in the clubhouse for these members. As a result many of them are able to keep their kayaks stored on a portage trolley where they can wheel it, often whilst in their wheelchair, out of the clubhouse and onto the landing stage and thence to the water.   I will be talking about their particular landing stage and its special features in Chapter 19.

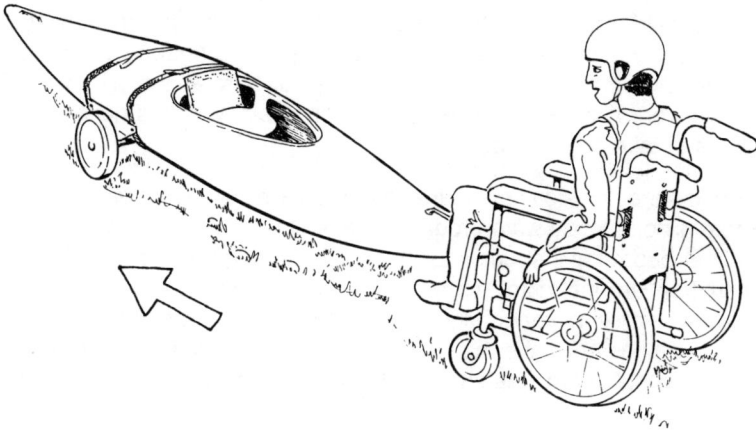

Fig 16:8 *The portage trolley*

There is a wide variety of trolleys available commercially, some of them small and light enough to be carried in the craft for use at the end of a trip, although for someone with a little engineering skill it would be possible to construct one by utilising the wheels used on golf trolleys.

Radio aids

The need for strategies to communicate with someone who has a sensory impairment has been referred to previously.   A radio link from the person to their buddy or instructor has proved to be a useful, and discreet, system of communication.

One of the most effective radio links I have used is a combined ear piece and microphone that comes on a simple headset with a small transceiver box.   I have one that I bought from *Tandy's* for about £45.

This system is designed for use by cyclists and has a range of about one hundred metres It is "voice operated" which means it is not switch on until one person or the other talks.

The only problem with most systems such as this is that they are not waterproof and would probably not survive a dunking! However, mine has survived for a few years now in regular use by paddlers in placid water situations.   It has been used particularly with paddlers with a visual impairment where the buddy needed to relay information about navigation.   It has also been used by people with a hearing impairment. The fact that the sound is being received directly at the person's ear seem to work in the same way as the hearing aid, which is generally too delicate to take on the water.

There is another device on the market called a *"Commlink"*   This system is completely waterproof. However it only allows communication from the buddy or instructor to the pupil, although with the switchable transmitter an instructor can communicate with up to nine pupils individually or simultaneously.   Furthermore the transmitter is quite bulky and does not have the "hands-free" potential of the other system. Finally, it costs approximately £350 for the transmitter and one receiver.

V.A.T.

Certain specialised items used exclusively for people with disabilities such as lifting aids or hoists can be zero rated for V.A.T.   Goods can only be zero rated if the supplier is registered for V.A.T. and if the person signs a declaration to say that he is disabled.   The form of declaration will usually be provided by the supplier.

For more information see the V.A.T. leaflet 701/7/86: *"Aids for Handicapped Persons"*

STRATEGIES for SAFE PRACTICE and RESCUES

Of course, the principles of these are generally a part of most canoeing or kayaking scenarios and feature within the training of all paddlers either for their tests of personal performance or as skills for those in the coaching scheme.

Importantly, the greatest contribution to safety and the success of any rescue is to follow the rule of always paddling with at least two other paddlers. The second most important rule is to practice and practice again those strategies that are essential to the paddler making a successful recovery from a capsize.

Its not a good time to try them when the wind is blowing, it's hailing, the water temperature is 48°, or two great white sharks are circling your yum yum yellow boat and you have heard they like yellow.

Webre and Zeller 1990

As mentioned previously, this book does not cover those skills of canoeing or kayaking that are common to all paddlers, the are covered already in such publications as the BCU's *"Canoeing Handbook"* Skills covered by this book are those pertinent because the paddler is disabled when canoeing or kayaking. Such special considerations may have to be given to the following.

- **Rafting up**
- **Towing**
- **Swimmer to Canoe Rescues**
- **Canoe to Canoe Rescues**
- **Deep water Rescues.**
- **Self Rescues**

A Note of Caution

Many rescues will involve the paddler moving in and out of the craft, often unavoidably scraping the legs on the inside of the craft or the cockpit rim or gunwale. People with reduced skin sensation can easily become injured during such manoeuvres. Therefore, care must be taken to ensure that all rough or sharp edges are smoothed down and that any likely injury points are padded. The edges of footrests, seats and cockpit rims are the most likely areas to cause problems. It also help to ensure that the paddler's danger areas are adequately covered or padded, clothes that cover the whole of the legs and shoes should always be worn.

Also be aware than for anyone the risk of hypothermia is greatly increased when in the water since the body loses heat 32 times faster than when out of the water. Coupled with the inability of some people to maintain their body temperature the need for speedy rescues when they are in the water is imperative.

Rafting up

Rafting up a number of canoes or kayaks can be useful to give a paddler some assistance or support in a relatively safe and stable situation.   The administration of first aid or medication, relief of cramp, putting on, or removing, clothing, or to have a rest,   are but a few reasons to form a raft.

In the right circumstances, a paddler can use the rafted situation to explore the potential for exiting and regaining access to their craft should they ever capsize.   Conditions such as the amount of support, particular strategies, numbers of and the role of assistants can all be investigated before such requirements are tested in a "real" rescue situation.

Towing

This is a skill used by instructors that needs to be practised since a poor towing technique or strategy can result in exhaustion for the person towing, and a state of nervous distress for the person being towed. Again, training for the leader appropriate to the type of water to be paddled is essential since it is during this training that the skills of rescue will be taught and practised for mastery.

Fig 16:9b The rafted tow

Fig 16:9a Towing

There are a number of towing techniques and strategies many with a specific purpose in mind.   However, in general I prefer a tow that uses a the shortest link between the two craft.   This allows the person being towed to lean on the towing craft to increase their stability.   If I have any need to maintain observation of the person I am towing I position their craft in front and facing me.   This method is more of a *push* than a *tow* but no more difficult.   This is usually referred to as the *rafted tow*.

Towing can cause an individual to be embarrassed.   This may be especially true if the person is disabled and perhaps more sensitive to being different.   Therefore, before taking someone in tow, discuss the situation with the individual and take every precaution to avoid embarrassment or distress.   Only tow for as long as is necessary and only when it is necessary.   If the group stop to play, disengage the towline.   Sometimes is only necessary to tow a tired paddler to the front of the group and then release the tow.   If you are tired it is harder to keep up with a group that appears to be pulling away from you.   Furthermore, from a group point of view, having the slower paddler at the front allows the rest of the group to take their pace from this person.

Fig 16:10 Swimmer to capsize rescue

Swimmer to Canoe Rescues

These rescues are used principally in swimming pool sessions. However, if contemplating such rescues as procedure, it is important to be aware of the necessity to have a particular strategy for use with people who have a physical disability.

The normal procedure is for the rescuer to grasp the extended arm of the capsized kayakist on the opposite side of the kayak and pull gently to restore the paddler to an upright position.   If the paddler has a physical disability then using this technique   it   is possible to either injure them, if they have poor upper body strength, or to pull them out of the kayak, if they have poor lower body strength.

A safer method of rescue is to get the paddler to put their arms round the hull of the kayak and concentrate on holding themselves in.   The rescuer rights the kayak, and the paddler, by reaching across and grasping the cockpit rim and pulls the kayak up with the paddler attached, rather than pulling the paddler up with the kayak attached.

You body should be over the front of the spraydeck so that you can have good eye contact with the paddler.   You will also be able to ensure that he does not capsize again on top of you.

This technique needs to be practised by the rescuer and the paddler. The technique will not work for someone who cannot hold themselves in the kayak when inverted.

Canoe to Canoe Rescues (The Eskimo Rescue)

Sometimes called the Eskimo Rescue this technique enables a capsized kayakist to right himself by using another kayakist or canoeist. It relies on the ability of the capsized paddler to locate the rescue kayak or canoe, and also their strength to pull themselves upright .

If working with a paddler with a sensory impairment the most sensible position for the rescue craft to take is alongside the capsized kayak. The rescuer can then indicate by tapping the upturned kayak that they are in position and then take the extended hands of the capsized paddler and guide them onto the rescuer's paddle, which is place at right angles to both craft and bridging the gap between them.

1

2

3

Fig 16:11 The "Eskimo" rescue

Deep Water Rescues.

If a paddler should fall out of her craft during a capsize then the easiest way to re-enter is to swim with the craft, or be towed, to the bank where the craft can be emptied of water and the paddler reseated.

However, there are occasions when this is not possible and the paddler must be returned to the craft whilst still in the water. These rescues are well documented in the *Canoeing Handbook* and are part of the repertoire taught to all instructors.

However, it is necessary to bear in mind that some physically disabled people may not be able to get back into their craft from the water without considerable assistance, perhaps even requiring someone in the water with them to help. This requirement obviously creates more risk for the party and such rescues must be practised thoroughly to avoid them turning into rescue "epics". As in *Fig 16:12* note the following:-

- The rescue kayak faces the opposite way to the rescued kayak.
- The paddler is assisted to the rear of her kayak so that her legs face the right way for re-entry.
- All the team maintain eye contact.
- The rescued can use her arms to assist.

Fig 16:12 *A deep water rescue*

Generally speaking when rescuing a paddler with a physical impairment and putting him back into his kayak in deep water you should be using the maximum number of people possible to assist.   It may be necessary to lift the person onto the back of a pair of rafted kayaks as a prelude to transferring them into their own kayak.   There are some deep water rescues that allow people to enter a partially swamped craft.   In this condition the craft sits much lower in the water and the person can be almost "floated" into their craft.   It should be noted that this type of rescue requires the rescued craft to be emptied of water. This can be achieved by using a pump, either one on the rescued craft or, with appropriate adaptations, one on the rescuer's craft.

There are also inflatable devices that fit to the end of a paddle that enable the paddle to be used as an outrigger support during rescues.

Self Rescues (Rolling)

As long as the paddler can hold herself in the craft when it is inverted there is always the possibility of a *self rescue* most times referred to as *rolling* the craft upright again.   Since rolling relies more on synchronised technique than strength it should always be considered as a potential skill within the capabilities of most paddlers.   Success in rolling can be facilitated by a developmental programme of instruction.

• Start in the swimming pool where the consequences of a "failed" roll are not serious.

• Initially use a kayak that is relatively easy to roll such as one of the specially designed pool kayaks or "bats".

• Always have plenty of human support to help right the kayak if the roll is unsuccessful.   This is much easier that having to exit, empty and re-enter the kayak.

• Use goggles to enable the paddler to find their orientation under the water.

• Use a nose clip to avoid gradually filling the sinuses with chlorinated water, this often brings a rolling session to a premature conclusion.

• Use a longer paddle.

Once the roll is successful and can be repeated as required, gradually reduce the artificial advantages of kayak, support, vision and paddle until the person is rolling the kayak she will use when on open water.

Paddlers with poor lower body strength may need to strap themselves into their craft to enable them to stay in whilst inverted. The use of such straps has been covered in Chapter Ten.   These references must be studied carefully since strapping someone into a craft is potentially very dangerous.   Furthermore, if such straps are used to help a person roll the escape strategy must be practised until considered to be foolproof.

Additional assistance can be provided by the use of kayaks with central buoyancy since this stops the legs from falling to one side thus upsetting the equilibrium of the craft.

Many kayaks have thigh braces. Whilst these can assist the paddler to brace herself in the craft they are also potential devices for scraping the legs should an exit be necessary.   A considered balance of advantage and disadvantage is required.   Note that even paddlers with weak lower body muscles will benefit from being able to brace themselves against a good footrest.   This is further assisted by using a backstrap.

Webre and Zeller advocate the use of the *Steyr* roll for people with a physical disability. They consider this roll to be more suitable since the body is kept closer to the rear deck which reduces the strength necessary to right the kayak. Since the paddler is facing away from the kayak during this roll, the usual concerns about shallow water and risk of facial injury have to be considered.

People with a physical disability may have difficulty after completing a Steyr roll and may need assistance to regaining an upright seating position. Some people may have spasms when they lean back onto the rear deck. Whilst you will need to be aware of this during instruction, after repeated practice these spasms should cease to occur.

Finally

There are a number of rescues techniques that are not described here. Indeed there are books written about nothing else! It is strongly recommended that the reader reads at least the relevant chapters in the *Canoeing Handbook* to supplement the information contained in this chapter. Furthermore, it must be emphasised once again that practice is the key to successful and trauma free rescues. Practice, not only in the warmth and safety of the swimming pool, but also in the open water situation that is the usual environment for the coaching sessions.

There is little doubt that once a paddler has taken part in a successful rescue he will feel more confident about his safety on the water.

CHAPTER SEVENTEEN

PROGRAMMES FOR PEOPLE WITH EPILEPSY

Acknowledgements

I am grateful to Carol Jobson of St Piers Lingfield on whose work much of this chapter is based. Also to Karin Wilkinson for her support and advice on the original chapter for the 1986 edition.

Introduction

The following guidelines have been produced with both general and specific considerations given to a variety of environments. All situations vary according to the weather, the group composition or the location, in addition all of these variables interact and affect the other. Each situation will need to be considered separately according to the conditions and the leaders and buddies available.

Group leaders will need to use their discretion and experience in applying these guidelines. However, in doing so they have the confidence of knowing that this is the code of practice recommended by the British Canoe Union and anyone following it will have the usual support of the BCU and the benefits of its insurance cover.

AT ALL TIMES SAFETY OF THE STUDENTS IS THE ULTIMATE AIM

Note: The advice in this chapter must be considered alongside advice and recommendations for canoeists found in other parts of this book.

Choice of craft

Where there is a risk of a paddler having a seizure, the craft used must be one that will allow the person to fall out of the cockpit if a kayak; or to fall off the craft if it is the sit-on type. In this respect, many craft previously mentioned in this book are potentially suitable. The open canoe is a very suitable craft, paddled either solo or by two or more paddlers.

However, when considering the situation of having someone experiencing a seizure whilst still in their craft, it is worth giving thought to the use of all plastic boats rather than glass-fibre or aluminium framed boats.

Geoff Smedley   Canoeing for Disabled People

A very stable set up for canoeing with people with epilepsy is that of two canoes rafted together, this allows for four, or more depending upon the size of the canoes, people to paddle.

However, the greater the risk of the participant having a seizure when on the water the more need there is for either:- a very stable craft, and/or one with the minimum restriction to a safe exit in an emergency.

Similar criteria must apply to the use of spray-decks, or in the case of canoes, knee straps or a saddle. Their use can only be recommended if the participant has a very low risk of seizure and if an emergency procedure to exit the kayak has been well rehearsed and everyone involved is confident of it's success in an emergency.

The first rule must be:- when there is any concern for the safety of the participant in the event of a seizure, an open cockpit craft, preferably an open canoe, with a buddy* and no restraints must be recommended.

* For information and advice about the buddy system see the latter part of chapter 18.

Personal Buoyancy

Participants must always wear a buoyancy aid that fits and is checked by the leader before each session. As stated previously buoyancy aids must be approved.

Life-jackets to B.S.I. 3595/81 or buoyancy aids approved by S.B.B.N.F. (now B.M.I.F.) or B.C.U./B.C.M.A. Standard B.A. 83 are normally suitable, although the new European Standards CE Mark will soon be obligatory.

You should look for the CE mark and the 50 Newtons as the standard

However, such a buoyancy aid, whilst it will support the person safely in the water will not keep the person floating on their back with their face, and airway, clear of the water. This situation is often exacerbated if the person is also wearing a wet-suit or a dry-suit since the buoyancy that these impart to the legs often results in the wearer's legs floating higher than their head.

Whilst this situation is of no consequence to the conscious person, who will still be able to keep their face clear of the water, it will have serious consequences for the unconscious person.

For these reasons it is recommended that people with epilepsy also wear a source of additional buoyancy. The best way to do this is to wear a buoyancy aid that can be manually triggered and inflated by means of a CO_2 bottle.

There is an automatic version; but since this "fires" when a paper washer gets wet it is likely to inflate under most canoeing situations, which would be both inconvenient and inappropriate.

This type of additional buoyancy is quite unobtrusive, relatively easy, and very fast to inflate and once inflated is capable of keeping the wearer floating on their back with their face, and airway clear of the water. Such buoyancy aids can give an extra 150N or more of additional buoyancy.

Programmes

The content and delivery of programmes for people with epilepsy is essentially no different than for any other canoeists. However, there are some factors related specifically to participation that may differ. The following advice is adapted from the Notes for Guidance of St Piers Lingfield as devised by Carol Jobson.

1. People with epilepsy can only participate on a 1:1 basis. Leaders and students both knowing with whom they are partnered or buddied.

2. All leaders and buddies, canoeing or support, must wear an approved buoyancy aid at all times when on or near the water.

3. In addition to an approved buoyancy aid, people with epilepsy must also wear a manually operated CO_2 buoyancy aid.

4. It may be advisable, in the interests of safety, for some people with epilepsy to wear a canoeing safety helmet. However, when such decisions are made on the basis of the medical condition rather than the canoeing situation, great care must be taken to avoid stigmatising the individual.

5. Careful thought should be given to the locations used with a group, especially if members of the group have epilepsy that is particularly difficult to manage . For example the following locations may require the use of a safety boat:-

- large lakes where the paddler may be beyond a reasonable swimming distance from the shore,

- rivers with banks which make landing difficult.

6. The safety boat may be either an open canoe, or, preferably an inflatable. It may also be motorised, this decision would depend on the ability of its users to make swift progress without a motor in the event of an emergency that required the use of the safety boat. If a decision is made to use such a location with a group and have a safety boat there are additional implications.

   - On some lakes, reservoirs and rivers motorised boats are not permitted.

   - In a motorised boat there must be one person exclusively in charge of the motor to ensure that it does not present a hazard to anyone in the water.

   - When using a motorised craft consideration must be given to the increased effect of wind chill caused by the speed of the craft. If speed of recovery is a factor then consideration must be given to sheltering the person being recovered from the wind.

   - Without a motor, or with the motor switched off, the safety boat can be a safe base to which people with epilepsy may be towed, in their craft or whilst in the water.

7. In most circumstances a safety boat will not be required, however, the use of a standby craft that can take a person who may need to recover after a seizure, and tow their craft, whilst maintaining contact with the rest of the group would be valuable. This may be particularly appropriate where the width of the stretch of water is beyond throwing line distance.

8. Since there is a possibility of the inhalation of water should a person with epilepsy have a seizure in the water, the person should be turned over and drained. Everyone should be told of the incident so that the possibility of secondary drowning is excluded. The person should be checked over the following two days.

9. People with epilepsy must always be at the front of the group and never allowed to lose contact with the group. In the event that a person should be separated from the group the leader should carry a means of attracting attention, with a whistle or a gas horn etc.

10. Once a seizure has run its course, depending on the individual and the circumstances, the individual may return to the shore, or continue canoeing as the instructor and the individual feel appropriate.

RESCUES   Seizure not involving a capsize

1.   The person having a seizure must be supported by the buddy in such a way that will maintain a clear airway.   *N.B. THIS IS A PRIORITY*

2.   The person must be supported by the buddy in such a manner that will minimise impact and abrasion injuries to the head and limbs.

Rescue Methods - person having the seizure and buddy in an open canoe (or a double open cockpit kayak).

The person with epilepsy must always be in the bow position.

In the event of a seizure the buddy moves forward and kneels behind the person having the seizure and holds them by the buoyancy aid, taking care to keep their head in a position that avoids them being hit. The buddy should leave her paddle behind the rear seat and, if possible secure the person having the seizure's paddle and place it with hers, failing this it should be put over the side for recovery by someone else in the group.

If the seizure will allow, the person having the seizure can be eased backwards until they are lying on the floor of the canoe/kayak.   In preparation for this it is a simple matter to have one or two carry-mats on the bottom of the canoe to protect the individual.   In this position or the previous sitting position it should not be necessary to inflate the CO_2 buoyancy aid.

Other craft can be paddled to the buddy's canoe/kayak and rafted up to the rear of the person having the seizure to stabilise the craft.   This position can be maintained whilst the person who has had the seizure recovers or is transferred to the safety craft.

Depending upon the need, the "craft" may be a pair of canoes rafted together; there may also be an additional paddler who takes the stern position leaving the buddy to position himself or herself immediately behind the person with epilepsy from which position they can paddle, coach and be ready for a possible seizure.

Rescue Methods - person having the seizure in a solo kayak.

The buddy must be a competent paddler who will position her kayak in a close paddling situation and be able to draw alongside the kayak of her buddy quickly and safely.

In the event of a seizure, she will paddle alongside the other kayak to support the person having the seizure to maintain the airway and minimise impact and abrasion injuries to head or limbs.

Whilst the person having a seizure remains in his kayak the above advice will best be achieved by the buddy rafting alongside and physically supporting the person having a seizure by the buoyancy aid.

If the seizure will allow, a greater level of control will be achieved by laying the person having the seizure sideways across the foredeck of the rescuer's kayak.

At this, or the previous stage, it will probably be unnecessary to inflate the CO_2 buoyancy aid.

Other canoe/kayaks can be paddled to the buddy's kayak and rafted up to the rear of the person having the seizure to stabilise the craft. This position can be maintained whilst the person who has had the seizure recovers or is transferred to the safety craft.

RESCUE   Seizure involving a capsize.

Should the person having a seizure capsize during the seizure then speed of rescue is of the essence. It must be assumed that the person involved is paddling a craft that they have fallen out and are not restrained in the craft by a small cockpit.

Once the person is in the water the rescue can be affected in one of two ways.

The rescuer remains in her canoe/kayak.

The rescuer pulls alongside the person in the water making contact with the back of the buoyancy aid and pulling the person up to clear the airway of the water. Once in a secure position the CO_2 buoyancy aid can be fired.

Since the buoyancy aid will now keep the airway of the person having the seizure clear of the water this position can be maintained whilst the seizure runs its course.

Again, others in the group can raft on the rescuer's craft to give additional support. This must be done on the side away from the person having the seizure.

When the person has recovered the gas cylinder can be replaced and he can either be returned to his craft to continue or placed in the safety craft.

Rescuer leaves her canoe/kayak.

Once the person having the seizure is in the water the rescuer exits her canoe/kayak leaving it the right way up in the water.   The rescuer makes contact with the person having the seizure from the rear and fires the CO_2 buoyancy aid.   The person can now be supported by the buoyancy aid and the rescuers craft until the seizure has run its course.

Others in the group can paddle to rescuer to give additional support. This must be done on the side away from the person having the seizure and only on the invitation of the rescuer.

When the person has recovered the gas cylinder can be replaced and he can either return to his craft to continue or rest in the safety craft.

SUGGESTED PADDLING LOCATIONS   Swimming Pool

This is an enclosed environment in which someone in difficulties is easy to get to from either in the water or from the pool side. The use of the swimming pool is essential for early capsize practice especially for the poor swimmer or nervous paddler.   It is also good environment for practising many paddling skills and to improve confidence and balance. It is also environment for the leaders and buddies to become familiar with rescue techniques and to practice locating quickly and surely the important release toggle to fire the CO_2 buoyancy aid.

All support staff should also practice the use of throw-lines, in particular the recovery and re-throwing of such lines.

Safety "safety"

Consideration must be given to the appropriate placement of leaders and buddies; in or on the water, on the pool side or a combination of all

Geoff Smedley   Canoeing for Disabled People

these according to the activity. For people with epilepsy the buddy ratio must be 1:1.

In the pool area the wearing of buoyancy aids is discretionary according to circumstances. CO_2 buoyancy aids and safety helmets will probably be unnecessary in most swimming pool environments

A useful aid is a large sheet (1m x 2m x 30 mm) of closed cell mat that will float on the pool and onto which someone having a seizure can be lifted.   Once on such a sheet they can be lifted to the pool side. The use of such a sheet depends largely on the severity of the seizure but has proved a useful aid in getting people out of the water during or after a seizure.

SUGGESTED PADDLING LOCATIONS Placid/sheltered water.

These are environments such as canals, small ponds or lakes and small slow flowing rivers. There should be little or no current and access to and from the bank should be easy. The site should be sheltered to keep any effects of the wind to a minimum. Participants can use the skills they have learned in the swimming pool in a real, but safe, environment.

Safety

Personal buoyancy as described previously will be worn on and off the water. The wearing of helmets is discretionary and dependent upon circumstances, again be cautious about stigmatising. The area for paddlers must be clearly defined. Leaders and buddies on the water will carry tow-lines. Leaders on the bank may be required to carry throw-lines.

SUGGESTED PADDLING LOCATIONS Moving water

These are waters such as rivers and lakes where the effects of currents or the wind have to be taken into account.   Participants will be able to put into practice more of the skills they have learned but will still be in a relatively safe environment.

Safety

Because of the possibility of capsize and the nature of the river banks and the river bottom, helmets and personal buoyancy will be worn at all times on or off the water. The area to be paddled will be clearly defined and all leaders and buddies on the water will carry tow-lines. A safety boat may be considered appropriate.

SUGGESTED PADDLING LOCATIONS Graded rivers.

Rivers are graded according to the level of difficulty (for more information about river grades see page 232 of the Canoeing Handbook). Consideration must be given to currents, rocks and trees that affect negotiation of the river.

Safety

Helmets and personal buoyancy must be worn at all times both on and off the water. Leaders and buddies on the water will carry tow-lines. A safety boat will not be practical in most cases, therefore, extra consideration needs to be given to the leader ratio and level of competence and the abilities of the group. At any rapids or weirs leaders must be on the bank with throw-lines. They must be belayed to a safe point and be prepared to go into the water with an additional throw line.

With these considerations in mind some river locations may not be appropriate to use.

Leader / Buddy Training

It must be fairly obvious after reading these notes that leaders and buddies working with people with epilepsy will need to have specific training and awareness.

- There can be no substitute to the experience of being with people who have epilepsy. It is strongly advised that anyone wishing to paddle with people with epilepsy should first gain experience of dealing with seizures on dry land before they consider paddling with people with epilepsy.

- Epilepsy is an "invisible" disability. Many famous people have had epilepsy without the general public being aware of their condition. Since you cannot tell by looking at a person what affect a seizure may have, you will need to take advice from the individual, or if appropriate, from his or her parents or carers.

- Many rescue techniques including exiting one's craft and using tow-lines or throwing-lines have a more fundamental role in the repertoire of skills for the leader or buddy. Therefore, these skills must be developed and rehearsed regularly.

- The deployment of the CO_2 buoyancy aid is a specific skill and the wearer, buddies and instructors must be conversant in their use and operation. Leaders should also carry spare bottles and clips with them for emergency replenishment.

In Conclusion

Epilepsy is no longer an automatic bar to water based activities such as canoeing or kayaking.

This chapter is here to encourage and support the involvement of people with epilepsy in canoeing. There is an additional responsibility in paddling with people with epilepsy that probably exceeds that of paddling with people with any other disability. Nevertheless, the achievements of people like Carol Jobson, with the canoeing programmes at St Piers and similar programmes at many other centres has demonstrated the possibilities and the great potential for success.

There are also specific guidelines available from the BCU, who wish to encourage and support paddlers with epilepsy who want to gain coaching qualifications, see Chapter 14.

CHAPTER EIGHTEEN

PROGRAMMES FOR PEOPLE WITH LEARNING DISABILITY

Acknowledgements

I am grateful for the help and advice of Roger Biggs, the Director and Mark Southam, the National Officer, of the United Kingdom Sports Association for People with Learning Disability.

Introduction

The terminology used to describe people who have some form of intellectual impairment is changing. The use of the term *Mental Handicap* is now replaced, generally, by the term *Learning Disability*. Whilst there are a number of alternative terms, this book uses the term Learning Disability.

It is still a fact that most people understand very little about people with learning disability since they probably have little contact them. Perhaps as a result of this, there is still a stigma attached to people with learning disability which can serve to exclude them from many opportunities that the rest of the population enjoy.

People with learning disability, and those concerned maximising opportunities for them are constantly looking for way to break down the barriers of prejudice. Canoeing, and physical activity in general, has a great deal to offer. However, it is recognised that many leaders and instructors view the prospect of coaching people with learning disability daunting. They should not be deterred or apprehensive, the challenge is there but the rewards are significant.

This chapter will, hopefully, give awareness, knowledge and confidence to those entering this field of coaching for the first time. It builds upon previous chapters and suggestions for coaching programmes and addresses particular considerations that coaching programmes need to address for people with learning disability , and focuses on the practical question - HOW?

By focusing upon the how, I hope to address some of the doubts and apprehensions that the reader may have and give encouragement to become involved, since only by getting involved can the confidence to develop the appropriate skills ultimately be achieved.

What is learning disability?

Learning disability is an impairment to the functioning of the brain. Making wide generalisations about people with learning disability is dangerous and potentially insulting. The term learning disability covers a wide range of abilities.

However, the term learning disability, as it suggests, refers to often wide ranging impairment in the individual's ability to understand and learn. The effect varies considerably from person to person but may influence the assimilation of knowledge, the acquisition of skills, memory and the retention of knowledge or skills, or the application of learning or previous experiences.

Approximately one million people have some form of learning disability but the majority of these are able to lead normal independent lives with only minimal assistance.   A further 160,000 are severely impaired, many of these needing special care and having multiple impairments. (Information taken from "Building on Ability", the report of the Minister of Sport's Review Group 1989).

The value of sport

By and large it can be assumed that the readers of this book are aware of the general advantages of sport. Many people with learning disability are already aware of the additional benefits that can be gained from participation in sporting opportunities.

Not only can general health and fitness be improved but independence, communication, friendships, self reliance, self esteem and integration are greatly enhanced. Most of us take such skills for granted, but for many people with a disability the capacity to acquire these skills requires guidance and support, and opportunities often need to be sought actively.

The information which follows must be seen as being supplementary to information already given about programmes and coaching in the previous chapters, and not as a substitute for this information.

Key considerations when developing the programme.

Give equal dignity and respect

People with learning disability should be accorded the same dignity, rights, respect and quality of life as everyone else. However, this does mean that there must be support from the community for the changes in attitudes and policies to reflect the right of all people to be a part of the community in which they live or in which they enjoy their leisure.

Focus on abilities

We all differ in those things we are good at and those skills we can develop better than others. When considering programmes for people with learning disability, look for the abilities and the strengths and build upon these. There is now a wide variety of craft available to encourage canoeing and kayaking. Therefore, matching the abilities of a particular individual to a paddling opportunity is significantly easier.

Consider the range of stability that is offered at one extreme by the rafted open canoes, and at the other by the sprint K1. Paddlers can, and have, learned their skills in the open canoe raft and with appropriate coaching progressed through to paddling the sprint K1, whilst others have developed skills in paddling that have been more appropriate for the rafted open canoe. Of course, a greater number of people have found an appropriate craft somewhere between these two extremes. Nevertheless, all still acquire skills that enable them to participate and contribute to the management of the craft they paddle. The sprint racer taking part in competition and the rafted open canoe paddler taking part in expedition canoeing.

However, do not consider each example as exclusive, there are also people with learning disability who are paddling in every section of canoeing and kayaking sport.

Use local community activity

Historically, many people with learning disability have been excluded from mainstream life activities; they have been segregated from the community and confined in institutions with little opportunity to be with non-disabled people and enjoy a similar lifestyle.

Having spent a lot of time in the company of other people with learning disability in special settings, they are often uncertain or anxious in new situations in the community. Often the effects of having been deprived of mainstream school and work environments, leads to them finding occasional difficulties in understanding what is the appropriate response in some new situations.

For these reasons your programme may be more successful if it commences within the known environment of the people with learning disability. Therefore, wherever possible take your programme to them in the early stages.   Many establishments such as schools and leisure centres have swimming pools and you may be able to move the programme onto the water whilst still remaining on familiar territory.

In particular you may find it useful to introduce the equipment in a "familiarisation" session, before the practical sessions on the water, when the prospective participants can explore, ask questions and generally become familiar with the equipment they will use.   Leaving a buoyancy aid and helmet with people so that they can learn in their own time how to put it on themselves, helps to give confidence when they attend the actual paddling sessions.

As confidence develops you will be able to move the programme to your more usual environment at the canoe club, and onto on the river or open water.

Seek age appropriate activity

It may appear that some people with learning disability are functioning and behaving at a level below their age. This can often have its origins in the situation they have found themselves as described in the previous paragraphs.   Limited opportunities, and in some cases restrictive attitudes, may have held back the potential to develop age appropriate behaviour for some people with learning disability.   Often the under-estimation of their potential development that has led to limited skill development.

Given the opportunity to extend beyond apparent limitations, people with learning disability have many more similarities with other people than they have differences. One way in which the canoeing programme can support these opportunities is to ensure that people with learning disability are given recognition and activities that are appropriate to their real age.

Making their own decisions about their activities

You may find that some people with learning disability are encouraged to come to your activities as part of an awareness raising programme set up by the individual's parents or carers. This may be a strategy to give people sufficient knowledge about potential sport and leisure opportunities to enable them to make an informed choice.

Once they have joined your programme you should make every effort to ensure that the people with learning disability have the opportunity to make choices about their activities. Give choices and options and allow people to make decisions, only consult with carers, parents or teachers if you feel you need their support specifically. Your skills as an instructor will ensure that your programme, and its implementation, is based on informed decisions and is within the potential of the individual.

Involvement in planning

Once people with learning disability have become a part of the club or group you are coaching, they should be involved in the planning of activities, committee meetings and discussion groups that are the essential features of programme development. They will probably not be able to do this without your support, and initially at least, will need your help in interpreting procedures and processes, until they gain confidence and knowledge.

This type of involvement needs careful planning if everyone is to feel that the process is mutually beneficial. Bear in mind that committee business can be, on one hand boringly routine and on the other, intellectually challenging; and that often the voluntary time of its members may be at a premium and so meetings need to be business-like and efficient.

Nevertheless, there are often agenda items, sub committees or members' groups that play a major part in the planning of activities. These will always benefit from representatives of the membership of club and may be the most valuable role to be assumed by people with learning disability.

Ensure high standards

If they have had little or no experience of canoeing, people with learning disability may place a great deal of trust in you as a leader, to give them guidance in the choice of equipment and in the coaching of appropriate skills.   Without your help they, like anyone else without the relevant knowledge or information, could easily select equipment or make decisions about their activities that are not of an appropriate standard.

All clubs or centres, tend to accumulate equipment of differing standards. Most people will seek the better equipment and only choose the lesser standard equipment as a last resort. As a leader you will need to ensure that people with learning disability are not always left with the lower standard equipment.   Sometimes the lower standard equipment should have been taken out of service completely.

A reasonable rule to apply to basic equipment (although not to any specific leaders equipment) is;

> "would I exchange my equipment for that which one of my students is using?" If the answer is "no", then the next question must be;

> "should they be using that equipment at all?"

The same rules could also apply to activities.   Questions such as; "would I do a capsize drill in that water?" should also be asked and the outcome acted upon.

Opportunities to mix and socialise

In the early stages of programme development you may find some people with learning disability have specific needs that are best addressed by them being taught collectively. This is to allow you, and them, to address the issues raised in the previous sections. However, many of the previously discussed issues have at their core the problems that arise from segregation. Therefore you should consider involving people with learning disability in integrated coaching and activity situations as much, and as early, as possible.

Only by giving people with learning disability the opportunities to mix and socialise with other people will the prejudices and myths that exist to their disadvantage be overcome.

Other disabilities

People with learning disability are liable to have any of the conditions which affect other people. However, the way in which they react may be different. In some cases it may be necessary for the leader or instructor to interpret a person's reaction to a situation. Sometimes a person with a learning disability seems to be unaware of pain or discomfort and they may continue in an activity even though they may be hurt or perhaps unwell. On the other hand some people with learning disability may have a low tolerance to pain or discomfort due to their having been over protected. The leader's knowledge of the individual and their observations are crucial in this respect.

Furthermore, people with learning disability are also as likely as anyone else to have sensory or physical disabilities, or to have medical conditions such as epilepsy, diabetes or asthma. Further notes regarding these conditions are in chapters 11 and 12. However, do not assume that people with learning disability will have an additional disability.

In Conclusion

As an instructor your aims for people with learning disability can be as broad as they are for the rest of the population. Although growing in popularity, canoeing for people with learning disability is still relatively new and there are exciting further developments to be made.

Putting the principles described in this chapter into the context of the rest of the book requires of the instructor, flexibility and responsiveness to individual needs, interests and abilities. Given time and appropriate coaching, there is almost no limit to what people with learning disability, and their instructors, can achieve.

Plate 18:a *Practical coaching*

Canoeing for Disabled People   Geoff Smedley

CHAPTER NINETEEN

FACILITATING ACCESS FOR PEOPLE WITH DISABILITIES

Acknowledgements

I have been guided in the advice offered in this chapter by the information contained in "Informal Countryside Recreation for Disabled People - A practical guide for countryside managers". This book is published by the Countryside Commission

Introduction

Throughout this book the theme of access has been fundamental. However, whilst access to the sport is facilitated by appropriate equipment and coaching programmes, of at least equal importance is access and mobility around the clubhouse and in the route to the paddling environment.

Although they are very important, access is more than providing ramps and having doorways with sufficient width for wheelchairs. The needs of people who experience mobility difficulties but not necessarily from a wheelchair, people with sensory impairments of vision or hearing, those with learning disability, all need to be catered for. You should also be aware that by providing an accessible resource for people with disabilities you often give improved access to other groups in the community such as the young or the elderly, and those with temporary special needs, such as parents with pushchairs.

Whilst we practice our sport in a natural environment, the rivers, lakes and sea, which present the same challenges to us all, disabled or non-disabled, the access to these areas has, on the whole, been designed and developed by non-disabled people for use by non-disabled people. Often it is the minor features of a situation that create the unnecessary barrier to access. Consider the lock to the door, why are so many latch type locks placed at chest level to the average standing person when they would be equally usable at a lower level that would also be accessible by someone in a wheelchair. These features, and others will be addressed later in this chapter.

The aim must be to provide facilities within the clubhouse or centre provision that are accessible by all people irrespective of their ability. Integration must be the aim so that facilities are developed for all people and, importantly, no more specifically, for the person with a disability

Geoff Smedley   Canoeing for Disabled People

than for the person without a disability.   Where-ever possible, all facilitates must be accessed equally by all people.

Often the provision of facilities that *enable* people with disabilities can be devised so that the special features are not glaringly obvious.   A clear and well lit notice board will be seen equally well by people with a visual impairment as it will by the rest of the members.

I frequently hear people say *"we would improve our provision, but we can't afford it"*.   By *afford* they usually mean *have the money*.   My response is usually two fold; firstly, not all changes require money and secondly, if we are to meet our intentions of an integrated sport we have to find the ways and means.

Many modifications and adaptations to existing facilities can be made simply by having a policy that resolves to address the needs of people with disabilities every time a change or renewal of any facility is considered in the usual cycle of repairs and maintenance.   Often the renewal or repair of a resource to incorporate integrated use is no more costly that to restore the facility to its original, but non-accessible, function.

In addressing the potential for integrated provision the following broad groups of people will be considered.

- Wheelchair users and the ambulant person with a disability

- People with a sensory impairment - vision or hearing

- People with a learning disability.

Conditions for accessibility to facilities

In this section I will look at:

- Car parks

- Facilities inside buildings

- Paths and path surfaces

- Handrails

- Steps

- Ramps

- Access within buildings

- Landing stages and jetties.

- An Access Check List

Car parks

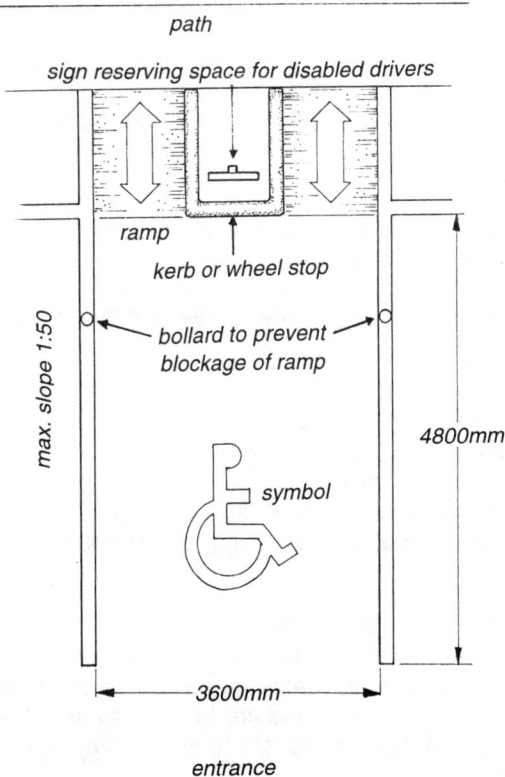

path

sign reserving space for disabled drivers

ramp

kerb or wheel stop

bollard to prevent blockage of ramp

max. slope 1:50

4800mm

symbol

3600mm

entrance

Fig 19:1 Parking space for a disabled driver

If you have a car park the provision of parking spaces for people with disabilities should be seriously considered. I am sure no-one will take the attitude that is immortalised in disability folk lore *"What do we need parking spaces for disabled people for? No disabled people ever come here!"*

The following guidelines should be applied to car parks.

- Mark out a "setting down" area adjacent to the entrance. This will assist not just drivers setting down people with disabilities before they park, but will also benefit other members who have boats to unload.

- Next to this area designate parking for drivers with a disability, one or more spaces depending upon the size of the car park.

Geoff Smedley   Canoeing for Disabled People

- This space should be wider than normal to allow the driver space to manoeuvre their wheelchair if necessary.   Fig 19:1 has the suggested dimensions.

- Use the international disability symbol to indicate the reservation place on this parking space.   See the diagram for an illustration of this.

- Include directions to the setting down area and the reserved parking spaces with any other directions or notices that you have.

Access into buildings

Consider the route that people will take from the car park, not necessarily from the reserved parking spaces - they may have been occupied! Ensure that there is:

- A level path with a smooth firm surface that is clear of any obstructions. (see the section on paths)

- Ramped provision at any steps or kerbs. (see the section on ramps)

- A minimum width of 900 mm.

- A level, or ramped access through the door.   If the main door has a large flight of steps then adapt another, more accessible entrance, and use clear signs to indicate where this alternative entrance is. Above all make this alternative entrance as inviting as you can so that it does not give the impression of being a "second class" entrance.

The wheelchair dimensions in Fig 19:2 may help you to plan routes that will enable someone in a wheelchair to access.   These dimensions may also help you to consider safe accommodation for wheelchairs whilst their owners are on the water.   If the paddlers are to be away from the club house for a long time you must give thought to the security of any wheelchairs.

See also the guidance in Fig 19:4 for the planning of routes.

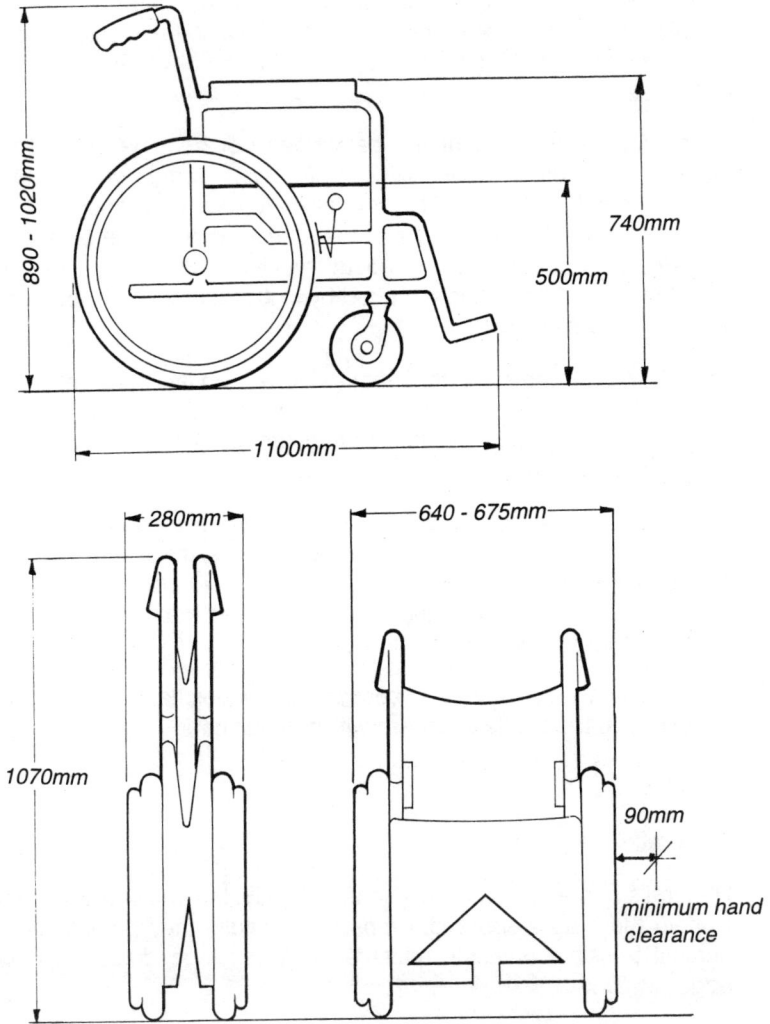

Fig 19:2 *Wheelchair dimensions*

Geoff Smedley   Canoeing for Disabled People

Paths and path surfaces

Paths should be 1200 mm wide as a minimum.   Paths this wide allow for wheelchair use and also for people using crutches sticks or frames. People move at different rates and this width also takes into account the possible need for overtaking of a person in a wheelchair, or by a person in a wheelchair!

Take care to ensure that the path does not become cluttered.   All manner of objects can litter pathways, some will accumulate environmentally such as litter or fallen leaves or branches.   Other objects may be deposited by members such as a paddle or boat.   You will need to educate members about this kind of cluttering. People with visual impairments will be hindered by clutter as much, if not more than people in wheelchairs.

The various parameters for features of a path and information about path surfaces can be obtained from   *"Informal Countryside Recreation for Disabled People - A practical guide for countryside managers" Countryside Commission*

It is important to mark the edge of the path to assist people who have a visual impairment.   Contrasts in colour and texture between the path and the adjacent area can be used.   You should also ensure that there are no obstructions overhanging the path that may be walked into by people with a visual impairment.

Note also the clearances necessary for wheelchairs in all routes as described in the section "Access within buildings".

Handrails

Handrails serve two basic functions.   Firstly, they help people to pull on to help them up steps and ramps.   Secondly, they provide protection against possible pathside hazards such as steep drops, or a waters' edge.

For specific details and advice about handrails study *"Informal Countryside Recreation for Disabled People - A practical guide for countryside managers" Countryside Commission*

Steps

Steps are made up of two parts: *goings* or the part of the step that you tread on, and *risers*, the height difference from one step to the next. When constructing steps the following advice is given.

- Steps should be at least 1.2 metres wide.

- Make the flight of uniform going depth and riser height.   The riser height is the most important.

- The going should be not less than 250 mm and the riser not more than 170 mm.

- Irregular or uneven steps should be avoided since these break the rhythm of walking.

- The edges of the steps should be rounded or chamfered to avoid people injuring themselves.

- Edges between each step and between the steps and their surroundings should be of a colour that is easily seen and that contrasts with the rest of the step to assist people with visual impairments.

- Treads must be non-slip, and open steps should be avoided since toes can easily be caught in them.

Ramps

Ramps need to be provided for people in wheelchairs but as an alternative to steps and not as a substitute.   Many ambulant people who have difficulties of balance or use callipers find ramps difficult to use. Recommended ramp gradients are given here.

Length of Ramp	Up to 3m	3.6m	over 6m
Ambulant with a disability	1:9	1:12	1:12
Independent wheelchair user	1:10	1:16	1:20
Wheelchair pushed by companion	1:9	1:12	1:20
Electric Wheelchairs	1:16	1:16	1:20

Advice on surfaces and handrails can be found earlier in this section.

top of slope

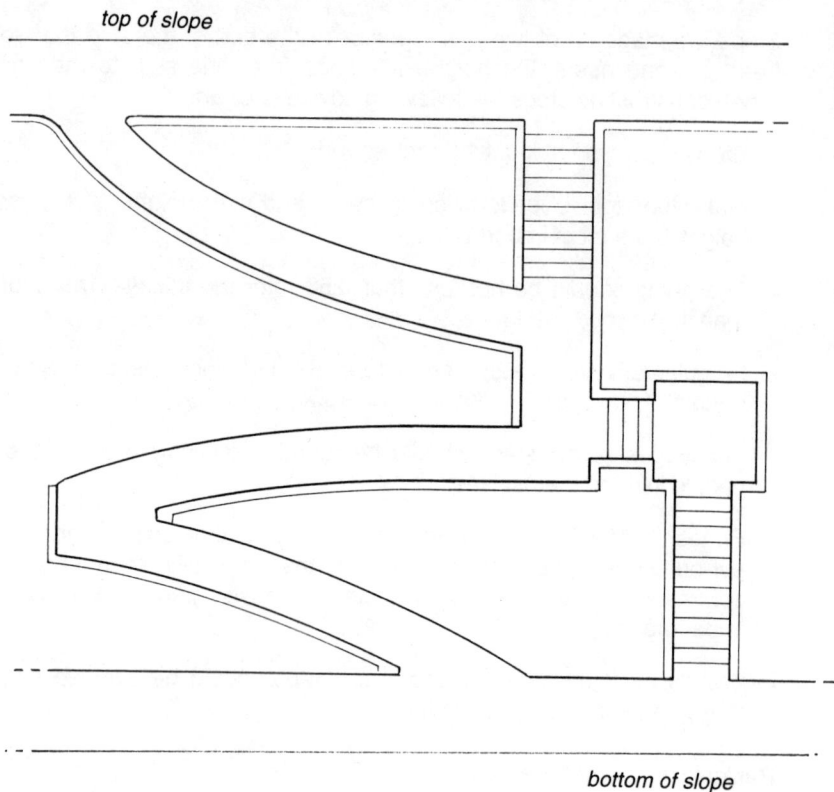

bottom of slope

Fig 19:3 *Steps supplemented by ramps*

Facilities inside buildings

Routes

The rules for ensuring routes are as described earlier for paths. Within the canoeing environment this requires exceptional housekeeping to persuade members not to leave equipment lying around on the floor and to ensure that boats are put away properly and not left overhanging routes.

The rules for steps, ramps and handrails apply equally indoors as well as outdoors. In addition where contrasting colours are used to identify edges on steps the provision of adequate lighting will also be important. Without lighting contrasting colours are of little use.

Where wheelchairs have to be manoeuvred the following diagrams give the appropriate dimensions.

Sounds can give useful clues to directions.   Different floor surfaces can give indications of the whereabouts of a person. and different surfaces on floors walls and ceilings reflect sounds in different ways.   You can also create sounds to aid direction.   I have previously made reference to the Sound Beacon that enables people with a visual impairment to locate direction.   Similar aids can be used around the club such as wind chimes at the door that leads outside.

Remember that many of the features of a building, that most people take for granted, can be a hazard if you have mobility or visual difficulties.

- Fire extinguishers

- Litter bins

- Notice boards that protrude

- Mats or carpets that are not fixed down.

However, there are also hazards that can be created by carelessness.

- Partially open doors or windows

- Canoe bags and paddles

- Trailing leads for electrical apparatus.

Everyone needs to be aware of the need to close doors and if windows have to be left open to ensure that they either open into an area which is not a route, such as over flower beds, or that they are so high that people cannot walk into them.

Where a route comes to a door or a step, or where deviation from the route may lead into hazards such as boat racks, clues can be build into the floor, rubber tiles, wooden blocks, strips of carpet or cork, all provide a different feel.   However, do ensure that such clues are set into the floor sufficiently for them not to be a hazard to other people walking or for people in wheelchairs.

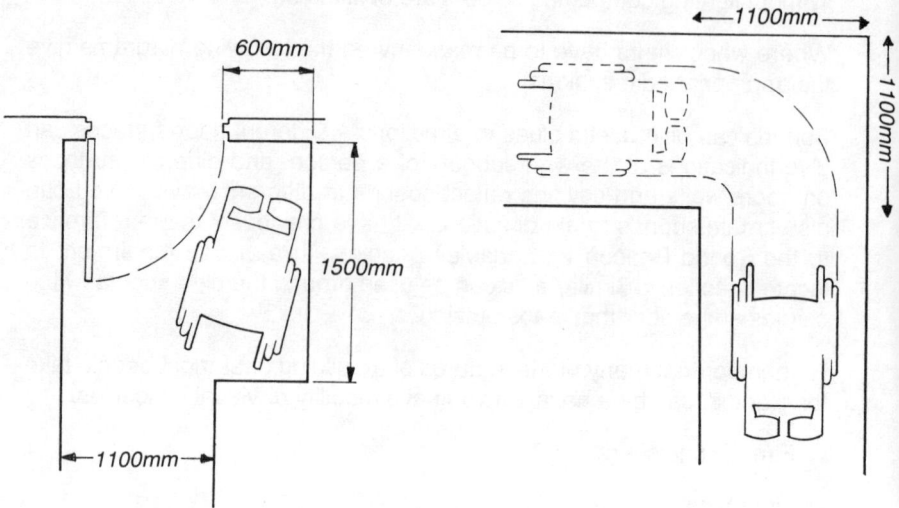

minimum clearance for door opening outwards

minimum space for a 90° turn

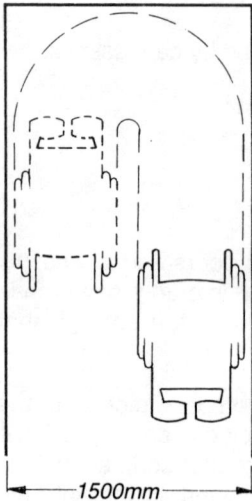

minimum width for door or between obstacles

minimum for a 180° turn

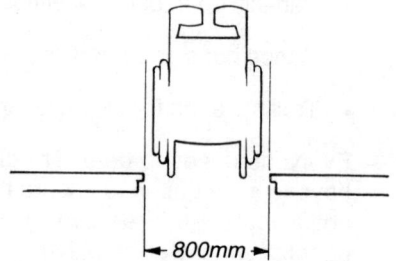

Fig 19:4 *Clearances for wheelchair access*

Canoeing for Disabled People   Geoff Smedley

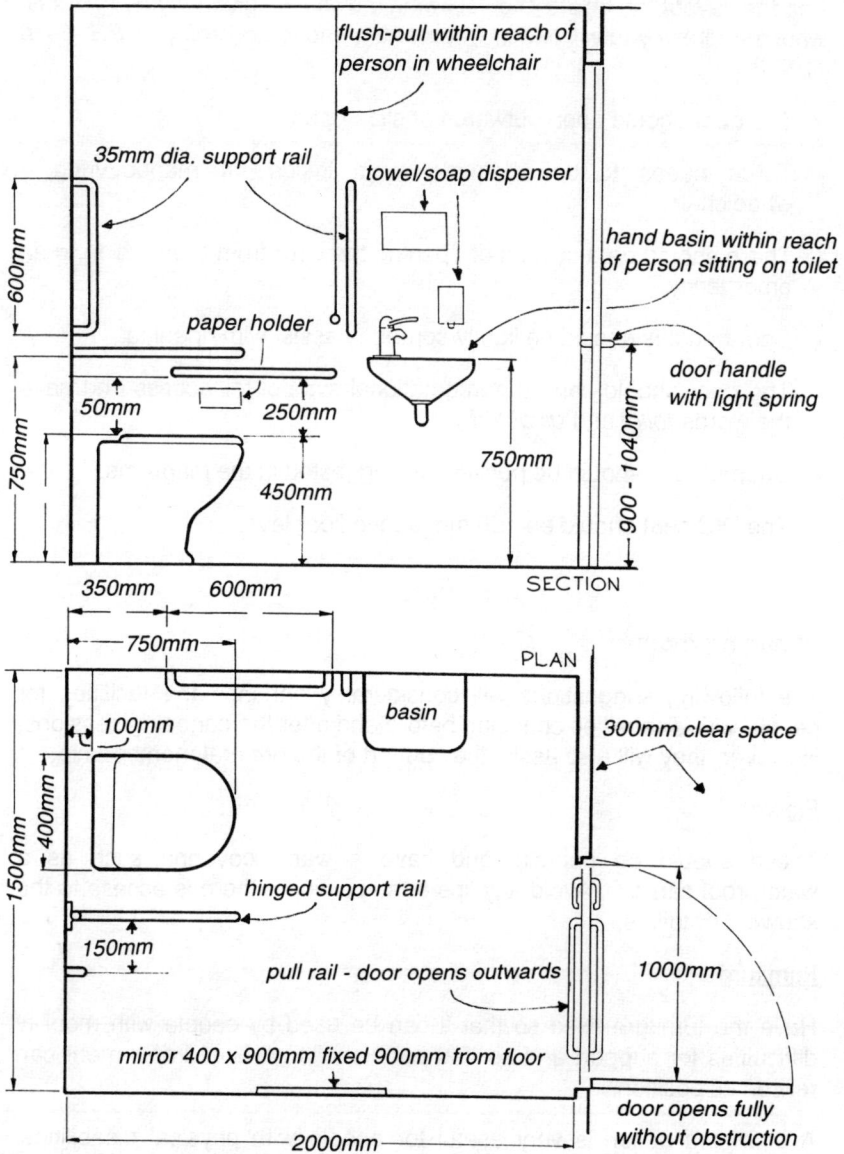

Fig 19:5 *Toilets for people with disabilities.*

Geoff Smedley   Canoeing for Disabled People

Toilets

For the layout of toilets the following advice is given by *R.A.D.A.R.* whose address you will find in Chapter 21, and is according to *BS. 5810 (1979)*.

• The door should open outwards or slide open.

• There needs to be adequate room inside for manoeuvring a wheelchair.

• There should be a system of opening the door from the outside in an emergency.

• Door handles should be lightly sprung to assist with opening.

• The door should carry the international symbol for access and have the words *toilet* and *disabled*

• Support rails should be position as suggested in the diagrams.

• The WC seat should be 450 mm above floor level.

Changing rooms

The following suggestions will considerably enhance the facilities for people with disabilities changing before and after the canoeing sessions. However, they will also assist the comfort of the general membership.

Floors

These should be non-slip and have a warm covering such as a waterproof carpet.   Avoid any lips or steps where there is access to the showers or toilets.

Furniture

Have the furniture fixed so that it can be used by people with mobility difficulties for support and so that people with a visual impairment can rely on its position.

A *changing bench* is very useful for people with physical disabilities. This should be of a height where easy transfer from a wheelchair is possible. It should have a padded surface and be long enough for a person to lie on it, a minimum of 2 metres long and 1 metre wide is recommended.

Always put coat hooks above fittings such as benches to reduce the possibility of someone walking into them.

If you have showers you should also have a *shower chair*. This is a plastic chair on wheels that enables someone with a physical disability to be seated in the shower.

A *lifting handle*, suspended from the ceiling or from a free standing frame, can help people to transfer independently from a wheelchair to a changing bench or shower chair and vice-versa. A transfer board can also be useful again in this situation.

Showers

The shower area should have easy access for the shower chair and be wide enough for its turning. The shower controls must be at a level that can be reached from the chair. The shower hose and head should have a fitting at about 1.5 metres to allow a person in a chair easy access. The shower head and hose should be detachable to allow it to be used by a person in a shower chair.

For people who wish to stand there should be handrails on all sides. See Fig 19:5 for details of these.

You should always have a non-slip mat in the shower area.

Building Features

Doors

All doors should be wide enough to take a wheelchair but you should also take care that the handles are of an appropriate height to be reached from a wheelchair. Try to avoid doors that have large glass panels, someone with a visual impairment may not realise that it is a glass panel and walk into it. Have glass panels in the top part of the door so that people can see if some one is on the other side. This is especially important for people who may not be able to open the door as quickly as others.

If doors lead to areas that have a specific purpose such as toilets or changing rooms. Make sure that the signs can be easily read and incorporate a tactile clue with either raised letters or a raised graphic.

Geoff Smedley   Canoeing for Disabled People

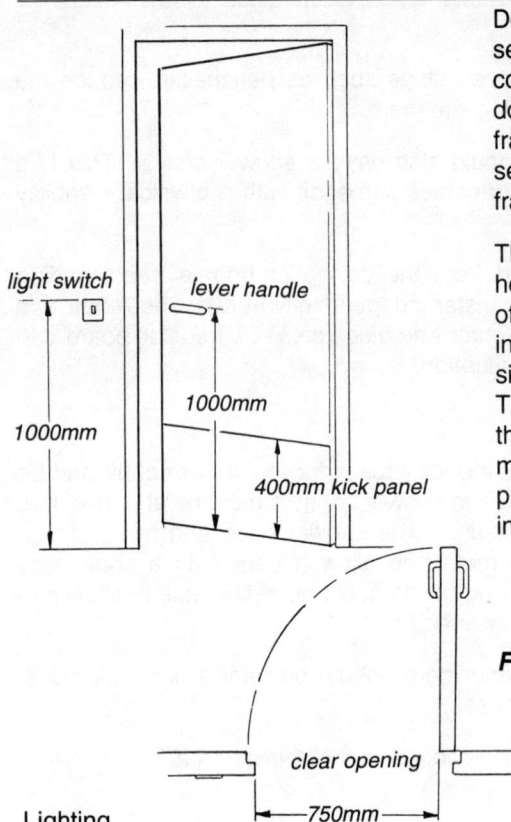

Doors can be more easily seen if the door frame is of a contrasting colour to the door. White doors in white frames are more difficult to see than white doors in red frames.

The diagram shows the heights for handle, the width of door necessary for people in wheelchairs and also the size of the "kick plates". These are important since the wheelchair's footplates may hit the door in the process of the person open in the door.

light switch

lever handle

1000mm

1000mm

400mm kick panel

Fig 19:6 *Door dimensions*

clear opening

750mm

Lighting

Try to ensure that lights cover the whole area in use. Sometimes the centrally placed light leaves dark corners. If there are specific areas that can be hazardous, such as stairs, or there are areas you wish to draw attention to, such as notices, look for ways of having direct lighting for them.

Glare can be a problem for people with visual impairments. Glare can come from glass panels in doors or above doors, polished or white surfaces on furniture can cause dazzle if there is a strong light on them. Matt surfaces can be kept just as clean and do not create glare.

Signs

It is quite usual to find a great deal of club information to be given in the form of notices. Apart from giving out general information, some notices are there for safety reasons. All notices should be readable by people with disabilities and this means giving consideration to their siting.   You should consider the following.

- Are notices lit adequately to allow easy reading?   Having large text also helps.

- Are they printed in colours that are easy to distinguish the print? Black on white, or yellow on dark blue or dark green works well.

- Have you considered using simple graphics or drawings to support the text.   This is especially important for notices that refer to safety when they may need to be read by people with learning difficulty? There are standard graphics for toilets.

- Are notices kept in good order and redundant notices removed to avoid confusion?

- Are they at the right height to be read by people in wheelchairs?

- If you have blind members, have you brought their attention to the notices and told them what they say, and provided a Braille copy?   If noties are very long, such as newsletters, it may be valuable to have them transferred to audio tape.   This system will also be of benefit to people who cannot read well.

- It is a good idea to position notices so that all the light, natural or artificial falls upon them.   Notices on windows are difficult to read. Notices are also best on non-reflective surfaces.

- To supplement notices and to ensure that everyone gets the message, consider repeating important messages in your newsletter and having a taped copy of this for your blind members.

- Provide alternative ways of indicating door bells, telephone or fire alarm audio warnings, with flashing lights or similar.   Similarly, if the warning is a visual one you should also have an audible warning.

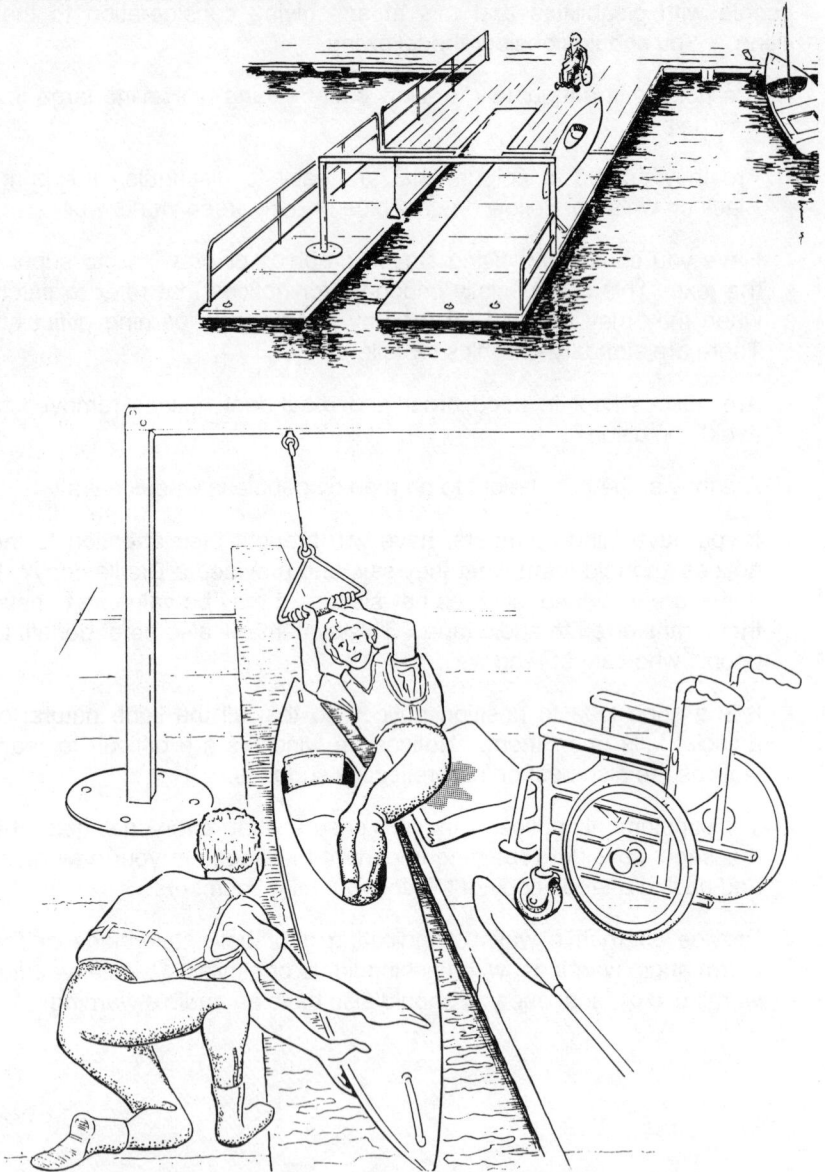

Fig 19:7 a & b A docking bay with frame to support the paddler's independent entry and exit.

Landing stages and jetties.

a

b

All of the previous sections need to be considered to give access to your landing stage. Also consider the following.

Since the provision of a handrail or raised edge is inappropriate for the launching and entry to boats special care needs to be given to the safety of disabled people whilst on the landing stage.

The edge should be clearly identified with a contrasting colour.

If the landing stage is made of wood:

- There should be gaps between the planks to give extra grip when wet

- Gaps should be not less than 6 mm to avoid them clogging with mud.

- Gaps should also be no greater than 10 mm to avoid wheels slipping between the boards.

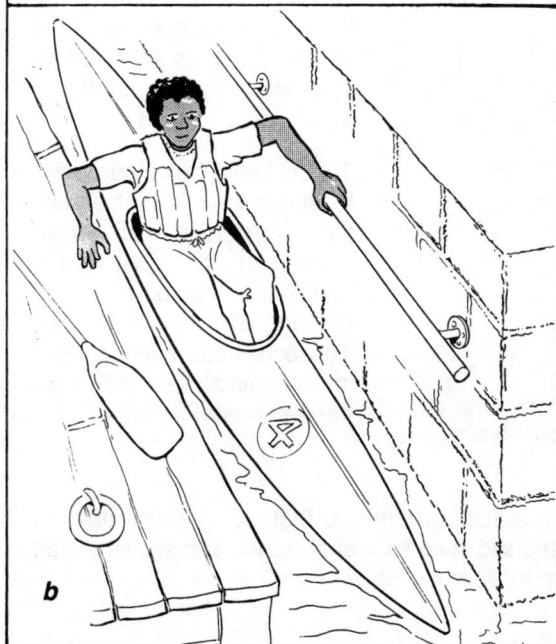

Fig 19:8 a & b
Docking bay and rail

- Algae growth can make surfaces slippery.   Therefore an algae inhibiting preservative should be used.   Surface can also be sprayed with a special tar coating.   However, take care that those that contain a grit do not make the surface to abrasive for people who may need to sit down for entry.

- Sometimes a plastic mesh can be fixed to give grip,   Again this should not be abrasive and needs regular maintenance to avoid it becoming loose and tripping people up.

If the landing stage is concrete it is a good idea to have a "friendly" surface such as rubber mats or even old towels handy to pad the surface and avoid injury from the rough surface.   Make sure such aids are picked up after use and do not become a hazard to other users.

If the design of the jetty or landing stage is right then many people can get into and out of their craft independently.   The main ways in which this can be facilitated is by the following provisions.

Fig 19:9 *Extended transfer board*

Docking Bays

As can be seen from the diagrams these can be constructed as a part of the landing stage to enable craft to be accesses from either side, either by the paddler or by any support craft.

These bays can incorporate hoists or frames that enable the   person   to   have something   to   give   them additional   support   when entering or exiting their craft These devices can be used in   conjunction   with   the transfer board.

The bay itself could have a sloping ramp so that craft can be entered when clear of the water and slid in as for a seal launch and similarly craft can be pulled up the ramp for safe exiting.

An Access Check List

Based on one devised by the Disabled Living Foundation.

General

- Is there wheelchair access?
- Are all routes safe?
- Are they clearly identified?
- Are routes clear of clutter?

Car Parking

- Are there some reserved spaces appropriate for disabled drivers?

Footpaths

- Are there paths without steps?
- Are paths wide enough?
- Are there ramps and handrails where necessary?
- Are surfaces smooth and level?
- Are the edges clearly defined by surface changes or colours?

Steps
- Are they of the appropriate dimensions?

Ramps

- Is the gradient appropriate?

Toilets

- Is there an accessible toilet?
- Is it clearly identified?

Signs

- Are signs clear and easy to read by people with visual impairments?
- Are they low enough to be read by people in wheelchairs?
- Are there visual warnings devices and audio warnings devices.
- Can blind people access information?

Landing stages

- Are the surfaces safe and not slippery?
- Are they abrasive, or is there appropriate padding?

Plate 19:a   *With the right access many people can achieve independence*

Canoeing for Disabled People   Geoff Smedley

CHAPTER TWENTY

THE INFORMATION ENQUIRY FORM

Acknowledgement

> *I am indebted to Clive Gritton for his advice and support in the preparation of this chapter.*

Introduction

I have stated previously that I believe we should focus on the abilities of people, not their disabilities. However, in supporting this view there is also a need to know about factors which may affect any individual's full access and enjoyment of a programme. The information that you may seek of participants to your programme should not be directed solely at people with disabilities. This makes the assumption that you know who has a disability, but more seriously unnecessary singles them out.

When asking for this information, it is important to reassure all the people you are asking that your enquiries are for positive reasons and that you are seeking to ensure that they have a successful experience and that, whatever they tell you, it will not prevent them from taking part.

Incoming information

With this previous declaration in mind, and to maximise opportunities and minimise risk, it is advisable for every programme leader and instructor to be aware of the special needs of all those people participating in their activity.   In most cases it may be left to the responsibility of the individual participant to organise what special care they require, when it is appropriate and by what means it is to be administered, be it medication or other special need.

However, when there are certain regular needs for which special care or medication is crucial to the individual's well being, it is advisable for the programme leader to be aware of these. There are also situations when special care will be needed to meet a crisis situation and the individual may be incapacitated and unable to administer that care themselves. In these circumstances it is essential that the group leader is aware of both the need and its treatment.

Readers should study Chapters 11 and 12 and especially those observations regarding medical conditions, and where special care is needed for people with impairments.

Sometimes it is the condition or impairment itself that the leader needs to be aware of since it may have a bearing on the duration or intensity of the activity.   Congenital Heart Disease, Diabetes and Asthma are examples.   Consideration may also have to be given to the equipment needed, such as the Co^2 buoyancy aid advised for people with epilepsy.

Other information may give the leader advance knowledge that will affect the programme structure.   An indication of the degree to which a participant may be ambulant, wear an appliance or be in a wheelchair, will have consequences with regard to the environmental conditions of the proposed programme.

Information should always be sought from the person first. Only if that person cannot explain to the leader the nature and implications of their impairment should the information be requested of a parent or carer. This latter approach should always be addressed sensitively and with consideration to the dignity of the person about whom the information is sought.

Disclosures

I have included a special section on disclosure, or the sharing of information, since it raises very important issues of confidentiality. This subject has two implications.

Firstly, the need for people to disclose to you that they have an impairment which may disable them when canoeing or kayaking. Secondly, whether information about participant's impairments should be disclosed to the rest of the group.

Disclosures to the leader.

The implications when information is not given about impairments can be potentially dangerous.   However, I believe that you should precede any request for the disclosure of information about impairment with the statement, *"It does not matter what you tell me, it will not stop you from participating"*.   Depending upon the response a suitable programme is always possible.

Disclosures to the group.

Of course any disclosures to you as the leader, must be treated as confidential. Nevertheless, it may be advisable to either ask the person if you can tell the rest of the group, or ask the person if they wish to tell the group personally, about their impairment and its implications. The reasons for this are to enable the group to understand when the person does not appear to respond as they expect.

Some examples of impairments that provoke this reasoning would be severe hearing or visual impairments, or conditions that prevent the individual from lifting or carrying anything heavy.

Non disclosure of these examples could lead the rest of the group wondering why individuals do not respond when spoken to, or appear to tread on anything left on the bankside, or do not appear to be taking a fair share of the loading and unloading of boats and equipment. Such impressions of individuals, without the knowledge that explains why they appear to behave in specific ways, can lead to dissent and frustration for the rest of the group and the possible alienation of the individual concerned.

Outgoing information

In addition to the information sought by the programme leader is the information required by the participant. There is a responsibility to inform participants about:-

- the nature of the activity,

- its duration,

- the venue and access conditions,

- changing and toilet facilities (or absence of),

- what you will provide,

- what they will need to provide,

- staffing available.

Individuals can then make informed decisions regarding appropriate actions they might take. E.g.:-

• To choose between using a wheelchair or crutches,

• Deciding what clothes to wear, considering such factors as warmth or ease of removal for changing,

• Whether or not to bring their medication or other medical aids.

The duration or physical demands of the programme will be determined by the level to which people may be able to participate. It is sometimes the case that some people with disabilities do not get the opportunity to exercise as frequently as they would like.   This has the result that coaching programmes will have to start with the intention of giving a basic level of fitness and only move to the more exacting exercises when this has been achieved.

It is not generally considered necessary for participants to consult their doctors before taking part in a canoeing programme. However, it may be advisable if the programme is to be significantly more strenuous that the person's usual lifestyle, or there is a higher level of risk involved than usually experienced by the individual.   If the doctor consulted is to understand the implications of the programme for her patient, then the information given by the programme leader is crucial to understanding and approval of participation in the intended programme.

In a similar way, some participants may wish to consult their physiotherapist or occupational therapist. Whilst physical activity is beneficial to most people, for some people there are implications regarding posture and the vulnerability to tissue damage or muscular injury.   If this is a problem, it is worthwhile discussing this with the participant and their therapist, since the problem can be minimised with the use of such support as aids or padding. Similarly, the style of craft or the choice of equipment may be determined by the special needs of the participant.

Where programme leaders and instructors are employed professionally their employers may have a form that they require and are almost certain to include a disclaimer section. This should not prevent the leaders having a supplementary form to request and give information.

The Enquiry Form Tool Box

What follows in the rest of this chapter should be considered as a suggestion tool box. Suitably modified these questions can be used to construct an enquiry form appropriate to your programme. _It is highly unlikely that you will need all of the questions suggested_, these have been selected from forms used by a number of people in a number of situations and are recommended for use with all participants, disabled or non disabled.

You should also be aware that all information can change. Therefore, when using information ensure it is current and still valid.

Information to be completed by the Participant

Personal
Name	Address
Age (date of birth)	Telephone number

Contacts
Next of Kin (Spouse, partner etc.)
_or_ Parent/Guardian	Address
Emergency contact	Address
Relationship	Telephone number

Medical
Blood group	N.H.S. number
G.P.s name	Address/telephone
Specialist doctor	Hospital & patient number

Special needs
Description of impairments	Primary
	Secondary

Mobility	Arms
	Legs
	Spine etc.

Speech	Clarity
	Sign languages

Hearing	Level
	Hearing aids

Vision	Range

Glasses

Appliances
Appliances   Type
Care (i.e. waterproof?)   Spare
Wheelchair - type

Medication

Type
Dose
Frequency
Emergency
Implications (Side Effects)

Special considerations
Epilepsy   Type
Frequency
Treatment

Asthma   Allergies
Medication

Diabetes   Medication
Diet

Dietary Needs
Coeliac   (Flour)
Diabetes   (Sugar)
Other   (i.e. Salt)
Vegetarian
Likes / Dislikes

Domestic needs
Assistance for   Eating
(Give specific details, i.e.   Dressing
tying shoelaces, etc.)   Toileting
Stomas

Night-time considerations   Continence
Medication

Appropriate skills

Canoeing	Level
	Craft used
	Special aids

Swimming   Level
                 Support
                 Confidence

Information to be completed by the Programme Leader

Activity   Description
                            Venue
                            Dates
                            Duration

Resources   Craft
                            Equipment

Staff   On water
                            Off water

Environmental   Access
                            Changing
                            Toilets

Recording Information

Forms can have sections that have conditional completion

- Complete this section if you are camping with us..
- If you have a wheelchair please complete the following..

Information can be given on a scale

Please circle which of these that applies;

good	poor	nil
strong	average	weak
high	moderate	low

Please score on a scale of 5(good) to 1(poor)

Levels can be charted

Mark at the appropriate point

MOBILITY

Good(100%)...(0%)Poor

FIELD OF VISION

*
*   *
*   *
*   *
*   *
*   *
*   *
*   *

Other information can be gathered by offering choices

yes/no
right/left
manual/electric

Or by ticking the boxes i.e.

Which limbs are affected?

	right	*left*
hand	[ ]	[ ]
foot	[ ]	[ ]

	upper	*lower*	*upper*	*lower*
leg	[ ]	[ ]	[ ]	[ ]
arm	[ ]	[ ]	[ ]	[ ]

To this system can be added a degree of response.
(Instead of a tick) put in a number i.e.

1 = v. weak   **2** = weak   **3** = average   **4** = strong   **5** = v. strong

Examples of information Enquiry Forms

The degree of complexity and the amount of information required will be determined by the activity and it's duration.

- A sampling activity may only require information supplied in Form 1.

- A continuous programme may require Form 2 and certainly should include the information to be given by the course organiser.

Of course, these forms are examples. It is possible to modify or extend these forms according to need. The implications of transport, providing meals, overnight accommodation and expeditions, especially abroad, will all add to the need for useful and appropriate information.

FORM 1

Name   Special Needs   Medication

Swimming Ability   Canoeing Ability

Other Notes

Alternative presentations

Forms can be Brailled, put onto audio tape or reprinted with a large script for people with a visual impairment. They can also be prepared with pictorial representation for people who have difficulties reading.

Give thought to who the form is for and then consider whether the individual can interpret and respond to the questions. If necessary adapt your form accordingly.

FORM 2

Information to be completed by the participant

Name	Age
Address	Tel
School	Tel

Special Needs   Medication
                     Diet

Mobility	Vision	Hearing

Water Confidence   Able to float   minutes

Able to Swim   yards

Contact Name   Tel   Address

Emergency Name   Tel   Address

Information completed by the activity organiser

Description of activity   Date   Time

Access Conditions

Site Conditions

Support Available (State Qualifications)

Instruction (State Qualifications)

Organiser's Name   **Tel.**

Signed Organiser   **Date**

Signed Participant   **Date**

CHAPTER TWENTY ONE

USEFUL INFORMATION

This chapter contains some information which might be useful to you as you progress through your coaching programmes people with disabilities. You will find information on:-

- **The BCU Standing Advisory Panel for Disability**

- **Addresses for;**

  - **National Sporting Organisations**

  - **National Disability Sports Associations Disability Specific Groups**

  - **Disability Sports Groups**

  - **Canoeing Equipment**

  - **Support Equipment**

  - **Adventure Centres with Facilities for Disabled People**

- **Useful Books**

- **Fund-raising Advice**

- **Fund Giving Contacts**

The BCU Standing Advisory Panel for Disability

The Standing Advisory Panel for Disability reports to the Access, Coaching, and Recreation Management Committee (A.C.R.M.C.). This Committee has representatives from the Coaching Committee, which has responsibility for the Training and Assessment of all members involved with teaching or leading, and other Technical committees concerned with Touring, Lifeguards and Access. The Disability panel is one of three panels that report to A.C.R.M.C., the others being for Women in Canoeing and Youth Canoeing.

Since A.C.R.M.C. reports to the BCU Executive, the Standing Advisory Panel influences policy and decision making throughout the Union, and significantly the BCU Development Plan.

The Panel is composed of a chairperson and twelve members (currently 1/3 are disabled) who are elected or co-opted annually during the A.G.M. held at the International Canoe Exhibition each February.

The role of the panel.

The panel is responsible for the management of the syllabus, approval of examiners, development and monitoring of the Disability Awareness Training Courses

It advises with regard to:-

• Specific advice for individuals with a disability

• Personal Tests and Awards.

• Appropriate entry to the Coaching Scheme for people with disabilities where their disability has implications for the fulfilment of their responsibilities.

• Re-entry to the Coaching Scheme after becoming disabled.

• Medical conditions and physical impairments where they have a bearing upon the entry of the individual to the Coaching Scheme.

• It also advises on matters of equal rights and opportunities by giving proactive encouragement to Technical Committees and reactive observations and advice to projects within the BCU, either regionally or nationally.

• The panel also manages the *Paddle-ability project*.

The aim of the project is:-

To facilitate further participation in canoe sport by all people regardless of ability.

It has implemented this by organising a conference for representatives of each Region to raise levels of awareness, assist in establishing Regional Development Plans, and plan for Regional activity and projects.

Outcomes of the project have been to support:-

- Regional try-it and sampler sessions.
- Regional Competitions for people with disabilities.
- National Competitions for:
  - People with learning disability.
  - People with physical disability.
- International Events for people with physical disability.
- World-wide expeditions.
- Regional Disability Awareness Training Courses
- Information about the opportunities for disabled people in canoeing.

Other aspects of the role of the panel have been the establishment of policies concerning:-

- Giving equal access by avoiding having any special awards or qualifications for people with disabilities.

- Indicating in the list of canoe clubs in the BCU Yearbook, which clubs welcome people with disabilities.

- Addressing the special access needs of people attending the International Canoe Exhibition.

- Administering grants made available from internal and external sources for equipment, programmes, activities.

The panel also gives support and advice on request to:-

- Manufacturers regarding the design of canoes and equipment.

- University and college projects to support imaginative projects for developing aids. backrests, stability enhancement etc.

Finally

It is of paramount importance that events for paddlers with disabilities are managed by the appropriate technical committee. However, within the structure of these committees it is hoped that the coaches concerned will attend Disability Awareness Training Courses. All new ideas tend to be disseminated via reports and reviews in "Canoe Focus", books such as this one and Disability Awareness Training Courses.

Geoff Smedley   Canoeing for Disabled People

Addresses

Note that whilst efforts were made to ensure that these addresses were correct at the time of going to press they cannot be guaranteed.

British Canoe Union
Adbolton Lane
West Bridgford
NOTTINGHAM   Tel: 0115 982 1100
NG2 5AS   Fax: 0115 982 1797

National Sporting Organisations

Central Council of Physical Recreation (C.C.P.R.)
Francis House
Francis Street
LONDON
WC1H 0QP

National Coaching Foundation (N.C.F.)
114 Cardigan Road
Headingley
LEEDS   Tel: 0113 274 4802
LS6 3BJ   Fax: 0113 275 5019

The Sports Council
Information Centre
16 Upper Woburn Place
LONDON   Tel: 0171 388 1277
WC1H 0QP   Fax: 0171 383 5740

Scottish Sports Council
Caledonia House
South Gyle
EDINBURGH
EH12 9DQ   Tel: 0131 317 7200

Sports Council for Wales
National Sports Centre for Wales
Sophia Gardens
CARDIFF
CF1 9SW   Tel: 0122 239 7571

Sports Council for Northern Ireland
House of Sport
Upper Malone Road
BELFAST
BT9 5LA   Tel: 0123 238 1222

National Disability Sports Associations

British Sports Association For The Disabled (B.S.A.D.)
Solecast House
13-27 Brunswick Place
LONDON   Tel: 0171 490 4919
N1 6DX   Fax: 0171 490 4914

FSAD (Wales)
c/o Deeside Leisure Centre
Chester Road West
Queensferry
Deeside   Tel: 01244 822600

Scottish Sports Association for People with a Disability
Fife Sports Institute
Viewfield Road
Glenrothes
Fife
KY6 2RA   Tel: 01592 771700

Northern Ireland Committee on Sport for People with Disabilities
Sports Council for Northern Ireland
House of Sport
Upper Malone Road
BELFAST
BT9 5LA   Tel: 0123 238 1222

United Kingdom Sports Association For People With Learning Disability (U.K.S.A.P.L.D.)
Solecast House
13-27 Brunswick Place
LONDON   Tel: 0171 250 1100
N1 6DX   Fax: 0171 250 0110

Scottish Sports Association for People with a Disability
MH Division
Outdoor Resource Centre
3 Martha Street
Glasgow   Tel: 0141 553 1225
G1 1JN   Fax: 0141 552 5440

Northern Ireland Sports Association for People with Learning Disability
1 Clare Hill Road
Moira
Northern Ireland
BT67 0PB   Tel: 01846 674110

Welsh Sports Association for People with Learning Disability
3 Heol Mair
Lichard Higher
Bridgend, Wales
CF31 1YE   Tel: 01656 660675

Disability Specific Groups

Arthritis
    Arthritis Care
    5 Grosvenor Crescent
    London SW1X 7ER
    Tel: 0171 235 0902

Asthma
    National Asthma Campaign
    Providence House
    Providence Place
    LONDON
    N1 ONT   Tel: 0171 226 2260

Asthma Help line   (staffed by fully trained asthma nurses)
Tel: 01345 010203   (open 9 am - 9 pm, calls charged at local rate)

Cerebral Palsy
Scope
12 Park Crescent
London
W1N 4EQ   Tel: 0171 636 5020

Diabetes
The British Diabetic Association
10 Queen Anne Street
London W1M 0BD   Tel: 0171 323 1531

Epilepsy
British Epilepsy Association
Anstey House
40 Hanover Square
LEEDS   Tel: 0113 243 393
LS3 1BE   Fax: 0113 242 8804

Haemophilia
The Haemophilia Society
123 Westminster Bridge Road
London SE1 7HR   Tel: 0171 926 2020

Hearing Impairment
Royal National Institute for the Deaf (RNID)
105 Gower Street   Tel: 0171 387 8033 (Voice)
London WC1E 6AH   Tel: 0171 387 3154 (Minicom)
                   Fax: 0171 388 6038

If you want to learn sign language write to;
Into-Sign
British Deaf Association
38 Victoria Place
CARLISLE CA1 1HU

Multiple Sclerosis
The Multiple Sclerosis Society
22 Effie Road
Fulham
London SW6 1EE   Tel: 0171 736 6267

Muscular Dystrophy
The Muscular Dystrophy Group
7-11 Prescot Place   Tel: 0171 720 8055
London SW4 6BS   Fax: 0171 498 0670

Spina Bifida
The Association for Spina Bifida & Hydrocephalus
42 Park Road
Peterborough PE1 BUG   Tel: 0173 355 5988

Spinal Injuries
The Spinal Injuries Association
Newpoint House
76 St James Lane
London LN10 3DF   Tel: 0181 444 2121

Visual Impairment
Royal National Institute for the Blind
224 Great Portland Street   Tel: 0171 388 1266
London W1N 6AA   Fax: 0171 388 8316

General

Centre for Accessible Environments
35 Great Smith Road
LONDON SW1P 3BJ   Tel: 0171 222 7980

Countryside Commission
John Dower House
Crescent Place
Cheltenham GL50 3RA   Tel: 01242 521381

Disabled Living Foundation (D.L.F.)
380/384 Harrow Road   Tel: 0171 289 6111
LONDON W9 2HU   Fax: 0171 266 2922

Fieldfare Trust
67a The Wicker
Sheffield S3 8HT   Tel: 0114 270 1668

National Federation of Gateway Clubs
117 Golden Lane
London EC1Y 0RT   Tel: 0171 454 0454

Physically Handicapped and Able Bodied (PHAB)
12 - 14 London Road
Croyden
Surrey   Tel: 0181 667 9443

REMAP UK
Hazledene
Ightham   Tel: 0173 288 3818
Sevenoaks TN15 9AD Fax: 0173 288 6238

Royal Association for Disability and Rehabilitation (RADAR)
25 Mortimer Street
LONDON W1N 8AB   Tel: 0171 637 5400

Disability Sports Groups

British Amputee and Les Autres Sports Association
30 Greaves Close
Arnold
NOTTINGHAM NG5 6RS

British Blind Sports
67 Albert Street
Rugby CV21 2SN   Tel: 0178 853 6142

British Association of Sporting and Recreational Activities for the Blind
156 Belle Lane
Byfield
Daventry WN11 6US   Tel: 0132 762 214

British Wheelchair Sports Federation
and British Paraplegic Sports
Ludwig Guttman Sports Centre
Harvey Road
Aylesbury HP21 8PP   Tel: 0129 684 848

Cerebral Palsy Sport
11 Churchill Park
Colwick
NOTTINGHAM
NG4 2HF   Tel: 0115 940 1202

British Deaf Sports Council
7a Bridge Street   Tel: 01943 850214 (voice)
Otley LS21 1BQ   Tel: 0194 385 0081 (DCT)

For canoeing specific enquiries regarding hearing impaired people
Simon Scandrett can be contacted at the:-
Centre for the Deaf,   Tel: 0117 924 9868
16-18 Kings Square,   Fax: 0117 922 44884
BRISTOL BS2 8JL.   Minicom: 0117 944 1344

International Diabetic Athletic Association
24 Eden Drive
Sedgefield
Cleveland TS21 3DX   Tel: 0174 062 1252

Canoeing Equipment

AC Canoe Products Ltd
PO Box 62
Chester
Cheshire CH1 3JX

Andrew Ainsworth Designs
76 The Green
Twickenham
TW2 5AG

Avoncraft
Burrowfield Industrial Estate
Welyn Garden City
Hertfordshire AL7 4SR

Buffalo Clothing
The Old Diary
Broadfield Road
Sheffield S8 0XQ

Capel Canoes Ltd
Badsell Road,
Five Oak Green
Near Tonbridge,
Kent TN12 6RN

Chang
Unit 1, Loxdale Ind Estate
Northcott Road,
Bilston,
West Mids WV14 0TP

Coleman UK
Parish Wharf Estate
Harbour Road
Portishead, Bristol BS20 9DA

Crewsaver
Crewsaver House
Mumby Road
Gosport
Hampshire PO12 1AQ

Chris Hare Marine
Unit 3A Ullswater Road
Longhill Industrial Estate
Hartlepool TS25 1UE

Desperate Measures
39-41 Trent Boulevard
West Bridgford
Nottingham NG2 5BB

Eurocraft Ltd
112 Clydesdale Place
Moss Side
Leyland PR5 3QS

Fladbury Canoeing Ltd
Craycombe Farm
Fladbury
Worcs

Gaybo
Bellbrook Business Park
Uckfield
East Sussex TN22 1QU

Granta
29 Great Whyte
Ramsey, Huntingdon
PE17 1EZ

Lendal
30 Hunter Street
Prestwick
KA9 1LG

Marsport Ltd
215 London Road
Reading
RG1 3NY

Mobile Adventure Ltd
Bridge Works
Knighton Fields Road West
Leicester LE2 6LG

Paddle Sport
Park Farm Estate
Compton Verney
Nr. Stratford Upon Avon
Warwickshire CV35 9HJ

Palm Canoe Products Ltd
Harbour Road
Portishead
Bristol BS20 9BL

The P & H Company
Station Road
West Hallam
Derbyshire DE7 6HB

Plastimo
Chandlers Ford Ind Est
Eastleigh
SO5 3DG

Pyranha
Marina Village
Preston Brook
Runcorn WA7 3DW

SDS Watersports Ltd
66-70 Station Road
Halfway,
Sheffield S19 5GW

Strand/Scott Bader
Wollaston
Wellingborough
NN8 7RJ

Suzy's
2 Victoria Close
East Molesley
KT8 1SQ

Twickenham Canoe Centre
Shepperton Marina
Felix Lane
Shepperton TW17 8NJ

Valley Canoe
Private Road No 4
Colwick Estate
Nottingham NG4 2JT

Wild Water
Glasshouses Mill
Pateley Bridge
Harrogate
HG3 5QH

West Midlands Canoe Centre
112 New Hall Street
Willenhall
West Midlands WV13 1LQ

Whitewater
Shepperton Marine
Felix Lane
Shepperton
Middlesex TW17 8NJ

Support Equipment Suppliers

CO_2 Buoyancy Aids
see Crewsaver

Commlink   (Communication aid)
Delph Tool Company Ltd
Slackcote Lane
Delph
Oldham OL3 5TW

Custom   Design   Buoyancy Aids
Canyon Leisure Gear
7 David Road
Bilton
Rugby CV22 7PX

Hoists
Consult "Hoists and Lifts"
Equipment for Disabled People
Mary Marlborough Lodge
Nuffield Orthopaedic Centre
Headington
Oxon OX3 7LD

MEDesign   Patient   Handling Sling
MEDesign Ltd
Clock Tower Works
Railway Street
Southport PR8 5BB

Adjustable Paddle Joint
see Andrew Ainsworth Designs

Shower Chair Arjo Mecanaids Ltd St Catherine Street Gloucester GL1 2SL	**Trans-sit Seat** Ellis Son & Paramore Spring Street Works Sheffield S3 8PB
Transfer Board Homecraft Supplies Ltd Low Moor Estate Kirkby-in-Ashfield Notts NG17 7JZ	**Waterproof Hearing Aid** **(Lotos)** Sietech Hearing Ltd Langley House Stanneylands Road Wilmslow Cheshire SK9 4HH
	Waterproof Clothing see Chang

Adventure Centres with Facilities for Disabled People

Badaguish (Speyside Handicapped Holiday Trust)
Badaguish Centre
Aviemore
Inverness-shire PH22 1QU   Tel: 01479 861285

Bendrigg Lodge
Old Hutton
Kendal
Cumbria LA8 0NR   Tel: 0153 972 3766

Calvert Trust, Keswick
Little Crosswaite
Keswick
Cumbria CA12 4QD   Tel: 0176 877 2254

Calvert Trust, Kielder
Kielder Water
Hexham
Northumberland NE48 1BS Tel: 01434 250232

Churchtown Farm
Lanlivery
Bodmin
Cornwall PL30 5BT   Tel: 01208 872148

Low Mill
Askrigg
Leyburn
North Yorkshire DL8 3HZ   Tel: 01969 650432

Millfield Activity Centre
Geldeston Road
Ellingham, Bungay
Norfolk NR35 2ER   Tel: 01508 518402

The Nancy Oldfield Trust
Irstead Road
Neatishead
Norfolk NR12 8BJ   Tel: 01692 630572

Queen Elizabeth II (Silver Jubilee Activities Centre)
Manor Farm Country Park
Pylands Lane
Burlesdon
Hampshire SO3 8BH   Tel: 01703 404844

Ranch Adventure Centre
Llanbedr
Gwynedd
North Wales LL45 2HS   Tel: 0134 123 358

The Red Ridge Centre
Cefn Coch
Welshpool
Powys SY21 0AZ   Tel: 01938 810821

The Stackpole Centre
Stackpole
Nr Pembroke
Pembrokeshire SA71 5DQ   Tel: 01646 661425

The Northern Ireland Mountain Centre
Tollymore
Bryansford
County Down   Tel: 0139 672 2158

Plas Menai National Watersports Centre
Llanfairisgaer
Caernarfon
Gwynedd LL55 1UE   Tel: 0124 867 0964

Sports Council National Centre
Plas y Brenin
Capel Curig
North Wales   Tel: 0169 04214

Useful Books

"A Challenge to the Individual"   1988
Duke of Edinburgh's Award Scheme

"A Resource Manual in Canoeing for Disabled People"
Arthur & Ackroyd-Stolarz   Canadian Recreation Canoeing Assoc.

"Advisory Panel on Water Sports for Disabled People, water recreation areas; "access for disabled people"   1975
Sports Council

"Aids for Handicapped Persons"   701/7/86
V.A.T. Office

Asthma   "Exercise and Asthma"
"Take Control of Asthma" "Secondary School Pack"
All from the National Asthma Campaign

"Atlanto-Axial Instability among People with Down's Syndrome"
Down's Syndrome Association, 155 Mitcham Road, London SW19 9PG

"Activities for People with a Multiple Disability"   1993
Ed. Mark Leach for Pro-Motion   Scope (Spastics Society)

"The Benefits of Exercise"   1990
Brian Hunter   NURSING March 8-21 1990 vol. 4 ;no 6

"Canoe Games"   1986
Dave Ruse   A & C Black

"Canoeing Handbook"   1989
                              Ed. Ray Rowe   British Canoe Union

"Canoeing and Kayaking for People with Physical Disabilities" 1990
                    Webre & Zeller   American Canoe Association

"Diabetes" and *"Diabetes and Hypoglycaemia"*
                    Published by the British Diabetic Association

"A Diabetics Guide to Health and Fitness",
                          Professor Kris E Berg.   Human Kinetics

"Equipment and Services - for people with disabilities"   H.M.S.O.

"Epilepsy - Sport and Leisure" and *"Living with Epilepsy"*
                                    British Epilepsy Association

"Give us the Chance"   1989
                                        Latto & Norrice   D.L.F.

"Informal Countryside Recreation for Disabled People"   1994
                                      Countryside Commission

"Information Service for the Disabled; Leisure Activities"   1975
                                    Disabled Living Foundation

"Kader Informatie Map"   1991
                          Stichting Watersport Gehandicapten

"Outdoor Opportunities"   Leaflet No. 2
                              Ed. Geoff Smedley   U.K.S.A.P.L.D.

"Outdoor Pursuits for Disabled People"   1981
                                    Norman Croucher   D.L.F.

"Safety in Outdoor Education"   1989
                    Department of Education and Science   H.M.S.O.

"Working with People with a Disability"
                                        Paul Burrows   N.C.F.

"Watersports are for Everyone"   1993
                                        Carol Blundell   R.Y.A.

"The Water Sports Code"   1988
                                                              C.C.P.R.

"Water Sports for the Disabled"   1983
                                              Ken Roberts   B.S.A.D.

FUND-RAISING ADVICE

If your club or organisation is considering fund-raising then the following notes may be useful.

Decide

First of all you need to decide what you are fund-raising for. Discuss this openly and fully with all your members. You never know, someone may already have what you want, knows where one can be found or can obtain a substantial discount. Once the plans are accepted elect a small committee to manage the rest of the project.

Plan

Now you know what you want you must plan the project. Consider not only the main points of your project but all the additional implications. For example if you want some boats, do they need buoyancy as an extra or will it be included? If it is building work, are you looking for the funds for both materials and labour? Is your project likely to take some time? Could you phase it and look for funds over a two or three year period?

If you are planning some building work, it is advisable to have the plans prepared professionally. This is because in most cases you will need to get your project approved by the Local Planning Officer for Planning Permission and possibly Building Regulations Approval. Badly prepared submissions will be returned and since Planning Committees usually only meet monthly there can be an unnecessary delay. If there is no-one in your organisation who can help, you may have to do some preliminary fund-raising to pay for this professional help.

Cost

Once the plans for what you want are complete you need to get the project costed. Be very specific about what you want. Obtain as much detail about the specification as you can, otherwise you will not be able to cost the complete project accurately. Seek expert advice for this costing, do not guess since this often leads to under-estimation.

Cost everything realistically, especially any labour or delivery costs. Good intentions from someone to do either for free can evaporate as time goes by.

Finally, build in a contingency amount to allow for increases in costs or those little forgotten items, and the very important presentation ceremony.

Fund-raising

One of the most useful assets you will have for your fund-raising is your properly costed project plan. Use this to prepare a prospectus. Include in it all the details of your planning. If possible have some pictures of the equipment you want or "before and after" views of your project. At the front of the prospectus have one page of A4 with a summary of your request. Many people will only have time for this. However, if they like your project then they will probably go on to read the whole prospectus.

Many Organisations such as Sports Councils and the Foundation for Sport and the Arts need to be approached well in advance and before any work has commenced. In making such submissions seek advice of your regional BSAD officer, or from the BCU. The presentation and wording of submissions can be quite crucial to success.

If you contact your local library you can obtain a list of all the local organisations who have charity funds. These are groups such as Rotary, Lions, Round Table and probably some local trust funds.

It is important to find out what they will give funds for. Some organisations would rather give you labour or materials. Some will arrange special fund-raising events specifically for your project.

It may be worthwhile to break down your project into a list of smaller projects, rather like a wedding gift list. For example you could list a canoe, buoyancy, and paddles, with their individual costs. Some of the smaller organisations may then offer to buy you one or two of the items you need.

If you are going to need such things as building materials, contact local companies. You may be able to persuade them to provide these at little or no cost.

The project

When you have the money you can start to spend it. To get the best value for your money you should contact a number of suppliers and ask for written quotations. Use the details of the plan you drew up initially to ensure you cover the required specifications. Mention what the project is for and ask for discounts.

Give a clear date for quotations to be in and also a reasonable date when you expect the project to commence. Tell your potential suppliers that you are getting in a number of quotations to encourage them to be competitive.

When the quotations are in, although the content should be treated as confidential, discuss each fully with your project committee.

The project in process

When the project starts, whether it is purchasing, building or whatever, you should nominate people to monitor progress. If the project is likely to be disruptive, warn the members and ask for their tolerance and co-operation.

This is the time to start planning the opening or presentations.

Presentations

This can be an important occasion. Remember that this may not be your last project and so the publicity could inspire someone to sponsor your next project.

Fix a date by which time the work or purchasing will be completed. Give everyone concerned as much notice of this date as possible.

Your invitation list may include:-

All the people who have helped with the project. Don't forget your own club members.

Representatives from the fund givers.

Any local organisation concerned with disabled people, to let them know what you are doing that may be of interest to them. Include the BSAD, UKSAPLD, Gateway, CP Sport and any other regional organisations.

Any BCU representatives, your local and regional coaching officers.

Organise:-

A celebrity for the ceremony. The BCU can help you find someone from the canoeing world.

Press statements. Have a simple, but comprehensive statement made will details of the project, who it will serve, the presentation date and who will be there. Have this typed clearly on one side of A4 paper with a name and telephone number to be contacted for more information.

Send this statement to:-

- Newspapers, national and local.
- Television and radio, national and local.
- BCU,
- Sports Council,
- BSAD for newsletters.
- Ministers for Sport and People with Disabilities
- Local MPs.
- Press office for the local council.

On the actual day:-
- Have a reception committee and an area for your guests.
- Provide light refreshments.
- Arrange vantage points for the media, photographers and the audience.
- Have some pre-planned displays to show the new equipment, new facilities and the clubs usual programme.
- Organise a programme of:-
  - Introductions.
  - Guests .
  - Club Chairman to talk about project.
  - Celebrity Opening Speech
  - "Cutting the Ribbon".
  - Thanks to everyone concerned.
- Enjoy the party.

After the event:-

Send a report of the project and the presentation, with photographs, to everyone who did not make the presentation, including the media.

Write thank you letters to everyone, including one to your own club members published in the newsletter.

Start planning your next project. The second and successive ones do get easier.

Fund Giving Contacts

Sportsmatch
Francis House
Francis Street
London SW1P 1DE   Tel: 0171 828 8771

This scheme will match pound for pound sponsorship with money from the Government.

Foundation for Sport and the Arts
PO Box 20   Tel: 0151 524 0235/6
Liverpool L9 6EE   Fax: 0151 524 0285

Send for the application form to apply for potentially very large sums of money (bids can be in tens of thousands of pounds). However, you may have to wait some time.

The Lottery Sports Fund
The Sports Council
PO Box 649
London WC1 0QP

At the time of writing money from this fund is only available for capital funding.   However, there are hopes that this will be extended to revenue funding.

Jubilee Canoeing Foundation
c/o the BCU
Adbolton Lane
West Bridgford
NOTTINGHAM   Tel: 0115 982 1100
NG2 5AS   Fax: 0115 982 1797

This is the BCU's own charity. It manages other charity funds such as the James Turner Legacy Fund. Send for an application form to apply. Amounts usually granted are in the region of two to three hundred pounds.

Directory of Social Change
Radius Works
Back Lane
London
NW3 1HL   Tel: 0171 284 4364

This is an advice agency for fund-raisers. It runs courses and provides factsheets/leaflets on (among others):-

> *"Making an Application"*
> *"Writing a Proposal"*
> *"Drawing up a Budget"*

Regional Sports Councils

Also ask your regional Sports Council to let you know of any funds you can apply for through them.

Your own efforts

Finally, on the basis that every little helps encourage your members to get involved with club based activities:-

- raffles,
- coffee mornings,
- competitions,
- social events.

Each event may only raise a few pounds, but a number of events can soon raise substantial amounts. Furthermore, involving the members encourages them to feel a part of the project.

INDEX

ILLUSTRATIONS